W9-BXP-920

Taste of Home

Down Home Cooking for
One or Two

Mixed Vegetable Soup
p. 86

Senior Editor: Mark Hagen
Art Director: Gretchen Trautman
Senior Layout Designer: Julie Wagner
Layout Designer: Kathy Crawford
Proofreaders: Linne Bruskewitz, Jean Steiner
Editorial Assistant: Barb Czysz
Associate Food Editors: Coleen Martin, Diane Werner
Assistant Food Editor: Karen Scales
Senior Recipe Editor: Sue A. Jurack
Senior Food Photographer: Rob Hagen
Food Photographers: Dan Roberts, Jim Wieland
Associate Food Photographer: Lori Foy
Senior Food Stylist: Joylyn Trickel
Food Stylists: Diane Armstrong, Sue Draheim, Sarah Thompson
Set Stylists: Jennifer Bradley Vent, Stephanie Marchese
Associate Set Stylist: Melissa Haberman
Photo Studio Coordinator: Suzanne Kern

Vice President/Executive Editor, Books: Heidi Reuter Lloyd
Creative Director: Ardyth Cope
Senior Vice President/Editor in Chief: Catherine Cassidy
President: Barbara Newton
Founder: Roy Reiman

© 2006 Reiman Media Group, Inc.
5400 S. 60th St., Greendale WI 53129

International Standard Book Number (10):
0-89821-543-9
International Standard Book Number (13):
978-0-89821-543-4
Library of Congress Control Number:
2006935714

Pictured on the front cover:
Stuffed Pork Tenderloin (p. 162), Ginger Veggie Stir-Fry (p. 204) and Frozen Raspberry Cheesecakes (p. 286).

Pictured on the back cover:
Pizza Macaroni Bake (p. 156).

For other *Taste of Home* books and products, visit *www.tasteofhome.com*.

TABLE OF CONTENTS

Farmhouse Omelets
p. 13

Hamburger Mac Skillet
p. 116

Cheesy Carrot Casserole
p. 210

Sugar Dusted Blueberry
Muffins p. 219

Down Home Cooking for One or Two

With this scrumptious collection of 446 small-serving recipes, setting a table for two has never been easier!

Creamy Chicken Corn
Chowder p. 77

Rack of Lamb
p. 164

Chicken Parmesan
p. 137

Quick Ambrosia
p. 292

"Dig in!" That's what many empty nesters, newlyweds and novice cooks across the country are saying, as they whip up all-time favorite dishes in single- and double-serving sizes. From coast to coast, folks are finding delicious new ways to scale back comfort foods that usually feed a crowd...and they have shared their best dishes in *Down-Home Cooking for 1 or 2*.

Nearly every recipe was submitted by a family cook who is accustomed to preparing meals for small households. These classic dishes were then reviewed by our Test Kitchen staff, who couldn't help but share some of their favorites as well.

This means that you can prepare anything in this handy cookbook, knowing that it's sized right for two. After all, each item was given the stamp of approval by *Taste of Home*... America's No. 1 cooking resource.

At Your Fingertips
Longing for old-fashioned staples such as hearty meat loaf, steaming chicken noodle soup, golden buttermilk biscuits or luscious chocolate cake? With the 446 recipes found here, you can relish every bite without worrying about lots of leftovers. In addition, you'll discover plenty of breakfast items, appetizers, salads and desserts—all of which yield the absolute perfect amount.

Whether your kids flew the coop or you simply find yourself eating fewer servings, you'll have the dinner bell ringing once again with four distinct entree chapters. Spirit-warming casseroles, juicy roasts and savory stir-fries are just a few of the main courses in sections devoted to beef (p. 94), chicken (p. 122), pork (p. 150) and even fish and seafood (p. 172).

You also won't want to miss the chapter "Table for Two" on page 234. There, you'll discover 15 complete menus, each featuring succulent recipes and gorgeous photos.

Finding the perfect supper accompaniment won't ever be a problem with "Scaled-Down Side Dishes" (p. 190). That's where more than 40 mouth-watering specialties await, featuring everything from Twice-Baked Sweet Potatoes (p. 201) to Macaroni 'n' Cheese for Two (p. 204).

Crave brownies, cookies or pies but don't want to face the extras for days on end? There are plenty of sweet sensations to choose from, including Coconut Macaroons (p. 276), Luscious Lemon Bars (p. 279) and Mini Apple Pie (p. 291). Each treat yields a small amount, as do the aromatic baked goods in the "The Bread Basket" (p. 216).

The Skinny on Cooking for 2
Because so many folks are watching what they eat these days, many of the recipes offer Nutrition Facts and Diabetic Exchanges. These dishes are highlighted with a red checkmark, indicating that they are lower in fat, sodium or carbohydrates.

When a choice of ingredients is given in a recipe, the first ingredient listed is generally the one calculated in the Nutrition Facts. When a range is given for an ingredient, the first amount is calculated. Only the amount of marinade that is absorbed during preparation is considered. Garnishes listed in recipes are typically included in calculations.

We've marked these recipes in two useful indexes as well. Turn to page 308 and you'll see an index of major ingredients and cooking methods followed by an alphabetical index.

To top everything off, the pages of *Down-Home Cooking for 1 or 2* are sprinkled with loads of tips to make your kitchen as efficient as possible. Get started with the ideas on the following pages. They'll help you pare down your favorite recipes, store leftovers and create a number of memorable menus. So what are you waiting for? It's time to turn the page and dig in!

DOWNSIZED KITCHEN STRATEGIES

Today, cooking for one or two is easier than ever!

Downsizing your favorite dish is a snap...once you have a few kitchen secrets stashed up your apron sleeve. Whether you're an empty nester or a newlywed, you'll find that a little cooking know-how goes a long way when creating small-serving menus.

Follow the ideas here and you won't have to deal with a variety of barely-used ingredients. In the event that supper leaves you with extras, finishing them up or storing them won't be a problem either.

Stocking the Pantry

These days, more food manufacturers are selling their products in small quantities. Applesauce, prepared pudding, cookies, dried fruit and pretzels are just some of the single serving items found on supermarket shelves.

These handy packages are ideal when cooking for one or two because the amounts don't result in lots of leftovers. For example, a small bag of cookies or graham crackers can be used in a dessert crust that's sized right for two.

Single-serve juice boxes allow you to spruce up smoothies without having to store a large, open bottle of juice in the refrigerator. Similarly, a small, disposable container of applesauce is the perfect amount to use in two-person baked goods, and a tiny bag of potato chips makes a great topping for a 1-quart casserole.

While these smaller-yield packages are often slightly more expensive than their larger counterparts, many family cooks are willing to pay for the convenience of having the items on hand.

Storage Made Simple

Boxed items and canned goods are great kitchen staples for small households because they keep for an extended period of time.

The U.S. Food and Drug Administration doesn't require an expiration date on many shelf-stable foods because they are safe to eat indefinitely. Flavor and nutritional values, however, can diminish if an item sits on the shelf too long. *(Continued on p. 8.)*

Cooking-for-Two FAQs!

Having trouble paring down a favorite recipe of your own? Here are the answers to some of the most common questions cooks ask when resizing an original dish.

Q. *If I cut a recipe down, how will the baking time be affected?*

A. The answer depends on what you're baking. Occasionally, the baking time is the same but sometimes it's a lot shorter. To make sure your dish bakes properly, consider purchasing an instant-read thermometer.

If the original recipe specifies a desired internal temperature, check the food regularly. Casseroles, for instance, are usually done when they reach 160° to 180° or when they are heated through, bubbling around the edges.

Steaks, chops, chicken pieces and fish fillets generally require the same amount of baking time for two items as for more since it's the thickness of the meat that determines the cooking time.

Q. *How can I cut a recipe in half when it calls for one egg?*

A. Lightly beat a large egg and measure out 2 tablespoons to be used in the recipe. You can store the remaining egg in a covered container in the refrigerator for 2 to 4 days.

Q. *Must I use a smaller skillet when scaling down a stovetop recipe?*

A. It's always best to use cookware that is appropriate to the size of the recipe you are preparing. Excessive evaporation may occur if a skillet or saucepan is too large for the amount of food you're cooking. This can cause sauces to burn and foods to dry out quickly.

The good news is that you can find smaller skillets and saucepans in many discount department stores and supermarkets today. Similarly, smaller baking pans and dishes are becoming widely available. The pans called for in this cookbook can be found at most discount department stores.

Q. *What do I do when the amount I'm cutting the recipe down by doesn't divide evenly?*

A. This is difficult for many family cooks. See the chart below to make things easier. Remember that when it comes to herbs and seasonings, it's best to start with less as you can always add more to taste.

Reducing Ingredients

Original Amount	Half of Recipe	One-Third of Recipe
1 cup	1/2 cup	1/3 cup
3/4 cup	6 tablespoons	1/4 cup
2/3 cup	1/3 cup	3 tablespoons plus 1-1/2 teaspoons*
1/2 cup	1/4 cup	2 tablespoons plus 2 teaspoons
1/3 cup	2 tablespoons plus 2 teaspoons	1 tablespoon plus 2-1/4 teaspoons*
1/4 cup	2 tablespoons	1 tablespoon plus 1 teaspoon
1 tablespoon	1-1/2 teaspoons	1 teaspoon
1 teaspoon	1/2 teaspoon	1/4 teaspoon*
1/2 teaspoon	1/4 teaspoon	1/8 teaspoon*
1/4 teaspoon	1/8 teaspoon	Dash

* amount is rounded down

See the chart below for recommended storage times, and keep the following pointers in mind:

- Store shelf-stable foods in a cool, dry place away from temperature extremes. Avoid keeping food above the stove or under the kitchen sink.
- Don't buy badly dented or bulging cans. Avoid packages that are dusty or appear to be old.
- Look for the "use before" or "best if used by" date, and purchase only what you plan to use within that timeframe.

Recommended Storage Times*

CANNED GOODS	UNOPENED IN PANTRY	OPENED AND REFRIGERATED
Low-Acid (Meat, poultry, fish, gravy, peas, most soups, beans, carrots, corn, pasta, potatoes, spinach)	2-5 Years	3-4 Days
High-Acid (Juices, fruit, pickles, sauerkraut, tomato soup, foods in vinegar-based sauces)	12-18 Months	5-7 Days

From date of purchase
Source: *Food Safety and Inspection Service, U.S. Department of Agriculture*

Frosty Facts

Stocking up on kitchen staples or storing leftovers for future meals is a cinch with a little help from your freezer. Whether you are dividing up a family-sized package of ground beef or preparing a make-ahead dinner, you can avoid freezer burn by wrapping the food tightly and pressing out any excess air.

Wrap foods in plastic wrap, aluminum foil or freezer paper. Smaller items can be wrapped and set in resealable freezer bags or durable, leak-proof containers. If a container's lid doesn't fit properly, don't use it.

Avoid freezing mayonnaise, yogurt, sour cream, milk sauces and gravies. Similarly, lettuce, citrus wedges and cucumbers are not ideal for the freezer. The same is true for cooked eggs and fried foods.

Most casseroles, soups and baked goods freeze well. Cooked meat and poultry keep in the freezer for 2 to 3 months, and bacon, lunch meats and sausages stay for 1 to 2 months.

Always defrost items in the refrigerator or microwave. This may take a little bit of planning on your part, but you'll find the delicious rewards well worth the effort.

Planning Pointers

Anyone who runs a household surely agrees...a little planning goes a long way. The same holds true when cooking for two. Whether you have a system for grocery shopping, recipes that take advantage of leftovers or a method for using up frozen fare, a smart kitchen strategy saves time, effort and money in the long run.

As mentioned earlier, single-serving items can be more costly than full-sized goods. Scan the newspapers for coupons and take advantage of any in-store discounts your supermarket offers. Watch for small-sized products. More manufacturers are catering to one- and two-person households, and new, pared-down items can be found on grocery shelves regularly.

Weekly menu planners are a lifesaver in several ways. For example, if you schedule a chicken entree early in the week and know you'll have leftovers, you can plan on whipping up a dish or two that calls for cooked chicken later in the week. You'll clean out the refrigerator and never waste time wondering what to make for dinner. You'll even avoid emergency trips to the supermarket.

When you decide to freeze leftovers, label them with the type of food you're freezing, the date and any reheating instructions. Set the leftovers at the back of your freezer, and move the older food to the front so you're more likely to use it first.

Meal Ideas for Two

With the 446 downsized dishes in this collection, the menu possibilities are endless. Consider the following ideas the next time you need a complete meal that's perfect for a pair.*

Early Morning Marvels

- Pancakes with Orange Syrup, p. 238
  Moist Bran Muffins, p. 220
  Fruity Red Smoothies, p. 18

- Hearty Ham Omelet, p. 244
  Honey-Nut Breakfast Twists, p. 232
  Fruit 'n' Cream Crepes, p. 17

- Hint-of-Orange French Toast, p. 21
  Spiced Apricots, p. 27
  Yogurt Parfait, p. 24

- Egg and Tomato Scramble, p. 20
  Potato Pancakes, p. 26
  Breakfast Banana Split, p. 22

Lively Lunches

- Sourdough Cheeseburgers, p. 55
  Summer Squash Salad, p. 70
  Lemon-Berry Pitcher Punch, p. 257

- Fruited Chicken Lettuce Salad, p. 67
  Chilled Strawberry Soup, p. 90
  Zucchini Muffins, p. 228

- Meatball Sub Sandwiches, p. 71
  Macaroni 'n' Cheese for Two, p. 204
  Quick Ambrosia, p. 292

- Spinach Turkey Wraps, p. 56
  Peanut Slaw, p. 62
  Coconut Macaroons, p. 276

Dinners for a Duo

- Oven-Barbecued Chicken, p. 141
  Tangy Potato Salad, p. 54
  Corn Medley, p. 197

- Old-Fashioned Swiss Steak, p. 120
  Dutch Potatoes, p. 193
  Whipped Cream Biscuits, p. 224

- Ham with Potatoes and Onions, p. 171
  Creamy Chicken Corn Chowder, p. 77
  Green Bean Fritters, p. 202

- Chicken Parmesan, p. 137
  Fettuccine Primavera, p. 210
  Garlic Crescent Rolls, p. 223

- Reuben Meat Loaf, p. 112
  Warm Spinach Salad, p. 50
  Rye Drop Biscuits, p. 227

- Stuffed Haddock, p. 185
  Cheesy Carrot Casserole, p. 210
  Glazed Pineapple Sundaes, p. 291

Special-Occasion Suppers

- Surf 'n' Turf Dinner, p. 109
  Parmesan Asparagus, p. 209
  Coconut Creme Brulee, p. 293

- Bacon-Wrapped Chicken, p. 137
  Tomato 'n' Cheese Pasta, p. 193
  Apricot Berry Shortcake, p. 297

- Rack of Lamb, p. 164
  Apricot-Ginger Asparagus, p. 198
  Minty Baked Alaska, p. 289

- Honey-Dijon Salmon and Asparagus, p. 174
  Simple Green Salad, p. 246
  Basil Garlic Bread, p. 223

*See page 234 for 15 additional menus that are made for a twosome.

BREAKFAST & BRUNCH

Just because there are only two of you in the house doesn't mean you have to start the day with cold cereal and toast. Consider these eye-opening ideas for pancakes, omelets, hash browns and more that are perfect for a pair.

Very Veggie Omelet
p. 22

Scrambled Egg Cups
For Two p. 19

Parmesan Ham Frittata
p. 12

Hint-of-Orange
French Toast p. 21

Baked Eggs and Ham
p. 15

Triple-Berry Wake-Up Breakfast

Leandra Holland • Westlake, California

*These golden sandwiches are filled with flavored cream cheese and a juicy layer
of strawberries. Serve them warm with syrup for an unforgettable treat.*

1 carton (8 ounces) strawberry cream
   cheese
4 pieces white bread, crusts removed
1/2 pint fresh strawberries, sliced
1 egg
2 tablespoons milk
1 tablespoon butter *or* vegetable oil
Strawberry syrup *or* confectioners' sugar

Spread some cream cheese on two pieces of bread. Top with sliced berries, making a complete blanket over the cheese. Top each with the remaining bread.

In a bowl, beat egg and milk. In a frying pan or griddle, melt butter or heat oil over medium-high. Dip the sandwich in the egg mixture and fry until golden on both sides. Top with strawberry syrup or confectioners' sugar and serve immediately. **Yield:** 2 servings.

Parmesan Ham Frittata

T. Lentini • Rogue River, Oregon

*This egg dish is true to my Italian heritage. I'm a creative cook, so I came up with this simple recipe based
on how I remember my grandma making it. Even at that, I'm not sure I make it the same each time.*

1/4 cup chopped onion
1/4 cup chopped green pepper
2 garlic cloves, minced
2 tablespoons olive oil
4 eggs
Salt and pepper to taste
1/2 cup cubed fully cooked ham
1/4 cup grated Parmesan cheese

In a 6-in. broiler-proof skillet, saute the onion, green pepper and garlic in oil. Reduce heat to medium. In a bowl, beat eggs, salt and pepper. Add egg mixture and ham to vegetables.

As eggs set, lift edges, letting the uncooked portion flow underneath. When eggs are nearly set, sprinkle with cheese. Broil 4-5 in. from the heat for 1-2 minutes or until eggs are completely set. **Yield:** 2 servings.

Shake and Scramble

Carla Reid • Charlottetown, Prince Edward Island

*This is a fast morning recipe. To make it even easier to prepare, I cut up the turkey
and the vegetables, shred the cheese and freeze it all in 1/2-cup portions.
So when I want to serve this dish, I simply take out the number of bags needed.*

4 eggs, lightly beaten
1/2 cup milk
1/2 cup chopped green *and/or* sweet red
   pepper
1/2 cup diced deli smoked turkey
1/2 cup shredded cheddar cheese
2 tablespoons butter
Salt and pepper to taste

In a container with a tight-fitting lid, combine the first five ingredients. Cover and shake until well mixed.

In a small skillet, melt butter over medium heat. Add egg mixture; cook and stir until eggs are completely set. Season with salt and pepper. **Yield:** 2 servings.

Farmhouse Omelets

Farmhouse Omelets

Roberta Williams • Poplar Bluff, Missouri

We look forward to brunch after church on Sundays, so I always make an effort to serve something special. These pretty omelets provide a pleasant blend of tastes and textures.

4   bacon strips, diced
1/4   cup chopped onion
6   eggs
1   tablespoon water
1/4   teaspoon salt, optional
1/8   teaspoon pepper
Dash hot pepper sauce
3   teaspoons butter, *divided*
1/2   cup cubed fully cooked ham, *divided*
1/4   cup thinly sliced fresh mushrooms, *divided*
1/4   cup chopped green pepper, *divided*
1   cup (4 ounces) shredded cheddar cheese, *divided*

In a skillet, cook bacon over medium heat until crisp. Remove with a slotted spoon to paper towels. Drain, reserving 2 teaspoons drippings. In drippings, saute onion until tender; set aside.

In a bowl, beat the eggs, water, salt if desired, pepper and pepper sauce. Melt 1-1/2 teaspoons butter in a 10-in. nonstick skillet over medium heat; add half of the egg mixture. As the eggs set, lift edges, letting uncooked portion flow underneath.

When eggs are set, sprinkle half of the bacon, onion, ham, mushrooms, green pepper and cheese on one side; fold over. Cover and let stand for 1-2 minutes or until cheese is melted. Repeat with remaining ingredients for second omelet. **Yield:** 2 omelets.

Maple Pancakes

Maple Pancakes

Mary Colbath • Concord, New Hampshire

We look forward to tapping the maple trees in March...and then enjoying pure maple syrup year-round. This is just one of the recipes I like to make that has maple syrup as a key ingredient.

1 cup all-purpose flour
1-1/2 teaspoons baking powder
1/2 teaspoon salt
1 egg
1 cup milk
2 tablespoons vegetable oil
1 tablespoon maple syrup
Additional maple syrup

In a bowl, combine flour, baking powder and salt. In another bowl, combine egg, milk, oil and syrup; stir into dry ingredients just until blended.

Pour batter by 1/4 cupfuls onto a lightly greased hot griddle; turn when bubbles form on top of pancakes. Cook until second side is golden brown (pancakes will be thin). Serve with additional maple syrup. **Yield:** 6-7 pancakes.

Baked Eggs and Ham

Carolyn Crump • Center, Texas

I give this single-serving dish southwestern zip by using cheese that's flavored with jalapeno peppers. Regular cheddar cheese also produces tasty results, so use whatever you have on hand.

1/4 cup seasoned croutons
2 tablespoons chopped fully cooked ham
1 tablespoon butter, melted
2 eggs
1 tablespoon shredded cheddar cheese

In a greased shallow 2-cup baking dish, toss the croutons, ham and butter. Break the eggs carefully on top. Sprinkle with cheese. Bake, uncovered, at 350° for 15-18 minutes or until eggs reach desired doneness. **Yield:** 1 serving.

Apple-Banana Oatmeal

Linda Hocking • Mackay, Idaho

This special oatmeal gets me going in the morning and makes me feel great all day. My husband and son race mountain bikes, so they need foods like this that provide energy.

✓ Uses less fat, sugar or salt. Includes Nutrition Facts or Diabetic Exchanges.

1 cup water
1 tablespoon orange juice concentrate
1/2 cup chopped unpeeled tart apple
1/4 cup sliced firm banana
1/4 cup raisins
1/4 teaspoon salt, optional
1/8 teaspoon ground cinnamon
2/3 cup quick-cooking oats
1/4 to 1/3 cup oat bran
Brown sugar, optional

In a saucepan, combine water, orange juice concentrate, apple, banana, raisins, salt if desired and cinnamon; bring to a boil. Stir in oats and oat bran. Cook for 1-2 minutes, stirring occasionally. Sprinkle with brown sugar if desired. **Yield:** 2 servings.

Nutrition Facts: One serving (prepared without salt and brown sugar) equals 235 calories, 3 g fat (0 saturated fat), 0 cholesterol, 4 mg sodium, 52 g carbohydrate, 7 g fiber, 7 g protein. **Diabetic Exchanges:** 2-1/2 starch, 1 fruit.

Oatmeal Pancakes

Florence Groves • Vancouver, Washington

This recipe makes two short stacks of oat pancakes. When we used to travel in our motor home, I'd measure out the dry ingredients for individual batches in resealable bags, then just combine with an egg, buttermilk and butter for a quick meal.

3/4	cup quick-cooking oats
1/2	cup all-purpose flour
1/2	teaspoon baking soda
1/2	teaspoon sugar
1	egg
1	cup buttermilk
3	tablespoons butter, melted

In a bowl, combine the oats, flour, baking soda and sugar. Combine the egg, buttermilk and butter; stir into the dry ingredients just until moistened.

Pour batter by 1/3 cupfuls onto a greased hot griddle. Turn when bubbles form on top; cook until second side is golden brown. **Yield:** 7 pancakes.

Cheesy Chive Omelet

Naomi Giddis • Two Buttes, Colorado

Fresh chives and cheddar cheese make this easy omelet a smart way to jump-start the day.

3	eggs
2	tablespoons water
1	tablespoon minced chives
1/8	teaspoon salt
Dash pepper	
1	tablespoon butter
1/4	to 1/2 cup shredded cheddar cheese

In a small bowl, beat eggs and water. Stir in chives, salt and pepper. In a small skillet, melt butter over medium heat; add egg mixture. As eggs set, lift edges, letting the uncooked portion flow underneath.

Just before eggs are completely set, sprinkle cheese over half of the omelet; fold in half. Cover and remove from the heat. Let stand for 1-2 minutes or until cheese is melted. **Yield:** 1-2 servings.

Tasty Eggs for Two

Deb Cornelius • Grant, Nebraska

I found this stovetop classic while looking for something quick to fix. My teenage son, who can be a picky eater, really likes the combination of hash browns, ham and broccoli, so I make it frequently.

1	cup frozen cubed hash brown potatoes, thawed
1/4	cup chopped onion
2	tablespoons butter
1	cup fresh *or* frozen broccoli florets
1/2	cup julienned fully cooked ham
4	eggs
1	tablespoon milk
1/4	to 1/2 teaspoon lemon-pepper seasoning
1/4	teaspoon dill weed, optional

In a skillet, cook the potatoes and onion in butter over medium heat until lightly browned, about 10 minutes. Add broccoli; cook until tender. Stir in ham.

In a bowl, beat eggs, milk, lemon-pepper and dill if desired. Pour over potato mixture; cook for 3-5 minutes or until eggs are completely set, stirring occasionally. **Yield:** 2 servings.

Fruit 'n' Cream Crepes

Ruth Kaercher • Hudsonville, Michigan

*Three types of berries, cream cheese and a hint of vanilla make these
tender and creamy crepes a hit whenever they appear on our breakfast table.*

1/3   cup milk
2   tablespoons beaten egg
1/4   teaspoon vanilla extract
1/4   cup all-purpose flour
1-1/2   teaspoons confectioners' sugar
1/4   teaspoon baking powder
Dash salt
2   teaspoons butter, *divided*
FILLING:
2   ounces cream cheese, softened
3   tablespoons plus 1/2 teaspoon confectioners' sugar, *divided*
4   teaspoons milk
1/8   teaspoon vanilla extract
1/3   cup *each* fresh blueberries, strawberries and raspberries

In a small bowl, combine the first seven ingredients. Cover and refrigerate for 1 hour.

In an 8-in. nonstick skillet, melt 1 teaspoon butter. Stir batter; pour about 2 tablespoons into the center of skillet. Lift and tilt pan to evenly coat bottom. Cook until top appears dry; turn and cook 15-20 seconds longer. Remove to a wire rack. Make three more crepes, adding remaining butter to skillet as needed.

For filling, in a small mixing bowl, beat the cream cheese, 3 tablespoons confectioners' sugar, milk and vanilla until smooth. Spread 1 rounded tablespoon on each crepe; top with 1/4 cup fruit and roll up. Sprinkle with remaining confectioners' sugar. **Yield:** 2 servings.

Fruit 'n' Cream Crepes

Egg Sandwich with Cilantro Lime Spread

Cindie Haras • Boca Raton, Florida

Turkey sausage, pepper Jack cheese, salsa and a lip-smacking cilantro spread are just some of the items that pump up the flavor of these bagel sandwiches.

- 2 tablespoons mayonnaise
- 1 teaspoon lime juice
- 1 teaspoon minced fresh cilantro
- 3 eggs
- 1 teaspoon finely chopped jalapeno pepper
- 1/4 teaspoon salt
- 1/8 teaspoon pepper
- 4 breakfast turkey sausage links
- 1 ounce pepper Jack cheese, sliced
- 2 plain bagels, split (4 inches *each*)

Dash chili powder

- 2 teaspoons salsa
- 2 slices red onion

In a small bowl, combine the mayonnaise, lime juice and cilantro; set aside. In another small bowl, combine the eggs, jalapeno, salt and pepper; set aside.

In a small nonstick skillet, cook sausage over medium heat for 10-12 minutes or until meat is no longer pink; drain. Remove from skillet and keep warm. In the same skillet over medium heat, add egg mixture. As eggs set, lift edges, letting uncooked portion flow underneath. When the eggs are set, place cheese over one side; fold omelet over cheese. Cover and let stand for 1-1/2 minutes or until cheese is melted.

Cut omelet in half; place on bagel halves. Cut sausage links in half lengthwise; layer over omelets. Sprinkle with chili powder. Spread with salsa; top with onion. Spread remaining bagel halves with mayonnaise mixture. Replace bagel tops. Broil 6 in. from heat for 2-3 minutes or until heated through. Serve immediately. **Yield:** 2 servings.

Editor's Note: When cutting or seeding hot peppers, use rubber or plastic gloves to protect your hands. Avoid touching your face.

Fruity Red Smoothies

Fruity Red Smoothies

Beverly Coyde • Gasport, New York

This thick beverage combines the refreshing flavors of cranberries, raspberries and strawberries. Once you start sipping it, you can't stop!

- 1 carton (8 ounces) strawberry yogurt
- 1/2 to 3/4 cup cranberry juice
- 1-1/2 cups frozen unsweetened strawberries, quartered
- 1 cup frozen unsweetened raspberries
- 1 to 1-1/2 teaspoons sugar

In a blender or food processor, combine yogurt and cranberry juice. Add strawberries, raspberries and sugar; cover and process until blended. Pour into glasses; serve immediately. **Yield:** 2 servings.

Individual Quiche

Laura Stoltzfus • New Holland, Pennsylvania

*This idea uses an 8-ounce custard cup to
bake up a wonderful quiche just perfect for one.
Feel free to add your favorite seasonings
to the egg and milk mixture.*

1/4   cup bulk pork sausage
  1   egg
1/3   cup milk
Dash *each* salt, pepper and ground mustard
  1   slice bread, crust removed
  1   green onion, sliced
  1   tablespoon shredded cheddar cheese

In a small skillet, brown sausage; drain. In a small
bowl, beat egg, milk, salt, pepper and mustard; set
aside. Cube bread; place in a greased 8-oz. custard
cup. Top with sausage and onion. Pour egg mixture
over top. Sprinkle with cheese.

Bake, uncovered, at 350° for 25-30 minutes
or until a knife inserted near the center comes
out clean. **Yield:** 1 serving.

Individual Quiche

Scrambled Egg Cups for Two

Dorothy Swanson • Affton, Missouri

*Here's a delightfully different way to enjoy eggs! These cute, little
bread cups go well with any type of breakfast meat. I found the recipe in my
newspaper's food section years ago, and it's been a favorite ever since.*

☑ **Uses less fat, sugar or salt. Includes Nutrition Facts
or Diabetic Exchanges.**

  4   slices bread, crusts removed
  2   tablespoons butter, softened, *divided*
  3   eggs
  1   tablespoon minced chives
1/4   teaspoon salt
1/8   teaspoon pepper
1/4   cup shredded cheddar cheese

Flatten bread with a rolling pin. Spread a scant
teaspoon of butter over one side of each slice.
Press bread buttered side down into four muffin
cups. Bake at 350° for 12-15 minutes or until
lightly toasted.

Meanwhile, in a bowl, beat eggs, chives, salt
and pepper. In a skillet, melt remaining butter over
medium-low heat. Add egg mixture; cook and stir
until eggs are completely set. Spoon into bread
cups; sprinkle with cheese. Bake 1-2 minutes
longer or until cheese is melted. **Yield:** 2 servings.

Nutrition Facts: 2 egg cups (prepared with reduced-
fat butter, egg substitute and reduced-fat cheese)
equals 234 calories, 13 g fat (7 g saturated fat), 31 mg
cholesterol, 747 mg sodium, 13 g carbohydrate, 1 g
fiber, 18 g protein.

Egg and Tomato Scramble

Ilva Jasica • St. Joseph, Michigan

*My mother used to make this for me as a special breakfast when
I was a little girl. I think of her when I prepare it these days.*

✓ **Uses less fat, sugar or salt. Includes Nutrition Facts or Diabetic Exchanges.**

- 1 **plum tomato, peeled and chopped**
- 1 **teaspoon chopped fresh basil *or* 1/4 teaspoon dried basil**
- 1 **egg *or* egg substitute equivalent**
- 1 **teaspoon water**
- 1 **garlic clove, minced**
- 1 **teaspoon olive oil, optional**

Salt and pepper to taste, optional

- 1 **slice bread, toasted**

Additional fresh basil, optional

In a small bowl, combine tomato and basil; set aside. In another bowl, beat egg, water and garlic. Heat oil if desired in a small nonstick skillet; add egg mixture. Cook and stir gently until egg is nearly set. Add tomato mixture and salt and pepper if desired. Cook and stir until egg is completely set and tomato is heated through. Serve with toast. Garnish with basil if desired. **Yield:** 1 serving.

Nutrition Facts: 1 recipe (prepared with egg substitute and without oil and salt) equals 152 calories, 4 g fat (0 saturated fat), 1 mg cholesterol, 289 mg sodium, 20 g carbohydrate, 0 fiber, 11 g protein. **Diabetic Exchanges:** 1 starch, 1 meat.

Pancakes for One

Ann Schenk • Winnett, Montana

As our kids grew up and left home, I scaled down our favorite pancake recipe. Now if my husband or I have a taste for pancakes, it's easy to make just a few.

1/2	cup all-purpose flour
2	teaspoons wheat germ
1/4	teaspoon baking soda
1/4	teaspoon baking powder
1/4	teaspoon salt
1	egg
1/2	cup buttermilk
1-1/2	teaspoons vegetable oil

Butter and maple syrup

In a bowl, combine flour, wheat germ, baking soda, baking powder and salt. In another bowl, beat egg; add buttermilk and oil. Stir into dry ingredients just until blended.

Pour the batter by 1/3 cupfuls onto a lightly greased hot griddle; turn when bubbles form on top of pancakes. Cook until the second side is golden brown. Serve with butter and syrup. **Yield:** 1 serving (3 pancakes).

Sunny Breakfast Special

Alberta Hanson • Cushing, Wisconsin

Get the day off to a great start with this wake-up treat. Orange marmalade and fresh pineapple lend a tangy twist to bacon, egg and cheese in this open-faced sandwich.

1	tablespoon butter, softened
1	English muffin half
1	slice Canadian bacon
1	pineapple ring
1	teaspoon orange marmalade
1	egg, *separated*
1	tablespoon shredded cheddar cheese

Spread butter over muffin half; place on a baking sheet. Broil 4-6 in. from the heat for 1-2 minutes or until butter is bubbly. Top with bacon and pineapple; spoon marmalade into center of pineapple ring. Brush egg white over top and sides of muffin. Sprinkle cheese on top.

With a spoon, make a well in cheese; place egg yolk in well. Bake at 375° for 15 minutes or until egg is completely set and top is golden brown. **Yield:** 1 serving.

Hint-of-Orange French Toast

Donna Warner • Tavares, Florida

Our daughter and son-in-law have their own sugar works in Vermont, so we always have a supply of maple syrup, which makes this breakfast specialty even better. This recipe can be expanded to feed a crowd, too.

4	slices French bread (3/4 inch thick)
2	eggs
1/2	cup milk
1	tablespoon orange juice
1/2	teaspoon grated orange peel
1/4	teaspoon vanilla extract
2	tablespoons butter

Confectioners' sugar *and/or* maple syrup, optional

Place the bread in an 11-in. x 7-in. x 2-in. baking dish. In a small bowl, beat the eggs, milk, orange juice, orange peel and vanilla. Pour over bread; turn to coat. Cover and refrigerate for 8 hours or overnight.

In a large skillet, cook French toast in butter over medium heat for 4 minutes on each side or until golden brown. Dust with confectioners' sugar and serve with syrup if desired. **Yield:** 2 servings.

Breakfast Banana Splits

Renee Lloy • Pearl, Mississippi

I can't help but share this recipe. It's elegant enough for a formal brunch, yet it's simple enough for busy weekdays. With different fruits and cereals, the variations are endless.

1 medium firm banana
1/3 cup *each* blueberries, halved seedless grapes, sliced kiwifruit and strawberries
1 cup vanilla yogurt
1/2 cup granola cereal with almonds
2 maraschino cherries with stems

Slice banana in half lengthwise; cut each in half widthwise. Place two pieces of banana in two individual bowls. Top each with 2/3 cup mixed fruit, 1/2 cup yogurt, 1/4 cup granola and 1 cherry. **Yield:** 2 servings.

Very Veggie Omelet

Jan Houberg • Reddick, Illinois

I enjoy serving this light, fluffy omelet to my husband, who always appreciates a different take on breakfast. It's chock-full of garden goodness.

✓ Uses less fat, sugar or salt. Includes Nutrition Facts or Diabetic Exchanges.

1 small onion, chopped
1/4 cup chopped green pepper
1 tablespoon butter
1 small zucchini, chopped
3/4 cup chopped tomato
1/4 teaspoon dried oregano
1/8 teaspoon pepper
4 egg whites
1/4 cup water
1/4 teaspoon cream of tartar
1/4 teaspoon salt
1/4 cup egg substitute
1/2 cup shredded reduced-fat cheddar cheese, *divided*

In a large nonstick skillet, saute onion and green pepper in butter until tender. Add the zucchini, tomato, oregano and pepper. Cook and stir for 5-8 minutes or until vegetables are tender and liquid is nearly evaporated. Set aside and keep warm.

In a mixing bowl, beat egg whites, water, cream of tartar and salt until stiff peaks form. Place egg substitute in another bowl; fold in egg white mixture. Pour into a 10-in. ovenproof skillet coated with nonstick cooking spray. Cook over medium heat for 5 minutes or until bottom is lightly browned.

Bake at 350° for 9-10 minutes or until a knife inserted near the center comes out clean. Spoon vegetable mixture over one side; sprinkle with half of the cheese. To fold, score middle of omelet with a sharp knife; fold omelet over filling. Transfer to a warm platter. Sprinkle with remaining cheese. Cut in half to serve. **Yield:** 2 servings.

Nutrition Facts: One serving (half an omelet) equals 197 calories, 9 g fat (5 g saturated fat), 21 mg cholesterol, 639 mg sodium, 10 g carbohydrate, 2 g fiber, 19 g protein. **Diabetic Exchanges:** 2-1/2 lean meat, 2 vegetable.

SUNRISE SOLUTION

Not only are fresh fruits delicious ways to start the day, but most are naturally sized right for one. The next time you need a simple morning treat, slice an orange or an apple and top it with flavored yogurt.

Breakfast Banana Splits

Yogurt Parfait

Jan Houberg • Reddick, Illinois

Beside being a popular breakfast or luncheon treat, this single-serving parfait makes a refreshing evening dessert.

Yogurt Parfait

✓ **Uses less fat, sugar or salt. Includes Nutrition Facts or Diabetic Exchanges.**

- **1** carton (6 ounces) flavored yogurt
- **1/4** cup granola
- **1/2** cup assorted fresh fruit

In a parfait glass or large glass mug, layer one-third of the yogurt, half of the granola and then half of the fruit. Repeat layers. Top with the remaining yogurt. **Yield:** 1 serving.

Nutrition Facts: 1 cup (prepared with reduced-fat, sugar-free yogurt) equals 209 calories, 5 g fat (0 saturated fat), 3 mg cholesterol, 171 mg sodium, 30 g carbohydrate, 0 fiber, 10 g protein. **Diabetic Exchanges:** 1 fat-free milk, 1 fat, 1/2 starch, 1/2 fruit.

Ham 'n' Cheese Crepes

Marion Lowery • Medford, Oregon

These thin pancakes are easy to freeze and thaw, so you can prepare a batch, enjoy a few and save the rest for another time.

- **1/3** cup cold water
- **1/3** cup plus 2 to 3 tablespoons milk, *divided*
- **1/2** cup all-purpose flour
- **1** egg
- **2** tablespoons butter, melted
- **1/8** teaspoon salt

ADDITIONAL INGREDIENTS
(for 4 crepes):
- **1** tablespoon Dijon mustard
- **4** thin slices deli ham
- **1/2** cup shredded cheddar cheese

In a blender, combine the water, 1/3 cup milk, flour, egg, butter and salt; cover and process until smooth. Refrigerate for at least 30 minutes; stir. Add remaining milk if batter is too thick.

Heat a lightly greased 8-in. skillet; add about 3 tablespoons batter. Lift and tilt pan to evenly coat bottom. Cook until top appears dry; turn and cook 15-20 seconds longer. Repeat with remaining batter, greasing skillet as needed. Stack four crepes with waxed paper in between; cover and freeze for up to 3 months.

Spread mustard over remaining crepes; top each with ham and cheese. Roll up tightly. Place in an 8-in. square baking dish coated with nonstick cooking spray. Bake, uncovered, at 375° for 10-14 minutes or until heated through.

To use frozen crepes: Thaw in the refrigerator for about 2 hours. Fill and bake as directed. **Yield:** 4 servings (8 crepes).

Cinnamon Pancake Cubes

Donna Bielenberg • Tabernash, Colorado

When I was young, my mother introduced our family to this delicious way to use up leftover pancakes. In fact, my father urged us not to eat all the pancakes in the morning so we could have these yummy cinnamon-and-sugar squares the next day.

1 tablespoon butter
2 to 3 pancakes (about 6 inches), cut into 1-inch pieces
1 tablespoon sugar
1/8 teaspoon ground cinnamon

In a skillet, melt butter. Add the pancakes, sugar and cinnamon. Cook over low heat until heated through, about 3 minutes. **Yield:** 2 servings.

Zucchini Frittata

Carol Blumenberg • Lehigh Acres, Florida

This recipe was always one of my family's favorites, and it remains so for my husband and me. When we plan a trip by car, I make the frittata the night before, stuff wedges into pita breads in the morning and microwave each one for a minute or two. Then I wrap them in plastic wrap, and we enjoy a still-warm breakfast on the road!

1/2 cup chopped onion
1 cup shredded zucchini
1 teaspoon vegetable oil
3 eggs, beaten
1/4 teaspoon salt
1 cup (4 ounces) shredded Swiss cheese

In an 8-in. ovenproof skillet over medium heat, saute onion and zucchini in oil for 2-3 minutes. Pour eggs over top; sprinkle with salt. Cook until almost set, about 6-7 minutes. Sprinkle with cheese. Bake at 350° for 4-5 minutes or until the cheese is melted. **Yield:** 2 servings.

Zucchini Frittata

Potato Pancakes

Ede Righetti • Hayward, California

Years ago, my grandson requested a special dish to be included in his class cookbook, and this is the recipe I gave him. It was his favorite whenever he ate at our house, so he was delighted. I often serve it as a morning side dish, but it's a good complement with any entree.

2 medium potatoes
1 egg
2 tablespoons all-purpose flour
1/2 teaspoon salt
1/4 teaspoon garlic salt
Vegetable oil

Peel the potatoes; shred and rinse in cold water. Drain thoroughly; place in a bowl. Add egg, flour, salt and garlic salt; mix well.

In a skillet over medium heat, heat 1/4 in. of oil. Pour batter by 1/4 cupfuls into hot oil. Fry for 5-6 minutes on each side or until potatoes are tender and pancakes are golden brown. Drain on paper towels. **Yield:** 2 servings.

Potato Pancakes

Mushroom Spinach Omelet

Arlene Hammonds • Gray, Tennessee

I lightened up this savory dish by using olive oil, one regular egg and three egg whites. For a change of pace, I like to mix in diced celery and parsley or try it with different cheeses.

✓ **Uses less fat, sugar or salt. Includes Nutrition Facts or Diabetic Exchanges.**

1 egg
3 egg whites
1 tablespoon grated Parmesan cheese
1 tablespoon shredded cheddar cheese
1/4 teaspoon salt
1/8 teaspoon crushed red pepper flakes
1/8 teaspoon garlic powder
1/8 teaspoon pepper
1/2 cup sliced fresh mushrooms
2 tablespoons finely chopped green pepper
1 tablespoon finely chopped onion
1/2 teaspoon olive oil
1 cup torn fresh spinach

In a small bowl, beat the egg and egg whites. Add cheeses, salt, pepper flakes, garlic powder and pepper; mix well. Set aside.

In an 8-in. nonstick skillet, saute the mushrooms, green pepper and onion in oil for 4-5 minutes or until tender. Add spinach; cook and stir until spinach is wilted. Add egg mixture. As eggs set, lift edges, letting uncooked portion flow underneath. Cut into wedges. Serve immediately. **Yield:** 2 servings.

Nutrition Facts: 1 serving equals 110 calories, 6 g fat (2 g saturated fat), 112 mg cholesterol, 489 mg sodium, 4 g carbohydrate, 1 g fiber, 11 g protein.
Diabetic Exchanges: 1-1/2 lean meat, 1 vegetable.

Southern Breakfast Skillet

James Newton • Minocqua, Wisconsin

I'd like to share a long tradition in our family. This was a special meal at my mother's table, and I cooked it for my seven children. Now they prepare it for their families. I'm glad this recipe was easy to adjust for the two of us. My wife and I enjoy it weekly.

1/4 pound sliced bacon, diced
1/4 cup chopped onion
  1 can (15-1/2 ounces) hominy, drained
  4 eggs, beaten
1/8 teaspoon pepper

In a skillet, cook bacon until almost crisp; drain. Add onion; continue cooking until bacon is crisp and onion is tender. Stir in hominy, eggs and pepper. Cook and stir until the eggs are completely set. **Yield:** 2 servings.

Toad in the Hole

Ruth Lechleiter • Breckenridge, Minnesota

This is one of the first recipes I had my children prepare when they were learning to cook. My little ones are now grown, but this continues to be a standby in my home and theirs.

1 slice of bread
1 teaspoon butter
1 egg
Salt and pepper to taste

Cut a 3-in. hole in the middle of the bread and discard the round. In a small skillet, melt the butter; place the bread in the skillet. Place egg in the hole. Cook for about 2 minutes over medium heat until the bread is lightly browned. Turn and cook the other side until egg reaches desired doneness. Season with salt and pepper. **Yield:** 1 serving.

Spiced Apricots

Trudy Barth • Niceville, Florida

I've been cooking for big gatherings for years...and now that I'm widowed, it's hard to cook for just one or two. That's why I appreciate simple recipes like this one, that turns canned apricots into a special side dish.

1 can (15 ounces) apricot halves
2 tablespoons cider vinegar
6 whole allspice
1 cinnamon stick (3 inches)

Drain apricots, reserving syrup. Set apricots aside. In a saucepan, combine the syrup, vinegar, allspice and cinnamon. Bring to a boil. Reduce heat; cover and simmer for 15 minutes. Remove from the heat; stir in apricots.

Cover and let stand for 30 minutes, stirring occasionally. Drain if desired. Serve warm or cold. **Yield:** 2 servings.

Spiced Apricots

Breakfast in a Mug

Susan Adair • Muncie, Indiana

Here's a great way to make a quick-and-easy breakfast for one. Not only does the flavorful dish cook in the microwave, but there's hardly anything to clean up!

2 eggs, beaten
2 to 3 tablespoons shredded cheddar cheese
2 tablespoons diced fully cooked ham
1 tablespoon diced green pepper
Salt and pepper to taste

In a microwave-safe mug coated with nonstick cooking spray, combine all ingredients. Microwave, uncovered, on high for 1 minute; stir. Cook 1 to 1-1/2 minutes longer or until eggs are completely set. **Yield:** 1 serving.

Cinnamon-Spice French Toast

Angela Sansom • New York, New York

Cinnamon and nutmeg give this French toast a tasty twist, which just goes to prove that breakfast for one can be fun!

1 egg
1/4 cup milk
1/2 teaspoon sugar
1/4 to 1/2 teaspoon ground cinnamon
1/8 teaspoon ground nutmeg
2 slices day-old whole wheat *or* white bread
2 teaspoons butter
Maple syrup

In a shallow bowl, beat egg, milk, sugar, cinnamon and nutmeg. Add bread, one slice at time, and soak both sides. Melt butter on a griddle over medium heat; cook bread until golden brown on both sides and cooked through. Serve with syrup. **Yield:** 1 serving.

Four-Berry Smoothies

Krista Johnson • Crosslake, Minnesota

This smoothie tastes even more scrumptious when I think of how much money I save by whipping up my own at home. As a breakfast, it keeps me satisfied and full of energy all morning. My husband and I appreciate the fact that it's nutritious, refreshing and fast.

✓ Uses less fat, sugar or salt. Includes Nutrition Facts or Diabetic Exchanges.

1-1/2 cups fat-free milk
1/2 cup frozen blackberries
1/2 cup frozen blueberries
1/2 cup frozen unsweetened raspberries
1/2 cup frozen unsweetened strawberries
2 tablespoons lemonade concentrate
1 tablespoon sugar
1/2 teaspoon vanilla extract

In a blender or food processor, combine all of the ingredients. Cover and process until smooth. Pour into glasses; serve immediately. **Yield:** 2 servings.

Nutrition Facts: One serving (1-1/2 cups) equals 172 calories, 1 g fat (1 g saturated fat), 4 mg cholesterol, 100 mg sodium, 36 g carbohydrate, 4 g fiber, 8 g protein. **Diabetic Exchanges:** 1-1/2 fruit, 1 fat-free milk.

Daddy's Omelet

Daddy's Omelet

Glenn Powell • Havana, Florida

*Omelets are one of my husband's specialties, and this fast-to-fix filling of
fresh-tasting vegetables adds a one-of-a-kind flavor we truly look forward to.*

1/4 cup *each* diced green pepper, onion and
mushrooms
  1 to 2 tablespoons butter
  2 eggs
1/8 teaspoon salt
Pinch pepper
1/4 cup shredded cheddar cheese

In an 8-in. skillet, saute green pepper, onion and
mushrooms in butter until tender. Remove with a
slotted spoon and set aside.

In a small bowl, beat eggs, salt and pepper.
Pour into the skillet. Cook over medium heat; as
eggs set, lift edges, letting uncooked portion flow
underneath. When the eggs are set, spoon vegetables and cheese over one side; fold omelet over
filling. Cover and let stand for 1-2 minutes or until
cheese is melted. **Yield:** 1 serving.

Hotcakes for a Pair
Zesty Poached Eggs

Hotcakes for a Pair

Annemarie Pietila • Farmington Hills, Michigan

You'll each get a hearty stack of pancakes with this down-home recipe!
The from-scratch, buttermilk flapjacks are always well received at the breakfast table.

1-1/4   cups all-purpose flour
1   tablespoon sugar
1   teaspoon baking powder
1/2   teaspoon baking soda
1/2   teaspoon salt
1-1/4   cups buttermilk
2   tablespoons vegetable oil
1   egg, beaten
1   cup fresh *or* frozen blueberries, optional

In a bowl, combine flour, sugar, baking powder, baking soda and salt. Combine buttermilk, oil and egg; stir into dry ingredients and mix well. Fold in blueberries if desired.

Pour batter by 1/4 cupfuls onto a lightly greased hot griddle; turn when bubbles form on top of pancakes. Cook until second side is golden brown. **Yield:** about 8 pancakes.

Zesty Poached Eggs

Kathy Scott • Hemingford, Nebraska

Here's a no-fuss favorite that's popular in my house. Loaded with
cheesy goodness, it's a delicious way to welcome the morning.

4   eggs, poached
2   slices whole wheat bread, toasted
1/4   cup process cheese sauce, melted
1/4   cup salsa

Place two eggs on each slice of toast. Top with cheese sauce and salsa. Serve immediately. **Yield:** 2 servings.

Deluxe Ham Omelet

Iola Egle • Bella Vista, Arkansas

Ham, vegetables and two cheeses are what make this omelet "deluxe." It's a satisfying morning main course
for one or two. Best of all, it's a great way to use up any leftover ham you might have in the refrigerator.

3   eggs
2   tablespoons half-and-half cream
2   tablespoons minced chives
1/2   teaspoon garlic salt
1/4   teaspoon pepper
1   tablespoon olive oil
1/2   cup finely chopped fully cooked ham
2   tablespoons chopped green pepper
2   tablespoons chopped tomato
2   fresh mushrooms, sliced
2   tablespoons shredded cheddar cheese
2   tablespoons shredded part-skim
mozzarella cheese

In a small bowl, beat the eggs, cream, chives, garlic salt and pepper. Heat oil in a large skillet over medium heat; add egg mixture. As eggs set, lift the edges, letting the uncooked portion flow underneath.

When the eggs are set, spoon the ham, green pepper, tomato, mushrooms and cheeses over one side; fold omelet over filling. Cover and let stand for 1-1/2 minutes or until cheese is melted. **Yield:** 1-2 servings.

SIZED-RIGHT SNACKS & BEVERAGES

Whether you're looking for something to munch on between meals, a savory hors d'oeuvre for a small dinner party or a satisfying late-night nibble, this chapter has you covered with plenty of appetizing options.

Deviled Eggs
p. 45

Cranberry Cooler
p. 45

Pesto Pita Appetizers
p. 46

Chocolate Marshmallow
Squares p. 41

Maple Walnut Fondue
p. 39

5-Minute Guacamole
Speedy Homemade Salsa

Speedy Homemade Salsa

Sarah Elizabeth Berger • Minneapolis, Minnesota

*I love Mexican food, and this refreshing salsa comes together in no time.
I think it tastes even better than the store-bought varieties, and there's never any leftovers.*

✓ Uses less fat, sugar or salt. Includes Nutrition Facts or Diabetic Exchanges.

- 1 can (14-1/2 ounces) whole tomatoes, drained
- 1/4 cup chopped red onion
- 1/4 cup chopped onion
- 1 jalapeno pepper, seeded
- 1 tablespoon cider vinegar
- 1 tablespoon minced fresh cilantro
- 1 garlic clove, peeled
- 1 teaspoon ground cumin
- 1/4 teaspoon salt

In a food processor, combine all ingredients; cover and process until chunky. Transfer to a small bowl. **Yield:** 1-1/3 cups.

Nutrition Facts: 1/3 cup equals 34 calories, trace fat (trace saturated fat), 0 cholesterol, 336 mg sodium, 7 g carbohydrate, 2 g fiber, 1 g protein. **Diabetic Exchange:** 1 vegetable.

Editor's Note: When cutting or seeding hot peppers, use rubber or plastic gloves to protect your hands. Avoid touching your face.

Bacon Cheese Stromboli

Abby Thompson • Madison Heights, Virginia

*Refrigerated pizza dough helps me speed up the preparation behind this bacon-filled stromboli.
Try the cheesy slices with sour cream for a hearty snack or even at lunch.*

- 1 tube (10 ounces) refrigerated pizza dough
- 3/4 cup shredded cheddar cheese
- 3/4 cup shredded part-skim mozzarella cheese
- 5 bacon strips, cooked and crumbled
- 1 jar (12 ounces) salsa

Sour cream, optional

On an ungreased baking sheet, roll the dough into a 12-in. circle. On half of dough, sprinkle cheeses and bacon to within 1/2 in. of edges. Fold dough over filling; pinch edges to seal.

Bake at 425° for 9-11 minutes or until golden brown. Serve with salsa and sour cream if desired. **Yield:** 4 servings.

5-Minute Guacamole

Sarah Elizabeth Berger • Minneapolis, Minnesota

This smooth avocado mix features salsa for a zesty dip that's excellent with chips.

✓ Uses less fat, sugar or salt. Includes Nutrition Facts or Diabetic Exchanges.

- 1 medium ripe avocado, peeled and cubed
- 1 tablespoon salsa
- 1 garlic clove, peeled
- 1/4 teaspoon salt

In a food processor, combine all ingredients; cover and process until smooth. Transfer to a small bowl; serve immediately. **Yield:** 3/4 cup.

Nutrition Facts: 2 tablespoons equals 53 calories, 5 g fat (1 g saturated fat), 0 cholesterol, 114 mg sodium, 2 g carbohydrate, 2 g fiber, 1 g protein. **Diabetic Exchange:** 1 fat.

Quesadilla

Amber Waddell • Grand Rapids, Michigan

This single-serving quesadilla is a snap to make. It is just as delicious whether you fill it with cooked and cubed chicken, turkey, pork or beef.

1 to 2 teaspoons vegetable oil
2 flour tortillas (6 inches)
1/2 cup shredded cheddar cheese, *divided*
1/2 cup cubed cooked chicken, turkey, pork *or* beef
1/4 cup sliced fresh mushrooms
1/2 cup shredded Monterey Jack cheese, *divided*
Sour cream and salsa, optional

Heat oil in a nonstick skillet; add one tortilla. Layer with half the cheddar cheese, all of the chicken and mushrooms and half the Monterey Jack cheese. Top with the second tortilla. Cover and heat until cheese melts and bottom tortilla is crisp and golden brown.

Turn over; sprinkle remaining cheese on top. Cook until bottom tortilla is crisp and golden brown and cheese is melted. Cut into wedges; serve with sour cream and salsa if desired. **Yield:** 1 serving.

Spicy Pinapple Spread

Mavis Diment • Marcus, Iowa

Want a snack that's both sweet and spicy? Try my one-of-a-kind spread. It features a mixture of warm preserves, zesty horseradish and mustard that you pour over cream cheese and serve with crackers.

1/4 cup apple jelly
1/4 cup pineapple preserves
4 to 5 teaspoons prepared horseradish
4 to 5 teaspoons ground mustard
1 package (8 ounces) cream cheese, softened
Assorted crackers

In a saucepan, combine jelly, preserves, horseradish and mustard. Cook and stir over medium-low heat until blended. Cover and refrigerate for 1 hour. Spoon over cream cheese. Serve with crackers. **Yield:** about 2/3 cup.

Salmon Puffs

Carolyn Moseley • Mount Pleasant, South Carolina

Convenient pastry shells turn salmon bits into an elegant, before-dinner appetizer. No one ever suspects how simple this comforting dish is to prepare.

2 frozen puff pastry shells *or* 2 slices toast
1/2 cup apricot preserves
1 tablespoon prepared horseradish
2 teaspoons cider vinegar
1 cup fully cooked salmon chunks *or* 1 can (7-1/2 ounces) salmon, drained, bones and skin removed

Bake pastry shells according to package directions. Meanwhile, combine the preserves, horseradish and vinegar in a saucepan. Cook over medium heat for 5 minutes or until heated through. Stir in salmon and heat through. Spoon into pastry shells or over toast; serve immediately. **Yield:** 2 servings.

Peachy Chicken Wings

Linda Walker • Dumfries, Virginia

I've been making small batches of these slightly sweet wings for 25 years, and folks still love them. The wings marinate overnight, then I bake them an hour before serving. The recipe is easy to double or triple when you're expecting a crowd.

2 tablespoons reduced-sodium soy sauce
2 tablespoons peach preserves
1-1/2 teaspoons lemon juice
1/4 teaspoon ground ginger
1/4 teaspoon minced garlic
8 chicken wingettes

In a large resealable plastic bag, combine the first five ingredients; add chicken wings. Seal bag and turn to coat; refrigerate for 8 hours or overnight.

Transfer wings to a 13-in. x 9-in. x 2-in. baking dish coated with nonstick cooking spray. Bake, uncovered, at 350° for 50-60 minutes or until chicken juices run clear, turning every 10 minutes. **Yield:** 2 servings.

Peachy Chicken Wings

Cheesy Zucchini Rounds

Taste of Home Test Kitchen • Greendale, Wisconsin

For a healthy alternative to high-calorie nachos, sprinkle zucchini slices with cheese, seasonings and bacon bits, then heat everything in the microwave. They're great for movie nights at home.

☑ **Uses less fat, sugar or salt. Includes Nutrition Facts or Diabetic Exchanges.**

1 medium zucchini, sliced
1/8 to 1/4 teaspoon dried basil
1/8 teaspoon onion powder
1/4 cup shredded reduced-fat cheddar cheese
1 bacon strip, cooked and crumbled
2 teaspoons grated Parmesan cheese

Place zucchini on a microwave-safe plate; sprinkle with basil and onion powder. Microwave, uncovered, on high for 1 minute or until hot. Sprinkle with the cheddar cheese, bacon and Parmesan cheese; microwave on high for 30-60 seconds or until cheese is melted. **Yield:** 2 servings.

Nutrition Facts: One serving equals 71 calories, 4 g fat (2 g saturated fat), 12 mg cholesterol, 240 mg sodium, 4 g carbohydrate, 1 g fiber, 7 g protein. **Diabetic Exchanges:** 1 lean meat, 1 vegetable.

Editor's Note: This recipe was tested in an 850-watt microwave.

Gingered Tea

Gingered Tea

Connie Lapp • Honey Brook, Pennsylvania

This is a wonderful tea to sip while you're home alone on a rainy day or when the chill of fall fills the air. It always gives me a boost of energy, plus its taste is so soothing.

1	cup water
2	teaspoons honey
3/4	teaspoon ground ginger
3	individual tea bags
3/4	cup milk

In a small saucepan, bring water to a boil. Add honey and ginger. Reduce heat; cover and simmer for 10 minutes. Remove from the heat; add tea bags.

Cover and steep for 5-7 minutes. Discard tea bags. Stir in milk; heat through (do not boil). **Yield:** 2 servings.

Parmesan Garlic Bread

Tracy Conley • Milwaukee, Wisconsin

I dress up ordinary French bread by topping it with butter, Parmesan cheese and seasonings. It's a quick side dish that complements most any meal. You can't stop after one slice.

1/4	cup butter, softened
1/4	cup olive oil
1/4	cup grated Parmesan cheese
2	garlic cloves
4	sprigs fresh parsley
1/2	teaspoon lemon-pepper seasoning
1	small loaf (8 ounces) French bread

In a mixing bowl or food processor, blend butter, oil and Parmesan cheese. Add garlic, parsley and lemon-pepper; mix or process until smooth.

Slice the bread on the diagonal but not all the way through, leaving slices attached at the bottom. Spread butter mixture on one side of each slice and over the top. Wrap in foil and bake at 400° for 15-20 minutes. **Yield:** 4 servings.

Maple Walnut Fondue

Angela Pohl • Marquette, Michigan

Sized right for a pair, this warm, praline-flavored mixture is great with cake cubes, strawberries, apple wedges and other delicious dippers.

1-1/2	teaspoons cornstarch
1/3	cup evaporated milk
1/4	cup maple syrup
3	tablespoons corn syrup
2	tablespoons finely chopped walnuts
1	tablespoon butter
1/4	teaspoon vanilla extract

Pound cake cubes and assorted fresh fruit

In a small saucepan, combine cornstarch and milk until smooth. Stir in maple syrup and corn syrup. Bring to a boil over medium heat; cook and stir for 2 minutes or until thickened. Remove from the heat.

Stir in walnuts, butter and vanilla. Transfer to a small fondue pot and keep warm. Serve with cake cubes and fruit. **Yield:** 1/2 cup.

Pepperoni Pizza Pita

Jeannette Derner • Newport News, Virginia

With its no-fuss pita crust, this pizza makes a small snack for two or even a quick meal for one. And if you're serving a family, the individual pizzas are perfect because everyone can choose their own toppings.

✓ Uses less fat, sugar or salt. Includes Nutrition Facts or Diabetic Exchanges.

2	tablespoons pizza sauce
1	whole pita bread (6 inches)
6	pepperoni slices
2	fresh mushrooms, sliced
1/4	cup shredded part-skim mozzarella cheese

Spread pizza sauce over pita bread. Top with pepperoni, mushrooms and cheese. Place on an ungreased baking sheet. Bake at 400° for 4-6 minutes or until the cheese is melted. **Yield:** 1 serving.

Nutrition Facts: One serving (prepared with turkey pepperoni) equals 275 calories, 6 g fat (3 g saturated fat), 25 mg cholesterol, 756 mg sodium, 38 g carbohydrate, 2 g fiber, 16 g protein. **Diabetic Exchanges:** 2 starch, 2 lean meat.

Granola Fruit Bars

Kim Finup • Kalamazoo, Michigan

We prefer these chewy wholesome treats to store-bought granola bars. They make a great anytime snack we like to keep on hand, particularly for grab-and-go breakfasts.

✓ **Uses less fat, sugar or salt. Includes Nutrition Facts or Diabetic Exchanges.**

- 1/2   cup chopped dried apples
- 1/3   cup honey
- 1/4   cup raisins
- 1   tablespoon brown sugar
- 1/3   cup reduced-fat peanut butter
- 1/4   cup apple butter
- 1/2   teaspoon ground cinnamon
- 1/2   cup old-fashioned oats
- 1/3   cup honey crunch *or* toasted wheat germ
- 1/4   cup chopped pecans
- 2-1/2   cups cornflakes

In a large saucepan, combine the apples, honey, raisins and brown sugar. Bring to a boil over medium heat, stirring often. Cook and stir 1 minute longer. Remove from the heat; stir in peanut butter until melted.

Add apple butter and cinnamon. Stir in the oats, wheat germ and pecans. Fold in cornflakes. Press firmly into an 8-in. square pan coated with nonstick cooking spray. Refrigerate for 1 hour or until set. Cut into bars. Store in an airtight container in the refrigerator. **Yield:** 8 bars.

Nutrition Facts: One bar equals 239 calories, 7 g fat (1 g saturated fat), 0 cholesterol, 160 mg sodium, 42 g carbohydrate, 3 g fiber, 6 g protein. **Diabetic Exchanges:** 2 fruit, 1 starch, 1 fat.

Editor's Note: This recipe was tested with commercially prepared apple butter.

Buttery Crab Bites

Buttery Crab Bites

Rebecca Young • Pleasant Hill, Missouri

These cheesy nibbles are easy but elegant. They're super as an hors d'oeuvre or even as a tasty, little snack.

- 2   English muffins, split
- 1/2   cup crabmeat, drained, flaked and cartilage removed
- 1/3   cup process cheese sauce
- 2   tablespoons butter, softened
- 1/2   teaspoon mayonnaise
- 1/8   teaspoon garlic powder

Paprika, optional

Toast English muffins in a toaster oven. Place muffin halves on toaster oven tray. In a small bowl, combine the crab, cheese sauce, butter, mayonnaise and garlic powder. Spread over the muffin halves. Cut each into four pieces.

Bake in toaster oven at 350° for 8-10 minutes or until lightly browned. Sprinkle with paprika if desired. **Yield:** 2 servings.

Old-Fashioned Chocolate Soda

Dawn Sams • Grayslake, Illinois

We enjoy making this classic soda fountain specialty at home. It's often requested by my grandchildren because they like to watch how the soda foams up as I prepare each glass.

6   tablespoons chocolate syrup
2   tablespoons whipped cream in a can
2-1/2   cups cold carbonated water
4   scoops ice cream of your choice
Additional whipped cream, optional

For each serving, place 3 tablespoons chocolate syrup in a 16-oz. glass. Stir in 1 tablespoon of whipped cream and 1-1/4 cups water until foamy. Add two scoops of ice cream. Top with additional whipped cream if desired. **Yield:** 2 servings.

Old-Fashioned Chocolate Soda

Walking Salad

Mrs. John Crawford • Barnesville, Georgia

This speedy stuffed apple is the perfect snack to take on a hike. In a brown-bag lunch, it's a nice change from the usual peanut butter and jelly sandwich.

2   tablespoons peanut butter
1   tablespoon raisins
1   teaspoon honey
1   medium apple, cored

In a small bowl, combine peanut butter, raisins and honey. Spoon into center of apple. **Yield:** 1 serving.

Chocolate Marshmallow Squares

Taste of Home Test Kitchen • Greendale, Wisconsin

You don't need to sit around the campfire to capture the popular taste of s'mores. Everyone will have fun covering the crackers with marshmallows, chocolate chips and ice cream topping.

8   whole graham crackers (about 5 inches x 2-1/2 inches)
1   cup miniature marshmallows
1/2   cup semisweet chocolate chips
2   tablespoons caramel *or* butterscotch ice cream topping

Place whole graham crackers 1 in. apart on a baking sheet. Top each cracker with marshmallows and chocolate chips. Drizzle with ice cream topping.
Bake at 350° for 5-7 minutes or until the marshmallows are puffed and the chips are slightly melted. Cool for 2-3 minutes before serving. **Yield:** 4 servings.

Chicken Croquettes

Carleen Mullins • Wise, Virginia

Here's a different recipe to try with leftover chicken. It has a terrific flavor that people seem to enjoy. The croquettes are fun to serve as an appetizer at friendly get-togethers.

2	tablespoons butter
3	tablespoons all-purpose flour
2	teaspoons ground mustard
1/4	teaspoon salt
1/8	teaspoon pepper
1	cup milk
2	cups chopped cooked chicken
1/4	cup chopped green pepper
1	tablespoon minced fresh parsley
1	tablespoon finely chopped onion
1	teaspoon lemon juice
1/4	teaspoon paprika
1/8	teaspoon cayenne pepper
1-1/2	cups dry bread crumbs
1	egg
2	tablespoons water

Oil for deep-fat frying

In a saucepan over medium heat, melt butter. Add flour, mustard, salt and pepper; stir until smooth. Gradually add milk; bring to a boil. Cook and stir for 2 minutes; remove from the heat.

Add chicken, green pepper, parsley, onion, lemon juice, paprika and cayenne; mix well. Refrigerate for at least 2 hours.

Shape into six 4-in. x 1-in. logs. Place bread crumbs in a shallow dish. In another dish, beat egg and water. Roll logs in bread crumbs, then in egg mixture, then again in crumbs.

Heat oil in an electric skillet or deep-fat fryer to 350°. Drop logs, a few at a time, into hot oil. Fry for 1-2 minutes on each side or until golden brown. Drain on paper towels. Serve immediately. **Yield:** 6 croquettes.

Chocolate Malts

Marion Lowery • Medford, Oregon

I can whip up this decadent, ice cream treat in just minutes. It's a favorite with kids of all ages, particularly after a day in the pool or at a hearty summer barbecue.

3/4	cup milk
1/2	cup caramel ice cream topping
2	cups chocolate ice cream, softened
3	tablespoons malted milk powder
2	tablespoons chopped pecans, optional

Grated chocolate, optional

In a blender, combine the first five ingredients; cover and process until blended. Pour into chilled glasses. Sprinkle with grated chocolate if desired. **Yield:** 2-1/2 cups.

TASTY TREAT FOR ONE

"For an easy snack, I freeze a container of yogurt, then let it thaw until just soft," says Lorelei Brashears of Hendersonville, North Carolina. "The result is just like sorbet! I like it as a topping for pound cake or Belgian waffles, too."

Chicken Croquettes

Greek Pizzas

Linda Lacek • Winter Park, Florida

Pita breads form quick crusts for these no-fuss, petite pizzas. Slice them into wedges for appetizers or enjoy them for lunch with a green salad and some fruit.

✓ Uses less fat, sugar or salt. Includes Nutrition Facts or Diabetic Exchanges.

2   whole pita breads (6 inches)
1   teaspoon olive oil, *divided*
4   cups torn fresh spinach
2   tablespoons chopped green onion
1   teaspoon minced fresh dill
4   tomato slices, halved
1/2 cup crumbled feta cheese
1/4 to 1/2 cup shredded part-skim mozzarella cheese
1/8 teaspoon dried oregano
1/8 teaspoon pepper

Place pita breads on a baking sheet. Brush each with 1/4 teaspoon oil. Broil 6 in. from the heat for 1-2 minutes or until lightly browned. Turn pitas over; brush with remaining oil. Broil 1-2 minutes longer.

In a microwave-safe dish, microwave spinach on high for 1 to 1-1/2 minutes or until wilted; drain well. Add onion and dill; mix well.

Top each pita with four tomato pieces, half of the spinach mixture and half of the cheeses. Sprinkle with oregano and pepper. Bake at 450° for 7-9 minutes or until cheese is lightly browned. **Yield:** 2 servings.

Nutrition Facts: One pizza (prepared with reduced-fat feta cheese and 1/4 cup part-skim mozzarella) equals 295 calories, 9 g fat (4 g saturated fat), 18 mg cholesterol, 810 mg sodium, 39 g carbohydrate, 4 g fiber, 17 g protein.

Fudgy Fruit Dip

Wilma Knobloch • Rock Rapids, Iowa

This rich, chocolaty dip is especially nice at holiday gatherings or served with fresh strawberries during the summer.

✓ Uses less fat, sugar or salt. Includes Nutrition Facts or Diabetic Exchanges.

1/3 cup fat-free sugar-free hot fudge topping
1/3 cup fat-free vanilla yogurt
1-1/2 teaspoons orange juice concentrate
Fresh strawberries

In a bowl, combine fudge topping, yogurt and orange juice concentrate. Cover and refrigerate for at least 30 minutes. Serve with strawberries. **Yield:** about 1/2 cup.

Nutrition Facts: One serving (2 tablespoons) equals 67 calories, 1 g fat (1 g saturated fat), 1 mg cholesterol, 32 mg sodium, 15 g carbohydrate, 1 g fiber, 1 g protein. **Diabetic Exchanges:** 1/2 starch, 1/2 fruit.

Fudgy Fruit Dip

Chocolate 'n' More Snack Mix

Karri Upchurch • Wichita, Kansas

With its nuts, sunflower kernels and dried fruits, this colorful snack mix tastes as good as it looks. Best of all, it makes a smaller yield than most such recipes, so I'm not stuck finding a place to store leftovers.

1	cup milk chocolate M&M's
1/2	cup semisweet chocolate chips
1/3	cup salted peanuts
1/4	cup raisins
1/4	cup dried banana chips, optional
2	tablespoons sunflower kernels

In a bowl, combine all of the ingredients. Store in an airtight container. **Yield:** about 2 cups.

Chocolate 'n' More Snack Mix

Cranberry Cooler

Carolyn Griffin • Macon, Georgia

I am a retired assistant luncheon manager for an elementary school. In addition to serving meals to the children, we were often called upon to create refreshments for school meetings and other occasions. Everyone always enjoyed this cranberry punch.

1	cup cranberry juice
1	cup pineapple juice
1/4	cup sugar
1/4	teaspoon almond extract
1-1/4	cups ginger ale, chilled

In a pitcher, combine the juices, sugar and extract. Stir until sugar is dissolved. Refrigerate for at least 2 hours. Just before serving, stir in ginger ale. **Yield:** 2 servings.

Deviled Eggs

Margaret Sanders • Indianapolis, Indiana

For variety, feel free to add some chopped, fresh herbs to the filling of these eggs. Or, experiment with the ingredients listed, increasing or decreasing the amounts to your personal taste.

6	hard-cooked eggs
2	tablespoons mayonnaise
1	teaspoon sugar
1	teaspoon white vinegar
1	teaspoon prepared mustard
1/2	teaspoon salt

Paprika

Slice eggs in half lengthwise; remove yolks and set whites aside. In a small bowl, mash yolks with a fork. Add the mayonnaise, sugar, vinegar, mustard and salt; mix well. Stuff or pipe into egg whites. Sprinkle with paprika. Refrigerate until serving. **Yield:** 6 servings.

Pesto Pita Appetizers

Lillian Julow • Gainesville, Florida

Bake these savory crisps the next time you're enjoying a creamy soup, chowder or even chili.

1   whole pita bread (6 inches)
3   tablespoons prepared pesto
3   tablespoons grated Parmesan cheese

Split pita bread into two rounds. Spread with pesto and sprinkle with cheese. Cut each into six wedges.
Place on an ungreased baking sheet. Bake at 350° for 10-12 minutes or until crisp. Serve warm. **Yield:** 2 servings.

Creamy Crab Spread

Norma Reynolds • York, Pennsylvania

This spread is so good that we never have extras. It's great for busy days because it's ready in a jiffy.

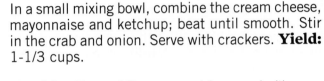 ✓ **Uses less fat, sugar or salt. Includes Nutrition Facts or Diabetic Exchanges.**

1   package (3 ounces) cream cheese, softened
1/4 cup mayonnaise
1   tablespoon ketchup
1   can (6 ounces) crabmeat, drained, flaked and cartilage removed
1   tablespoon grated onion

Assorted crackers

In a small mixing bowl, combine the cream cheese, mayonnaise and ketchup; beat until smooth. Stir in the crab and onion. Serve with crackers. **Yield:** 1-1/3 cups.

Nutrition Facts: 1/3 cup spread (prepared with reduced-fat cream cheese and fat-free mayonnaise) equals 111 calories, 5 g fat (3 g saturated fat), 54 mg cholesterol, 396 mg sodium, 4 g carbohydrate, trace fiber, 11 g protein.

Creamy Hot Cocoa

Creamy Hot Cocoa

Sara Swyers • Fayetteville, Georgia

Hot cocoa made school days memorable for me. Mom had it ready when I came home, and it was always a part of our special time together. The warm sipper is not overly sweet, but it's oh, so comforting.

4   teaspoons sugar
2   teaspoons baking cocoa
1-1/3 cups boiling water
2/3 cup evaporated milk
1/4 teaspoon vanilla extract
2   tablespoons marshmallow creme

Divide sugar, cocoa and water between two mugs; stir until dissolved. Stir in milk, vanilla and marshmallow creme; mix well. Serve immediately. **Yield:** 2 servings.

Smoked Salmon Spread

Smoked Salmon Spread

Judith Mason • Bismarck, North Dakota

We're empty nesters now, and I've been experimenting to downsize recipes. This is a favorite. You can mix together the tasty topper in just 5 minutes, then pop it in the fridge a few hours before snacktime.

☑ Uses less fat, sugar or salt. Includes Nutrition Facts or Diabetic Exchanges.

3   ounces reduced-fat cream cheese
1-1/2   teaspoons lemon juice
1   can (6 ounces) boneless skinless salmon, drained
2   tablespoons finely chopped onion
1/2   teaspoon prepared horseradish
1/4   teaspoon Liquid Smoke
Assorted crackers

In a small mixing bowl, beat cream cheese and lemon juice until fluffy. Stir in the salmon, onion, horseradish and Liquid Smoke until blended. Cover and refrigerate for at least 2 hours. Serve with crackers. Refrigerate leftovers. **Yield:** 3/4 cup.

Nutrition Facts: 2 tablespoons (calculated without crackers) equals 70 calories, 4 g fat (2 g saturated fat), 28 mg cholesterol, 155 mg sodium, 1 g carbohydrate, trace fiber, 9 g protein. **Diabetic Exchanges:** 1 lean meat, 1/2 fat.

SALADS & SANDWICHES

For no-fuss convenience, few things beat a crisp salad alongside a well-stacked sandwich. Stop here the next time you need a smart spinach salad, creamy pasta creation, refreshing wrap or crusty sub sandwich.

Spinach Turkey Wraps
p. 56

Tangy Potato Salad
p. 54

Greens with Mustard
Vinaigrette p. 69

Cheese Steak Subs
p. 50

Ranch-Style Pork Burgers
p. 60

Cheese Steak Subs

Taste of Home Test Kitchen • Greendale, Wisconsin

I like to stack peppers, onions and cheese over thin slices of roast beef for this satisfying sandwich. Along with some potato salad or frozen French fries, it's a great supper or hearty lunch.

1/2 cup julienned sweet red pepper
1/2 cup julienned green pepper
1/2 cup sliced onion
1/2 teaspoon vegetable oil
  2 slices part-skim mozzarella cheese
  4 ounces thinly sliced deli roast beef
  2 submarine sandwich buns, split

In a small skillet, saute the peppers and onion in oil until tender. Cut cheese slices in half. Place beef and cheese on the bottom of each bun. Broil 4 in. from the heat for 1-2 minutes or until cheese is melted. Top with pepper mixture and bun tops. **Yield:** 2 servings.

Warm Spinach Salad

Helen Ward O'Key • Torrington, Connecticut

In addition to being a yummy salad, this side dish is one of my favorites to have for lunch. It makes just the right amount for two.

  2 onion slices, separated into rings
1/4 teaspoon garlic powder
  1 tablespoon butter
  1 cup sliced fresh mushrooms
  4 cups torn fresh spinach
Salt to taste
  2 tablespoons raspberry vinaigrette
    or vinaigrette of your choice
1/2 cup salad croutons

In a skillet, saute onion and garlic powder in butter until onion is tender. Add mushrooms; cover and cook for 1 minute or until tender. Add spinach; sprinkle with salt and vinaigrette. Cover and cook for 1 minute or until spinach is wilted. Serve warm with croutons. **Yield:** 2 servings.

Apple-Herb Club Sandwiches

Taste of Home Test Kitchen • Greendale, Wisconsin

Sliced apple and a dill spread give these club-style sandwiches a boost of flavor. Filled with turkey, ham and cheese, they're perfect for a hungry twosome.

1/4 teaspoon dried tarragon
1/4 teaspoon dried thyme
1/8 teaspoon dill weed
  2 tablespoons mayonnaise
1/8 teaspoon lemon juice
  4 slices rye bread
  4 thin slices deli turkey
1/2 cup thinly sliced peeled tart apple
  4 slices Colby-Monterey Jack cheese
  4 thin slices deli ham
  2 lettuce leaves
  2 teaspoons prepared mustard

In a spice grinder or with a mortar and pestle, grind the tarragon, thyme and dill until mixture becomes a fine powder. Transfer to a small bowl; add the mayonnaise and lemon juice. Spread on two slices of bread. Layer each with turkey, apple, cheese, ham and lettuce. Spread mustard on remaining bread; place over lettuce. **Yield:** 2 servings.

Grilled Chicken
Pasta Salad

Grilled Chicken Pasta Salad

Leanne Royce • Appleton, Wisconsin

*My local supermarket deli carried a great pasta salad but kept the recipe a secret.
I was determined to duplicate it at home and created this delightful version for two.*

✓ Uses less fat, sugar or salt. Includes Nutrition Facts
or Diabetic Exchanges.

1   cup uncooked rigatoni *or* large tube
     pasta
1   boneless skinless chicken breast half
     (6 ounces)
1/4 teaspoon lemon-pepper seasoning
1   cup fresh broccoli florets
1/4 cup chopped sweet red pepper
1/4 cup chopped red onion
1/4 cup Parmesan peppercorn ranch salad
     dressing
1   tablespoon grated Parmesan cheese
1-1/2 teaspoons lemon juice

Cook pasta according to package directions.
Meanwhile, sprinkle the chicken with lemon-
pepper. Coat grill rack with nonstick cooking spray
before starting the grill. Grill chicken, covered,
over medium heat for 7-8 minutes on each side or
until juices run clear. Cut into 1-in. cubes.
   Drain pasta. In a bowl, combine the pasta,
chicken, broccoli, red pepper, red onion, salad
dressing, Parmesan cheese and lemon juice; toss
to coat. Serve immediately or cover and refrigerate until serving. **Yield:** 2 servings.

Nutrition Facts: One serving: 1-1/2 cups (prepared
with fat-free salad dressing) equals 300 calories, 4 g fat
(1 g saturated fat), 49 mg cholesterol, 488 mg sodium,
42 g carbohydrate, 4 g fiber, 24 g protein.

Southwest Pork and Bean Salad

Southwest Pork and Bean Salad

Lynn Biscott • Toronto, Ontario

This cool salad is very tasty on its own, but we also like it as a filling in tacos or tortillas for a hearty lunch.

✓ Uses less fat, sugar or salt. Includes Nutrition Facts or Diabetic Exchanges.

1 cup cubed cooked pork
1/2 medium sweet red pepper, chopped
3/4 cup frozen corn, thawed
1/2 cup canned kidney beans, rinsed and drained
1/4 cup chopped green onions
2 tablespoons balsamic vinegar
1 tablespoon water
1 tablespoon olive oil
1 garlic clove, minced
1/4 teaspoon salt
1/4 teaspoon pepper

1/4 teaspoon hot pepper sauce
Lettuce leaves, optional

In a small bowl, combine the first five ingredients. In another bowl, whisk the vinegar, water, oil, garlic, salt, pepper and hot pepper sauce. Pour over pork mixture and toss to coat. Cover and refrigerate for at least 30 minutes. Serve on lettuce-lined plates if desired. **Yield:** 2 servings.

Nutrition Facts: 1-1/4 cups equals 336 calories, 14 g fat (3 g saturated fat), 63 mg cholesterol, 453 mg sodium, 29 g carbohydrate, 6 g fiber, 26 g protein. **Diabetic Exchanges:** 3 lean meat, 2 vegetable, 1 starch, 1 fat.

Mini Orange Gelatin Molds

Taste of Home Test Kitchen • Greendale, Wisconsin

These pretty, layered gelatin molds use half a package of gelatin.
Save the other half for use in another downsized dessert.

✓ Uses less fat, sugar or salt. Includes Nutrition Facts or Diabetic Exchanges.

3 tablespoons plus 1 teaspoon orange gelatin
1/3 cup boiling water
1/2 cup cold water
1 can (11 ounces) mandarin oranges, drained
1 package (3 ounces) cream cheese, softened
1/2 cup whipped topping, *divided*

In a small bowl, dissolve gelatin in boiling water. Stir in cold water. Set aside 3 tablespoons gelatin at room temperature. Cover and refrigerate remaining gelatin for 30 minutes or until partially set.

Set aside six mandarin oranges for garnish and pat dry. Fold the remaining oranges into partially set gelatin. Divide between two individual fluted tube pans coated with nonstick cooking spray; cover and refrigerate for 30 minutes or until firm.

In a small mixing bowl, beat the cream cheese, 1/4 cup whipped topping and reserved gelatin until smooth. Carefully spread over gelatin molds. Refrigerate for 1 hour or until set. Invert molds onto a plate; garnish with remaining whipped topping and reserved oranges. **Yield:** 2 servings.

Nutrition Facts: 1 serving (prepared with 1-3/4 teaspoons sugar-free gelatin, reduced-fat cream cheese and reduced-fat whipped topping) equals 224 calories, 11 g fat (8 g saturated fat), 30 mg cholesterol, 235 mg sodium, 22 g carbohydrate, 0 fiber, 6 g protein.

Italian Sausage and Peppers

Claire Arrico • Portsmouth, Rhode Island

My mother used to make these full-flavored subs regularly and I can see why. They are easy and convenient, thanks to the purchased spaghetti sauce the recipe calls for.

2 Italian sausage links, casings removed
1 small onion, chopped
1 medium green pepper, cut into 3/4-inch chunks
1 medium sweet red pepper, cut into 3/4-inch chunks
1-1/4 cups spaghetti sauce
1-1/2 teaspoons sugar
1/4 teaspoon garlic powder
1/4 teaspoon onion powder
1/4 teaspoon dried oregano
1/4 teaspoon dried parsley flakes
2 Italian sandwich rolls *or* submarine buns, split

Cut sausage into 3/4-in. pieces. In a skillet, cook sausage and onion over medium heat until sausage is browned; drain. Stir in the peppers, spaghetti sauce, sugar, garlic powder, onion powder, oregano and parsley.

Place in a greased 1-qt. baking dish. Bake, uncovered, at 350° for 50-60 minutes or until sausage and peppers are tender, stirring every 20 minutes. Serve on rolls. **Yield:** 2 servings.

Tangy Potato Salad

Ruth Towle • Belmont, New Hampshire

I downsized a recipe to come up with this creamy picnic favorite that serves just two. My sister visits often, and this is one of our favorite dishes to enjoy together...especially with chicken and green beans.

✓ Uses less fat, sugar or salt. Includes Nutrition Facts or Diabetic Exchanges.

2 medium potatoes, peeled
1/2 teaspoon cider vinegar
2 tablespoons diced sweet red pepper
2 tablespoons frozen peas, thawed
2 tablespoons chopped cucumber
1 tablespoon finely chopped onion
1/3 cup mayonnaise
1/3 cup sour cream
1/2 teaspoon prepared horseradish
1/8 teaspoon salt
1/8 teaspoon pepper

Place potatoes in a small saucepan and cover with water. Bring to a boil. Reduce heat; cover and cook for 15-20 minutes or until tender. Drain. Sprinkle with vinegar.

When potatoes are cool enough to handle, cube and place in a small bowl. Add the red pepper, peas, cucumber and onion; toss gently to combine. In a small bowl, combine the mayonnaise, sour cream, horseradish, salt and pepper. Pour over potato mixture and toss to coat. Cover and refrigerate until serving. **Yield:** 2 servings.

Nutrition Facts: 1 cup (prepared with fat-free mayonnaise and reduced-fat sour cream) equals 204 calories, 5 g fat (3 g saturated fat), 18 mg cholesterol, 515 mg sodium, 36 g carbohydrate, 4 g fiber, 6 g protein.

NEXT-DAY DISH

Don't know what to do with a leftover piece of fish? Follow Jean DeGennaro's lead. She flakes extra fish over a bed of greens tossed with tomatoes, sliced cucumber and a vinaigrette in her North Haven, Connecticut home.

Sourdough Cheeseburgers

Sourdough Cheeseburgers

Michelle Dommel • Quakertown, Pennsylvania

Here's a mouth-watering cheeseburger that's as fast as it is juicy.
I came up with it one night when I realized I ran out of hamburger buns.
My husband loved the toasty crunch of the sourdough bread.

3   tablespoons mayonnaise
1   tablespoon ketchup
1   tablespoon sweet pickle relish
1/2   pound ground beef
Salt and pepper to taste
1   small onion, sliced and separated into rings
4   tablespoons butter, *divided*
4   slices sourdough bread
4   slices Swiss cheese

In a small bowl, combine the mayonnaise, ketchup and relish; cover and refrigerate.

Shape beef into two oval patties. In a large skillet, cook burgers over medium heat for 4-5 minutes on each side or until a meat thermometer reads 160°. Season with salt and pepper; remove and keep warm. In the same skillet, saute onion in 1 tablespoon butter until tender. Remove and keep warm.

Using 2 tablespoons butter, butter one side of each slice of bread. Melt remaining butter in the skillet. Place bread, buttered side up, in the skillet; cook for 2-3 minutes or until golden brown. Turn; top two of the bread slices with the cheese. Cook 2 minutes longer or until cheese is melted.

To serve, place toast, cheese side up, on a plate. Top with a burger, relish mixture, onion and remaining toast. **Yield:** 2 servings.

Spinach Turkey Wraps

Trixie Ferguson • Bennett, Colorado

Since getting married, I have been learning to pare down recipes for the two of us...and I have created a few small-size dishes such as these wraps. Cream cheese makes them a bit more filling than you'd expect.

1/4 cup spreadable chive and onion cream cheese
 2 flour tortillas (8 inches)
1/4 teaspoon garlic powder
 2 cups loosely packed fresh baby spinach
 5 ounces thinly sliced deli turkey
1/2 to 1 cup shredded Monterey Jack cheese
3/4 cup julienned sweet red pepper
1/4 cup chopped green onions
 2 tablespoons prepared ranch salad dressing

Spread 2 tablespoons of cream cheese over each tortilla. Sprinkle with garlic powder. Layer each with 3/4 cup spinach, turkey, cheese, red pepper and onions. Top with remaining spinach. Drizzle with dressing.

Roll up tightly jelly-roll style; wrap in plastic wrap. Refrigerate until serving. **Yield:** 2 servings.

Watermelon Grape Salad

Watermelon Grape Salad

Sue Gronholz • Beaver Dam, Wisconsin

This salad is easy to make and it also tastes great. I recommend it on a summer day when watermelon is at its best, or serve it with lemon sherbet for an easy, change-of-pace dessert.

✓ Uses less fat, sugar or salt. Includes Nutrition Facts or Diabetic Exchanges.

 1 cup cubed seeded watermelon
 1 cup seedless red grapes
 2 tablespoons white grape juice
1/2 teaspoon finely chopped fresh tarragon
1/2 teaspoon honey

In a small bowl, combine watermelon and grapes. In another bowl, whisk the grape juice, tarragon and honey. Pour over fruit and toss to coat. Serve immediately. **Yield:** 2 servings.

Nutrition Facts: 1 cup equals 92 calories, trace fat (trace saturated fat), 0 cholesterol, 5 mg sodium, 25 g carbohydrate, 1 g fiber, 1 g protein. **Diabetic Exchange:** 1-1/2 fruit.

Chocolate Fluffernutter Sandwiches

Taste of Home Test Kitchen • Greendale, Wisconsin

These fun sandwiches will be met with smiles when they're served with sliced bananas and a glass of milk for lunch. Kids of all ages gobble them up!

1/4   cup chunky peanut butter
4   thick slices white bread
1   tablespoon chocolate syrup
1/4   cup marshmallow creme

Spread peanut butter on two slices of bread. Drizzle with chocolate syrup; spread with marshmallow creme. Top with remaining bread. **Yield:** 2 servings.

Chocolate Fluffernutter Sandwiches

Chicken Strip Salad

Clara Coulston • Washington Court House, Ohio

Filled with chicken and good-for-you vegetables, this salad is coated in a tangy balsamic-and-mustard dressing. As a variation, you can try using turkey tenderloins and arugula instead of the chicken and mixed greens.

✓ Uses less fat, sugar or salt. Includes Nutrition Facts or Diabetic Exchanges.

6   ounces boneless skinless chicken breast, cut into thin strips
1/8   teaspoon salt
1/8   teaspoon pepper
1/4   cup chicken broth
3-1/2   cups torn mixed salad greens
1/4   cup sliced fresh mushrooms
1/4   cup chopped red onion
1   small carrot, julienned

DRESSING:
2   tablespoons balsamic vinegar
1   tablespoon water
1   tablespoon canola oil
1-1/2   teaspoons Dijon mustard
1/4   teaspoon sugar
1/8   teaspoon salt
1/8   teaspoon pepper

Sprinkle chicken with salt and pepper. In a small skillet, cook and stir chicken in broth for 4-6 minutes or until no longer pink. Meanwhile, in a bowl, combine the salad greens, mushrooms, onion and carrot.

In a jar with a tight-fitting lid, combine the dressing ingredients; shake well. Drizzle over salad and toss to coat. Divide between two serving plates; top with chicken. Serve immediately. **Yield:** 2 servings.

Nutrition Facts: 1 serving equals 209 calories, 10 g fat (1 g saturated fat), 47 mg cholesterol, 585 mg sodium, 11 g carbohydrate, 3 g fiber, 20 g protein.
Diabetic Exchanges: 3 very lean meat, 2 vegetable, 1 fat.

Egg Salad English Muffins

Egg Salad English Muffins

Deborah Flora • Sawyer, Kansas

These toasty breakfast muffins help you get a jump-start on brisk autumn mornings. I make the egg salad ahead of time, then assemble them as needed. They're also good with leftover ham piled on top.

3	hard-cooked eggs
1/4	cup mayonnaise
1/4	teaspoon prepared mustard
2	English muffins, split and toasted
4	slices Canadian bacon
1/4	cup shredded cheddar cheese

In a bowl, combine the eggs, mayonnaise and mustard. Place English muffins cut side up on an ungreased baking sheet. Top each with a slice of Canadian bacon, 1/4 cup egg mixture and cheddar cheese. Bake at 350° for 6-8 minutes or until cheese is melted. **Yield:** 2 servings.

Warm Tuna Pita Pockets

Marge Nicol • Shannon, Illinois

I like to tuck this cheesy tuna filling into a warm pita pocket for a fun, grab-and-go lunch. The celery is a nice addition.

1	can (6 ounces) water-packed tuna, drained and flaked
1/2	cup shredded cheddar cheese
1/3	cup chopped celery
2	tablespoons chopped onion
1/4	cup mayonnaise
1	pita bread (6 inches), halved

In a small bowl, combine the tuna, cheese, celery, onion and mayonnaise. Spoon into pita halves. Place on an ungreased baking sheet. Bake at 400° for 8-10 minutes or until heated through and cheese is melted. **Yield:** 2 servings.

Marinated Mushroom Salad

Dorothy Pritchett • Wills Point, Texas

These mushrooms get their flavor from a special vinaigrette made with Dijon mustard, vinegar and herbs. It's a tart medley that really complements the flavor of the mushrooms.

✓ Uses less fat, sugar or salt. Includes Nutrition Facts or Diabetic Exchanges.

1	tablespoon white wine vinegar
1	tablespoon Dijon mustard
1/4	teaspoon dried oregano
1/4	teaspoon dried tarragon
1/8	teaspoon salt
1/8	teaspoon pepper
2	to 4 tablespoons olive oil
1-1/2	cups sliced fresh mushrooms
1/2	cup cherry tomatoes, halved
8	pitted ripe olives, halved
	Lettuce leaves

In a small bowl, combine the first six ingredients. Gradually whisk in oil until blended. Add the mushrooms, tomatoes and olives; toss to coat. Cover and refrigerate for 2 hours. Serve in a lettuce-lined bowl. **Yield:** 2 servings.

Nutrition Facts: 1 cup (prepared with 2 tablespoons oil) equals 176 calories, 16 g fat (2 g saturated fat), 0 cholesterol, 497 mg sodium, 7 g carbohydrate, 2 g fiber, 3 g protein.

Ranch-Style Pork Burgers

Kathleen Benner • Williamsville, Illinois

We use our grill all year, and this recipe is quick and easy enough for busy weeknights. I think you'll agree that the hefty burgers make a nice alternative to ground beef, and the ranch salad dressing really punches up the flavor.

1/2	pound ground pork
1	tablespoon ranch salad dressing mix
1	teaspoon dried minced onion
1/4	teaspoon pepper
2	slices Swiss cheese
2	hamburger buns, split

Lettuce leaves and tomato slices, optional

In a small bowl, combine the pork, dressing mix, onion and pepper. Shape into two patties. Grill, uncovered, over medium heat for 7-8 minutes on each side or until a meat thermometer reads 160°.

Top each patty with a cheese slice; cover and grill just until cheese begins to melt. Serve on buns with lettuce and tomato if desired. **Yield:** 2 servings.

Old-Fashioned Egg Salad Sandwiches

Linda Braun • Park Ridge, Illinois

Here's a pared-down version of a longtime staple. You can also add a little cream cheese to the recipe for an extra-creamy sandwich if you'd like.

1/4	cup mayonnaise
2	teaspoons lemon juice
1	teaspoon dried minced onion
1/4	teaspoon salt
1/4	teaspoon pepper
6	hard-cooked eggs, chopped
1/2	cup finely chopped celery

Lettuce leaves *or* bread

In a large bowl, combine the mayonnaise, lemon juice, onion, salt and pepper. Stir in eggs and celery. Cover and refrigerate.

For each serving, spoon about 1/2 cup onto a lettuce leaf or spread on bread. **Yield:** 3 servings.

Speedy Steak Sandwiches

Ruth Page • Hillsborough, North Carolina

You can each enjoy two of these meaty, open-faced sandwiches. Toasted to perfection under the broiler, the warm bites are a great way to chase the chill as the temperature drops outside.

4	slices French bread (3/4 inch thick)

Butter, softened

Prepared mustard

1/2	pound uncooked lean ground beef
1/4	cup milk
1	tablespoon minced onion
1	tablespoon steak sauce
1/2	teaspoon garlic salt
1/4	teaspoon pepper

In a broiler, toast one side of the bread. Spread untoasted sides with butter and mustard.

In a small bowl, combine remaining ingredients; spread evenly over buttered side of bread. Broil 6 in. from the heat for 5-7 minutes or until beef is no longer pink. **Yield:** 2 servings.

Pineapple Turkey Salad

Stephanie Bremson • Kansas City, Missouri

It never ceases to amaze me what you can do with a fresh pineapple!

2 teaspoons canola oil, *divided*
1 teaspoon minced fresh gingerroot
1 garlic clove, minced
1 turkey breast tenderloin (1/2 pound), cut into 1/2-inch slices
1 cup fresh cauliflowerets
1/2 medium sweet red pepper, chopped
3 green onions, sliced
1 fresh pineapple
2 cups chopped fresh spinach
2 tablespoons apricot nectar
1 tablespoon white wine vinegar
1/4 teaspoon pepper

In a large nonstick skillet, heat 1 teaspoon oil, ginger and garlic. Add turkey; stir-fry for 8-10 minutes or until no longer pink. Remove turkey and keep warm. Add remaining oil to the skillet; stir-fry cauliflower for 3 minutes. Add red pepper and onions; stir-fry 1 minute longer.

Cut pineapple in half and remove fruit, leaving 1-in. shells; set shells aside for serving. Cut fruit into cubes; set aside 1-1/2 cups (refrigerate remaining pineapple for another use). In a large bowl, combine the turkey, vegetables, spinach and reserved pineapple. In a small bowl, whisk the apricot nectar, vinegar and pepper; add to turkey salad and toss to coat. Serve in pineapple shells. **Yield:** 2 servings.

Pineapple Turkey Salad

Peanut Slaw

Edie Farm • Farmington, New Mexico

To dress up everyday coleslaw, I add a little bit of a crunch with cucumber, peanuts and celery. I then sprinkle some Parmesan cheese over the top for extra flavor.

✓ **Uses less fat, sugar or salt. Includes Nutrition Facts or Diabetic Exchanges.**

1	cup shredded cabbage
1/4	cup thinly sliced celery
1/4	cup chopped cucumber
2	tablespoons chopped green onion
2	tablespoons chopped green pepper
2	tablespoons mayonnaise
2	tablespoons sour cream
1/8	teaspoon salt, optional
2	tablespoons chopped salted peanuts
4	teaspoons grated Parmesan cheese

In small bowl, combine the cabbage, celery, cucumber, onion and green pepper. In another bowl, combine the mayonnaise, sour cream and salt if desired. Top with peanuts and Parmesan cheese. **Yield:** 2 servings.

Nutrition Facts: 3/4 cup (prepared with fat-free mayonnaise and reduced-fat sour cream) equals 119 calories, 8 g fat (2 g saturated fat), 12 mg cholesterol, 251 mg sodium, 9 g carbohydrate, 3 g fiber, 5 g protein.

Barbecue Ham Sandwiches

Constance Eddy • Fogelsville, Pennsylvania

The tangy sauce for these ham sandwiches freezes well and is even better when it's reheated. It's great on hot dogs, too! You can also fix it ahead...and keep it warm in the slow cooker if you make a larger amount for a picnic or party.

1/4	cup chopped celery
2	tablespoons chopped onion
2	teaspoons butter
2/3	cup reduced-sodium tomato juice
4-1/2	teaspoons ketchup
1	tablespoon brown sugar
2	teaspoons lemon juice
1	teaspoon Worcestershire sauce
1	teaspoon prepared mustard
1	to 2 drops hot pepper sauce
1-1/2	teaspoons cornstarch
1	tablespoon water

1/4	pound shaved lean deli ham
2	sandwich rolls, toasted

In a small saucepan, saute celery and onion in butter. Add the tomato juice, ketchup, brown sugar, lemon juice, Worcestershire sauce, mustard and hot pepper sauce. Bring to a boil. Reduce heat; simmer, uncovered, for 5 minutes.

Combine the cornstarch and water until smooth; stir into tomato mixture. Bring to a boil; cook and stir for 1 minute or until thickened. Add ham; stir until coated. Cook 5 minutes longer or until heated through. Serve on rolls. **Yield:** 2 servings.

LIGHT LUNCH

In Grass Valley, California, Susan Allen creates a healthy, no-stress lunch by topping rice cakes with tuna salad. "You can also use chicken salad," she notes. "It's a refreshing bite!"

Peanut Slaw
Barbecue Ham Sandwiches

Toasted Swiss Deli Sandwich

Carol Bradley • Sun City West, Arizona

Paired with a salad or soup, this chicken and ham sandwich makes a tasty lunch.
It's really simple because it takes advantage of deli meats.

1   **to 2 tablespoons butter, softened**
2   **slices whole wheat bread**
1   **tablespoon sour cream**
2   **slices Swiss cheese**
1   **thick slice deli chicken breast**
1   **slice deli ham**

Spread butter over one side of each slice of bread. Spread sour cream over unbuttered sides. On one slice, layer one piece of cheese, chicken, ham and remaining cheese; top with remaining bread, buttered side up. In a small skillet, toast sandwich over medium heat until bread is lightly browned on each side. **Yield:** 1 serving.

Grilled Cheese with Tomato

Tricia Curley • Joliet, Illinois

Featuring mozzarella, tomato slices, oregano and basil, this skillet sandwich puts
an Italian twist on lunch time. Sizzle one up and see for yourself.

1   **tablespoon butter, softened**
2   **slices Italian bread**
1/3 **cup shredded part-skim mozzarella cheese**
2   **slices tomato**
1/4 **to 1/2 teaspoon dried oregano**
1/4 **to 1/2 teaspoon dried basil**

Spread butter on one side of each slice of bread. Place one slice, butter side down, in a skillet; top with half of the cheese. Layer with tomato and remaining cheese; sprinkle with oregano and basil. Top with remaining bread, butter side up. Cook over medium heat until golden brown on both sides. **Yield:** 1 serving.

Grilled Cheese with Tomato

Cheesy BLT Salad

Cheesy BLT Salad

Maxine Wheeler • Columbus, Indiana

"Frank's Salad" is what this was called at a cafe that my husband and I often visited when we were just out of college. With little money for entertainment or dining out, we enjoyed it regularly. This homemade version has remained a favorite of ours.

3	cups torn mixed salad greens
8	cherry tomatoes, halved
6	bacon strips, cooked and crumbled
3	tablespoons chopped sweet pickles
1/4	cup cubed Monterey Jack cheese
1/4	cup mayonnaise
1/2	cup French salad dressing

In a salad bowl, toss the greens, tomatoes, bacon, pickles and cheese. In a small bowl or pitcher, combine mayonnaise and French dressing; serve with the salad. **Yield:** 2 servings.

Fruited Chicken Lettuce Salad

Margaret Wilson • Hemet, California

*Here's a colorful yet simple salad that's super on warm days.
To speed up the preparation, I like to use bagged lettuce greens.*

1-1/2	cups torn salad greens
1	package (6 ounces) ready-to-serve grilled chicken breast strips
1/3	cup julienned sweet red *or* yellow pepper
1/3	cup sliced fresh peach
1/3	cup fresh raspberries
1/3	cup fresh blueberries

DRESSING:

2	tablespoons olive oil
4	teaspoons lime juice
1-1/2	teaspoons honey
1	tablespoon minced fresh cilantro
1/4	teaspoon ground cumin
1/8	teaspoon salt
1/8	teaspoon garlic powder

Dash pepper

In a large bowl, combine salad greens, chicken, red pepper and fruit. In a jar with a tight-fitting lid, combine dressing ingredients; shake well. Pour over salad; toss to coat. **Yield:** 2 servings.

Fruited Chicken Lettuce Salad

Crunchy Chicken Salad

Crunchy Chicken Salad

Margaret McNeil • Germantown, Tennessee

Water chestnuts and pecans dress up this creamy chicken salad as well as adding a welcomed crunch to each bite. It looks especially pretty nestled on a bed of lettuce leaves, but it also makes a fun sandwich filling.

✓ Uses less fat, sugar or salt. Includes Nutrition Facts or Diabetic Exchanges.

1-1/2	cups cubed cooked chicken
3	tablespoons chopped celery
3	tablespoons mayonnaise
2	tablespoons chopped water chestnuts
4	teaspoons sweet pickle relish
4	teaspoons diced pimientos, drained
1	tablespoon chopped pecans
1/4	teaspoon salt
1/8	teaspoon pepper
2	lettuce leaves
1	hard-cooked egg, sliced

In a bowl, combine the first nine ingredients. Serve on lettuce-lined plates. Garnish with egg slices. **Yield:** 2 servings.

Nutrition Facts: 1 cup (prepared with fat-free mayonnaise) equals 304 calories, 14 g fat (3 g saturated fat), 202 mg cholesterol, 692 mg sodium, 10 g carbohydrate, 2 g fiber, 34 g protein.

Tuna Patty Sandwiches

Ruth Wimmer • Bland, Virginia

Here's a tasty way to dress up canned tuna for a warm sandwich you'll want time and again. The patties are a snap to make, too.

1	egg
1/2	teaspoon prepared mustard
1/4	cup dry bread crumbs
1	can (6 ounces) tuna, drained and flaked
1	tablespoon vegetable oil
2	sandwich rolls, split

In a bowl, combine the egg, mustard, bread crumbs and tuna; mix well. Shape into four patties (mixture will be soft). In a skillet over medium heat, fry patties in oil on both sides until lightly browned. Place two patties on each roll. **Yield:** 2 servings.

Greens with Mustard Vinaigrette

Shirley Glaab • Hattiesburg, Mississippi

You only need a handful of items to toss together this delightful dressing. A bit of apple juice gives it a lovely flavor that's perfect with the mixed greens of your choice.

1	tablespoon olive oil
2	teaspoons apple juice
1	teaspoon red wine vinegar
1/2	to 1 teaspoon lemon juice
1/2	teaspoon Dijon mustard
1	cup torn mixed salad greens

Tomato wedges

In a small bowl, combine oil, apple juice, vinegar, lemon juice and mustard; mix well. Serve over greens and tomatoes. **Yield:** 1 serving.

Summer Squash Salad

Lois Gelzer • Oak Bluffs, Massachusetts

I'm so glad that my mother shared this five-ingredient recipe with me. It is very colorful, and it's a great way to use up whatever squash you may have on hand.

☑ **Uses less fat, sugar or salt. Includes Nutrition Facts or Diabetic Exchanges.**

- 2 cups torn Boston lettuce
- 1/3 cup thinly sliced zucchini
- 1/3 cup thinly sliced yellow summer squash
- 3 radishes, sliced
- 1/4 cup reduced-fat Italian salad dressing

In a bowl, toss the lettuce, zucchini, yellow squash and radishes and serve with dressing. **Yield:** 2 servings.

Nutrition Facts: 1 cup equals 67 calories, 5 g fat (trace saturated fat), trace cholesterol, 233 mg sodium, 5 g carbohydrate, 2 g fiber, 2 g protein. **Diabetic Exchanges:** 1 vegetable, 1 fat.

Sausage Sloppy Joes

Dixie Terry • Marion, Illinois

I came up with this barbecued burger recipe using pork sausage when I ran out of ground beef one night. It's one of our grandkids' favorites, and my husband likes it, too.

- 1/2 pound bulk pork sausage
- 1/3 cup chopped onion
- 1/2 cup tomato sauce
- 1/4 cup water
- 2 tablespoons ketchup
- 1-1/2 teaspoons Worcestershire sauce
- Dash to 1/8 teaspoon hot pepper sauce
- 2 hamburger buns, split

In a skillet, cook sausage and onion over medium heat until meat is no longer pink; drain. Stir in tomato sauce, water, ketchup, Worcestershire sauce and hot pepper sauce. Bring to a boil. Reduce heat; cover and simmer for 30 minutes. Serve on buns. **Yield:** 2 servings.

Cold Vermicelli Salad

Susan Miller • West, Texas

This recipe makes a light lunch for a pair on a hot day, but it can easily be increased for a potluck. I like to make it a day ahead so the flavors have time to blend.

☑ **Uses less fat, sugar or salt. Includes Nutrition Facts or Diabetic Exchanges.**

- 1 cup cooked vermicelli
- 1/4 cup chopped green pepper
- 1/4 cup chopped green onions
- 1/4 cup pickled whole mushrooms, sliced
- 1/4 cup fat-free Italian salad dressing
- 2 tablespoons sliced ripe olives
- 1 tablespoon diced pimientos
- 1 teaspoon Salad Supreme Seasoning

In a serving bowl, combine all of the ingredients; toss to coat. Cover and refrigerate for at least 4 hours. **Yield:** 2 servings.

Nutrition Facts: 3/4 cup equals 144 calories, 2 g fat (trace saturated fat), 1 mg cholesterol, 628 mg sodium, 27 g carbohydrate, 3 g fiber, 5 g protein. **Diabetic Exchanges:** 2 vegetable, 1 starch.

Editor's Note: This recipe was tested with McCormick's Salad Supreme Seasoning. Look for it in the spice aisle of your grocery store.

Meatball Sub Sandwiches

Meatball Sub Sandwiches

Kim Marie Van Rheenen • Mendota, Illinois

These heartwarming sandwiches are terrific for weekends and watching football games. I simmer the meatballs in a tangy barbecue sauce rather than the traditional Italian red sauce to give them a little bit more flair than expected.

2	submarine buns (about 6 inches)
1/2	pound lean ground beef
2	tablespoons beaten egg
2	tablespoons milk
1	teaspoon diced onion
1/8	teaspoon salt

Dash pepper

1/2	medium green pepper, julienned
1/4	cup sliced onion
2	teaspoons canola oil
1	teaspoon all-purpose flour
1/3	cup chili sauce
1/3	cup water
1	teaspoon brown sugar
1/4	teaspoon ground mustard

Cut a thin slice off the top of each bun; scoop out bread from inside. Cover buns and tops with plastic wrap; set aside. Crumble 1/3 cup of the removed bread and place in a bowl. Add the beef, egg, milk, diced onion, salt and pepper; mix well. Shape into eight meatballs, about 1-1/2 in. each.

In a nonstick skillet, cook meatballs for 15-20 minutes or until no longer pink. Remove with a slotted spoon; set aside. In the same skillet, saute green pepper and sliced onion in oil until tender. Remove with a slotted spoon; set aside. Stir flour into skillet. Add chili sauce and water. Bring to a boil; cook and stir for 1-2 minutes.

Stir in brown sugar and mustard. Add meatballs, green pepper and onion; cover and simmer for 15 minutes. Meanwhile, warm buns at 325° for 8-10 minutes. Spoon meatballs and sauce into buns; replace tops. **Yield:** 2 servings.

Soup's On!

Few things chase cold-weather chills like a steaming bowl of soup. Even seasoned cooks, however, can feel intimidated by paring down a soup recipe that feeds a crowd. Featuring the comforting flavor you expect, all of the recipes in this chapter are perfect for small households. Old-fashioned chicken noodle soup, beefy chili and hearty seafood chowders are just some of the satisfying varieties you'll turn to time and again.

Beefy Mushroom Soup
p. 90

Two-Potato Soup
p. 87

Flavorful Italian Soup
p. 84

Pretty Pepper Soup
p. 91

Autumn Chowder
p. 75

Southwestern Bean Soup

Southwestern Bean Soup

Grace Nordang • Methow, Washington

My daughter gave me this hearty soup recipe, and I'm glad she did—it's become
a household staple. You can't beat it on a cold winter day!

4	bacon strips
3/4	cup chopped onion
3/4	cup chopped celery
1/8	teaspoon garlic powder
1	can (16 ounces) refried beans
1/4	cup picante sauce *or* salsa
1	can (14-1/2 ounces) chicken broth
1	tablespoon chopped fresh parsley

Hot pepper sauce, optional
Shredded cheddar cheese
Tortilla chips

In a medium saucepan, cook bacon until crisp; remove to paper towel to drain. Crumble and set aside. In the drippings, saute the onion and celery; sprinkle with the garlic powder. Cover and simmer for 10 minutes or until vegetables are tender.

Add beans, picante sauce, broth, parsley and bacon; bring to a boil. Reduce heat and simmer, uncovered, for 5-10 minutes. Season to taste with hot pepper sauce if desired. Ladle into bowls and top with cheese. Serve with tortilla chips. **Yield:** 4 servings.

Autumn Chowder

Sheena Hoffman • North Vancouver, British Columbia

When the weather gets chilly, we enjoy comfort foods like this hearty chowder. It's easy
to prepare, and the aroma of it as it simmers makes my mouth water.

2	bacon strips, diced
1/4	cup chopped onion
1	medium red potato, diced
1	small carrot, halved lengthwise and thinly sliced
1/2	cup water
3/4	teaspoon chicken bouillon granules
1	cup milk
2/3	cup frozen corn
1/8	teaspoon pepper
2-1/2	teaspoons all-purpose flour
2	tablespoons cold water
3/4	cup shredded cheddar cheese

In a saucepan, cook bacon over medium heat until crisp; remove to paper towels. Drain, reserving 1 teaspoon drippings. In the drippings, saute onion until tender. Add the potato, carrot, water and bouillon. Bring to a boil. Reduce heat; cover and simmer for 15-20 minutes or until the vegetables are almost tender.

Stir in the milk, corn and pepper. Cook 5 minutes longer. Combine the flour and cold water until smooth; gradually whisk into soup. Bring to a boil; cook and stir for 1-2 minutes or until thickened. Remove from the heat; stir in cheese until melted. Sprinkle with bacon. **Yield:** 2 servings.

FREEZING FOODS

Hot food must be allowed to cool to room temperature before it is frozen. Once it's cool, freeze it immediately. Be sure to set items in the freezer in a single layer and then stack them once they are frozen solid.

Kielbasa Potato Soup

Beverlee Deberry • Hempstead, Texas

This is a delicious soup recipe. Combined with a nice, crusty loaf of French bread, it's a complete and satisfying meal. It's become a classic at our house.

Kielbasa Potato Soup

1   medium leek (white portion only), halved and sliced
1   tablespoon butter
1-3/4   cups chicken broth
1   medium potato, peeled and diced
1/3   pound fully cooked kielbasa *or* Polish sausage, cut into bite-size pieces
1/4   cup heavy whipping cream
1/8   teaspoon *each* caraway and cumin seeds, toasted
1/3   cup thinly sliced fresh spinach

In a large saucepan, saute leek in butter until tender. Add broth and potato; bring to a boil. Reduce heat; cover and simmer for 15-20 minutes or until potato is tender.

Stir in the sausage, cream caraway and cumin; heat through (do not boil). Just before serving, add the spinach. **Yield:** 2 servings.

Red Pepper Shrimp Bisque

Stephanie Buttars • Phoenix, Arizona

Here's a bisque that goes nicely with a steak and salad. It's also a tasty way to use up any extra cooked shrimp you might have.

1   cup chicken broth
1   jar (7 ounces) roasted sweet red peppers, drained
1/2   teaspoon sugar
1/2   teaspoon paprika
1   cup coarsely chopped cooked shrimp (6 ounces)
1/2   cup heavy whipping cream
1/4   cup grated Romano cheese, *divided*
1/4   teaspoon salt
1/8   teaspoon pepper
Dash hot pepper sauce

In a small saucepan, bring broth and roasted peppers to a boil. Reduce heat; cover and simmer for 5 minutes. Remove from the heat and cool slightly.

Transfer to a blender or food processor; cover and process until pureed. Return to the saucepan. Add sugar and paprika; bring to a boil. Reduce heat; simmer, uncovered, for 5 minutes. Add the shrimp, cream, 2 tablespoons cheese, salt, pepper and hot pepper sauce. Cook and stir for 2 minutes or until heated through. Garnish with remaining cheese. **Yield:** 2 servings.

Creamy Chicken Corn Chowder

Terrie Sowders • Carthage, Indiana

My 10-year-old son and I devised the recipe for this comforting chowder. Now it's one of our favorites.

1 cup chicken broth
2/3 cup cubed peeled potato
1/2 cup frozen corn
1/4 teaspoon minced garlic
1/8 teaspoon dried marjoram
1/8 teaspoon dried thyme
1/8 teaspoon pepper
2 tablespoons all-purpose flour
2/3 cup milk

2 ounces process cheese (Velveeta), cubed
2/3 cup cubed cooked chicken breast

In a large saucepan, combine the broth, potato, corn, garlic, marjoram, thyme and pepper. Bring to a boil. Reduce heat; cover and simmer for 15-20 minutes or until potatoes are tender.

Combine flour and milk until smooth; gradually add to vegetable mixture. Bring to a boil; cook and stir for 2 minutes or until slightly thickened. Reduce heat; stir in cheese until melted. Add the chicken; heat through. **Yield:** 2 servings.

Creamy Chicken Corn Chowder

Creamy Asparagus Soup

Adele Long • Sterling Heights, Michigan

Perfect for spring, asparagus is pureed to a smooth and creamy texture in this soup that's nicely seasoned with thyme. I bet it will please any asparagus lovers in your home.

✓ Uses less fat, sugar or salt. Includes Nutrition Facts or Diabetic Exchanges.

- 2 green onions, chopped
- 1 garlic clove, minced
- 1 tablespoon butter
- 2 cans (14-1/2 ounces *each*) reduced-sodium chicken broth *or* vegetable broth
- 1 pound fresh asparagus, trimmed and cut into 1-inch pieces
- 1/2 teaspoon salt
- 1/2 to 3/4 teaspoon dried thyme
- 1/8 teaspoon pepper
- 1 bay leaf
- 2 tablespoons all-purpose flour
- 3 tablespoons water
- 1/4 cup reduced-fat sour cream
- 1 teaspoon grated lemon peel

In a large saucepan, saute onions and garlic in butter. Add the broth, asparagus, salt, thyme, pepper and bay leaf. Bring to a boil. Reduce heat; cover and simmer for 8-10 minutes or until asparagus is tender. Drain asparagus, reserving cooking liquid. Discard bay leaf. Cool slightly.

In a food processor, combine asparagus and 1/2 cup cooking liquid; cover and process until smooth. Return pureed asparagus and remaining cooking liquid to pan.

Combine the flour and water until smooth; stir into soup. Bring to a boil; cook and stir for 1-2 minutes or until thickened. Garnish each serving with sour cream and lemon peel. **Yield:** 4 servings.

Nutrition Facts: 1 cup soup (calculated with 1 tablespoon sour cream) equals 107 calories, 4 g fat (3 g saturated fat), 13 mg cholesterol, 876 mg sodium, 11 g carbohydrate, 3 g fiber, 7 g protein. **Diabetic Exchanges:** 1 vegetable, 1 fat, 1/2 starch.

Cream of Spinach Soup

Cream of Spinach Soup

Patricia Bradley • Rohnert Park, California

This rich delight tastes like it's made by a professional chef. You can prepare it with frozen spinach or drain a can of spinach if you have that on hand.

- 1 package (1.8 ounces) leek soup and dip mix
- 1 package (10 ounces) frozen leaf spinach, thawed, drained and chopped
- 1 cup (8 ounces) sour cream
- 1/4 teaspoon ground nutmeg

Lemon slices

Prepare soup mix according to package directions. Stir in spinach. Cover and simmer for 2 minutes. Remove from the heat; stir in sour cream and nutmeg. Garnish with lemon slices. **Yield:** 4 servings.

Grandma's Tomato Soup

Gerri Sysun • Narragansett, Rhode Island

This recipe is my grandmother's. Originally Gram even made the tomato juice in it from scratch! Every time I return to Massachusetts for a visit home, Gram has this soup simmering on the stove. She's always loved to cook and still enjoys making tomato soup and other favorite dishes.

Grandma's Tomato Soup

2	tablespoons butter
1	tablespoon all-purpose flour
2	cups tomato juice
1/2	cup water
2	tablespoons sugar
1/8	teaspoon salt
3/4	cup cooked wide egg noodles

In a saucepan over medium heat, melt butter. Add flour; stir to form a smooth paste. Gradually add tomato juice and water, stirring constantly; bring to a boil. Cook and stir for 2 minutes or until thickened. Add sugar and salt. Stir in egg noodles and heat through. **Yield:** 2 servings.

Soup for Two

Margery Bryan • Royal City, Washington

Comforting and colorful, this soup is loaded with old-fashioned goodness. The flavorful broth is chock-full of chicken and macaroni, and by changing the vegetables, you can make it different every time.

✓ Uses less fat, sugar or salt. Includes Nutrition Facts or Diabetic Exchanges.

1/2	cup chopped onion
1/2	cup chopped carrot
1	tablespoon butter
1	can (14-1/2 ounces) chicken broth
2/3	cup cubed cooked chicken
1/2	cup cauliflowerets
1/2	cup canned kidney beans, rinsed and drained
1/4	cup uncooked elbow macaroni
1	cup torn fresh spinach
1/8	teaspoon pepper

Seasoned salad croutons, optional

In a saucepan, saute onion and carrot in butter for 4 minutes. Stir in the broth, chicken, cauliflower, beans and macaroni. Bring to a boil. Reduce heat; cover and simmer for 15-20 minutes or until macaroni and vegetables are tender. Add spinach and pepper; cook and stir until spinach is wilted. Garnish with croutons if desired. **Yield:** 2 servings.

Nutrition Facts: One 1-1/2-cup serving (calculated without croutons) equals 263 calories, 7 g fat (4 g saturated fat), 48 mg cholesterol, 888 mg sodium, 28 g carbohydrate, 5 g fiber, 22 g protein. **Diabetic Exchanges:** 2 lean meat, 1-1/2 starch, 1 vegetable.

Florentine Chicken Soup

Cindie Henf • Sebastian, Florida

My husband loves Alfredo sauce, so I'm always looking for new variations.
This easy-to-make soup is wonderful with Italian bread and a
tomato-mozzarella salad. Best of all, it's the perfect amount for a small household.

✓ **Uses less fat, sugar or salt. Includes Nutrition Facts or Diabetic Exchanges.**

- 1 cup uncooked penne pasta
- 1 package (6 ounces) ready-to-use chicken breast cuts
- 4 cups chopped fresh spinach
- 1 jar (7-1/4 ounces) roasted sweet red peppers, drained and sliced
- 3 fresh rosemary sprigs, chopped
- 1/2 teaspoon garlic powder
- 1/4 teaspoon pepper
- 1 tablespoon butter
- 1-1/2 cups reduced-sodium chicken broth
- 3/4 cup Alfredo sauce
- 3 tablespoons prepared pesto
- 2 tablespoons pine nuts, toasted
- 1 tablespoon shredded Parmesan cheese

Cook pasta according to package directions. Meanwhile, in a large saucepan, saute the chicken, spinach, red peppers, rosemary, garlic powder and pepper in butter until spinach is wilted.

Stir in the broth, Alfredo sauce and pesto; cook for 4-5 minutes or until heated through. Drain pasta and add to the soup. Garnish with pine nuts and Parmesan cheese. **Yield:** 5 cups.

Nutrition Facts: 1 cup equals 275 calories, 14 g fat (6 g saturated fat), 44 mg cholesterol, 865 mg sodium, 21 g carbohydrate, 2 g fiber, 17 g protein. **Diabetic Exchanges:** 2 lean meat, 1-1/2 fat, 1 starch, 1 vegetable.

Mexican Shrimp Bisque

Karen Harris • Castle Rock, Colorado

I enjoy both Cajun and Mexican cuisine, and this rich, elegant soup combines the best of both worlds.
I serve it with a crispy green salad and glass of white wine for a simple but special meal.

- 1/2 cup chopped onion
- 2 garlic cloves, minced
- 1 tablespoon olive oil
- 1 tablespoon all-purpose flour
- 1 cup water
- 1/2 cup heavy whipping cream
- 1 tablespoon chili powder
- 2 teaspoons chicken bouillon granules
- 1/2 teaspoon ground cumin
- 1/2 teaspoon ground coriander
- 1/2 pound uncooked medium shrimp, peeled and deveined
- 1/2 cup sour cream

Fresh cilantro and cubed avocado, optional

In a large saucepan, saute onion and garlic in oil until tender. Stir in flour until blended. Stir in the water, cream, chili powder, bouillon, cumin and coriander; bring to a boil. Reduce heat; cover and simmer for 5 minutes.

Cut shrimp into bite-size pieces; add to soup. Simmer 5 minutes longer or until shrimp turn pink. Gradually stir 1/2 cup hot soup into sour cream; return all to the pan, stirring constantly. Heat through (do not boil). Garnish with cilantro and avocado if desired. **Yield:** 3 cups.

Florentine Chicken Soup
Mexican Shrimp Bisque

Creamy Wild Rice Soup

Creamy Wild Rice Soup

Marilyn Ausland • Columbus, Georgia

My husband and I consider this our favorite soup.
Featuring ham, mushrooms and a garnish of almonds, it's a heartwarming treat.

✓ Uses less fat, sugar or salt. Includes Nutrition Facts or Diabetic Exchanges.

1/4   cup chopped onion
1/4   cup thinly sliced celery
1/4   cup sliced fresh mushrooms
  1   green onion, thinly sliced
1/4   cup reduced-fat butter
1/4   cup all-purpose flour
1/8   teaspoon pepper
  1   can (14-1/2 ounces) reduced-sodium chicken broth
  1   cup cooked wild rice
1/4   cup diced fully cooked lean ham
1-1/2   teaspoons diced pimientos

1/2   cup fat-free half-and-half
  1   tablespoon sliced almonds, toasted, optional

In a saucepan, saute the onion, celery, mushrooms and green onion in butter until tender. Stir in the flour and pepper until blended. Gradually stir in broth. Bring to a boil; cook and stir for 1-2 minutes or until thickened.

Reduce heat. Stir in the rice, ham and pimientos; heat through. Stir in half-and-half; heat through (do not boil). Sprinkle with almonds if desired. **Yield:** 3 servings.

Nutrition Facts: 1 cup equals 221 calories, 9 g fat (6 g saturated fat), 30 mg cholesterol, 640 mg sodium, 27 g carbohydrate, 2 g fiber, 11 g protein. **Diabetic Exchanges:** 1-1/2 starch, 1 lean meat, 1 fat.

Creamy Vegetable Soup

Valerie Jones • Portland, Maine

Loaded with carrots, celery and potatoes, this blended soup makes a great first course for a special meal.

☑ **Uses less fat, sugar or salt. Includes Nutrition Facts or Diabetic Exchanges.**

3	cups thinly sliced carrots
1	cup chopped onion
2/3	cup chopped celery
1-1/2	cups diced peeled potatoes
1	garlic clove, minced
1/2	teaspoon sugar
2	teaspoons vegetable oil
4	cups chicken broth

Dash ground nutmeg

Pepper to taste

In a Dutch oven or soup kettle over medium-low heat, saute carrots, onion, celery, potatoes, garlic and sugar in oil for 5 minutes. Add broth, nutmeg and pepper; bring to a boil. Reduce heat; cover and simmer for 30-40 minutes or until vegetables are tender.

Remove from the heat and cool to room temperature. Puree in batches in a blender or food processor. Return to the kettle and heat through. **Yield:** 4 servings.

Nutrition Facts: One serving (prepared with reduced-sodium chicken broth) equals 136 calories, 3 g fat (0 saturated fat), 0 cholesterol, 116 mg sodium, 23 g carbohydrate, 0 fiber, 5 g protein. **Diabetic Exchanges:** 2 vegetable, 1 starch, 1/2 fat.

Hearty Hamburger Soup

Diane Mrozinski • Essexville, Michigan

When I served this soup to my family the first time, I got a thumbs-up from everyone. You can substitute ground turkey for the beef, if you like, and easily double or triple the recipe to serve more people.

1/4	pound ground beef
1/4	cup chopped onion
1-1/2	cups water
1/4	cup thinly sliced carrot
1-1/2	teaspoons beef bouillon granules
1	can (5-1/2 ounces) V8 juice
1/4	cup frozen corn
1/4	cup frozen peas
1/4	cup sliced fresh mushrooms
1/4	cup sliced zucchini
1/8	teaspoon dried basil

Dash pepper

1/2	cup cooked elbow macaroni

Hearty Hamburger Soup

In a small saucepan, cook beef and onion over medium heat until meat is no longer pink; drain. Add water, carrot and bouillon. Bring to a boil. Reduce heat; simmer, uncovered, for 5 minutes. Add the V8 juice, corn, peas, mushrooms, zucchini, basil and pepper. Simmer 6-8 minutes longer or until vegetables are tender. Add macaroni; heat through. **Yield:** 2 servings.

Chili for Two

Norma Grogg • St. Louis, Missouri

Not only is this chili thick and hearty, but it makes a very small batch. I enjoy it with a grapefruit and avocado salad.

Chili for Two

1/4	pound ground beef
1/4	cup chopped onion
1	garlic clove, minced
1	can (15-1/2 ounces) chili beans, undrained
1	can (14-1/2 ounces) diced tomatoes, undrained
1-1/2	teaspoons chili powder
1/2	teaspoon ground cumin

In a saucepan, cook beef, onion and garlic over medium heat until meat is no longer pink; drain. Stir in the remaining ingredients; bring to a boil. Reduce heat; cover and simmer for 10-15 minutes or until heated through. **Yield:** 2 servings.

Flavorful Italian Soup

Shirley Taylor • Russiaville, Indiana

I first tasted a soup similar to this at a restaurant. They wouldn't give me the recipe, so I went home and created my own. I like to serve the spicy soup with biscuits, breadsticks or corn bread.

✓ Uses less fat, sugar or salt. Includes Nutrition Facts or Diabetic Exchanges.

1	Italian sausage link, casing removed
1	can (14-1/2 ounces) chicken broth
1/2	cup water
1/2	cup cubed peeled potatoes
1/4	cup chopped carrot
1/4	cup chopped onion
1/4	cup canned sliced mushrooms
1/4	teaspoon dried basil
1/8	teaspoon Italian seasoning
1/8	to 1/4 teaspoon hot pepper sauce

Dash celery seed

Dash garlic salt

1/3	cup broken uncooked spaghetti (2-inch pieces)

Crumble sausage into a large saucepan; cook over medium heat until no longer pink. Drain. Add the broth, water, vegetables and seasonings; bring to a boil. Reduce heat; cover and simmer for 30 minutes.

Add spaghetti. Cover and simmer 8-10 minutes longer or until spaghetti and vegetables are tender. **Yield:** 2 servings.

Nutrition Facts: 1-1/2 cups (prepared with turkey Italian sausage and reduced-sodium chicken broth) equals 213 calories, 7 g fat (2 g saturated fat), 29 mg cholesterol, 571 mg sodium, 25 g carbohydrate, 3 g fiber, 14 g protein.

Dilly Tomato Soup

Patty Kile • Greentown, Pennsylvania

This soup is particularly good to take along for lunch with a sandwich or salad.
Most often, I make the recipe ahead and keep it in the fridge for myself.

✓ **Uses less fat, sugar or salt. Includes Nutrition Facts or Diabetic Exchanges.**

1	small onion, thinly sliced
1/4	teaspoon minced garlic
1	tablespoon canola oil
1	teaspoon butter
2	medium tomatoes, sliced
1	teaspoon sugar
1/4	teaspoon salt

Dash pepper

1/3	cup tomato paste
2	tablespoons all-purpose flour
1-1/4	cups cold water, *divided*
1/3	cup fat-free half-and-half
1	to 2 teaspoons minced fresh dill

In a small saucepan, cook onion and garlic in oil and butter over low heat until tender. Add the tomatoes, sugar, salt and pepper; cook over medium-high heat for 3 minutes. Remove from the heat; stir in tomato paste.

Combine flour and 1/4 cup of water until smooth; stir into tomato mixture. Gradually stir in remaining water until smooth. Bring to a boil; cook and stir for 2 minutes.

Place a sieve over a bowl; pour tomato mixture into sieve. Press with the back of a spoon to remove tomato seeds and skin. Return puree to pan. Add half-and-half and dill; cook over low heat just until heated through (do not boil). **Yield:** 2 servings.

Nutrition Facts: 1 cup equals 224 calories, 10 g fat (2 g saturated fat), 5 mg cholesterol, 393 mg sodium, 30 g carbohydrate, 4 g fiber, 5 g protein. **Diabetic Exchanges:** 2 vegetable, 2 fat, 1 starch.

Pantry-Shelf Salmon Chowder

Kathryn Awe • International Falls, Minnesota

I always joke that if you can open a can, you can prepare this comforting chowder! It takes mere minutes to make but tastes like you fussed a lot longer.

1	small onion, thinly sliced
1	tablespoon butter
1	can (10-3/4 ounces) condensed cream of celery soup, undiluted
1-1/3	cups milk
1	can (7-1/2 ounces) salmon, drained, bones and skin removed
1	can (15 ounces) cream-style corn
1	tablespoon minced fresh parsley

In a large saucepan, saute onion in butter until tender. Stir in remaining ingredients; heat through. **Yield:** 4 servings.

Pantry-Shelf Salmon Chowder

Mixed Vegetable Soup

Mixed Vegetable Soup

Lucille Franck • Independence, Iowa

*My sister, who worked as a dietitian for years, gave me this recipe.
I sometimes double or triple the hearty soup when my family gathers for the holidays.*

✓ **Uses less fat, sugar or salt. Includes Nutrition Facts or Diabetic Exchanges.**

- 1/2 small carrot, grated
- 1/2 celery rib, chopped
- 2 tablespoons chopped green pepper
- 1 tablespoon chopped onion
- 1 tablespoon butter
- 1 cup reduced-sodium chicken broth
- 1 can (14-1/2 ounces) diced tomatoes, undrained
- 3/4 teaspoon sugar

Dash pepper

- 1-1/2 teaspoons cornstarch

In a small saucepan, saute the carrot, celery, green pepper and onion in butter until tender. Set aside 2 tablespoons broth. Add the tomatoes, sugar, pepper and remaining broth to vegetable mixture; bring to a boil. Reduce heat; cover and simmer for 10 minutes.

Combine cornstarch and reserved broth until smooth; gradually add to the soup. Bring to a boil; cook and stir for 2 minutes or until slightly thickened. **Yield:** 2 servings.

Nutrition Facts: 1 cup equals 124 calories, 6 g fat (4 g saturated fat), 15 mg cholesterol, 642 mg sodium, 16 g carbohydrate, 4 g fiber, 4 g protein. **Diabetic Exchanges:** 2 vegetable, 1 fat, 1/2 starch.

Two-Potato Soup

Pamela Reiling-Kemp • Roselle, Illinois

*Potato chunks, Swiss cheese and onions fill this creamy soup that's a must-have on
crisp autumn afternoons. For variety, I sometimes add chopped celery and
a dash of green hot sauce to the recipe that was originally my mother's.*

✓ **Uses less fat, sugar or salt. Includes Nutrition Facts or Diabetic Exchanges.**

- 1/2 pound small unpeeled red potatoes, cut into chunks
- 1/2 pound medium russet potatoes, peeled and cut into chunks
- 1 can (14-1/2 ounces) reduced-sodium chicken broth
- 1 cup water
- 1/4 cup chopped onion
- 2 teaspoons canola oil
- 1 tablespoon all-purpose flour
- 1/4 cup 2% milk
- 2 tablespoons evaporated milk
- 3 tablespoons cream cheese, cubed
- 1 tablespoon minced fresh parsley
- 1/4 teaspoon salt
- 1/8 teaspoon white pepper
- 1/3 cup shredded Swiss cheese

Place the potatoes in a large saucepan; add broth and water. Bring to a boil. Reduce heat; cover and cook for 10-15 minutes or until almost tender. Meanwhile, in a small skillet, saute onion in oil until tender; add to potatoes.

In a bowl, combine the flour, milk and evaporated milk until smooth; add to potato mixture. Bring to a boil; cook and stir for 2 minutes or until thickened. Reduce heat; stir in the cream cheese, parsley, salt and pepper. Cover and simmer for 5-10 minutes or until cream cheese is melted and potatoes are tender, stirring occasionally. Garnish with Swiss cheese. **Yield:** about 3 cups.

Nutrition Facts: 1 cup (prepared with reduced-fat cream cheese, fat-free evaporated milk and reduced-fat Swiss cheese) equals 245 calories, 8 g fat (3 g saturated fat), 17 mg cholesterol, 689 mg sodium, 33 g carbohydrate, 3 g fiber, 12 g protein.

Golden Carrot Soup

Golden Carrot Soup

Aline Winje • Slocan, British Columbia

This is a great-tasting soup to warm you up on a chilly day.
It's easy to fix, too, with a mild chicken flavor and hint of garlic.

✓ Uses less fat, sugar or salt. Includes Nutrition Facts or Diabetic Exchanges.

1/2	cup chopped onion
1/4	teaspoon minced garlic
2	tablespoons reduced-fat butter
2	cups water
1	cup sliced carrots
2	tablespoons uncooked long grain rice
2	teaspoons chicken bouillon granules
2	tablespoons minced fresh parsley

In a small saucepan, saute onion and garlic in butter until tender. Add the water, carrots, rice and bouillon; bring to a boil. Reduce heat; cover and simmer for 20-25 minutes or until carrots and rice are tender.

Remove from the heat; cool slightly. Transfer to a blender or food processor; cover and process until pureed. Return to the saucepan; heat through. Sprinkle with parsley. **Yield:** 2 servings.

Nutrition Facts: 1-1/3 cups equals 126 calories, 4 g fat (3 g saturated fat), 10 mg cholesterol, 442 mg sodium, 20 g carbohydrate, 3 g fiber, 2 g protein.
Diabetic Exchanges: 1 starch, 1 vegetable, 1/2 fat.

Cream of Broccoli Soup

Eileen Claeys • Long Grove, Iowa

Frozen vegetables make this a quick soup to stir up. The turkey ham makes a hearty addition to the green beans, broccoli and cheese.

✓ Uses less fat, sugar or salt. Includes Nutrition Facts or Diabetic Exchanges.

- 1 package (10 ounces) frozen chopped broccoli
- 3/4 cup finely chopped cooked turkey ham
- 1/2 cup water
- 1/4 cup frozen cut green beans
- 1 tablespoon chopped onion
- 2 tablespoons all-purpose flour
- 1 cup fat-free milk
- 1/3 cup cubed reduced-fat process American cheese

In a large saucepan, combine the first five ingredients; cover and cook over medium heat until vegetables are tender, about 5 minutes (do not drain). Combine flour and milk until smooth; gradually add to the vegetable mixture. Bring to a boil; boil for 1-2 minutes, stirring constantly. Remove from the heat.

Stir in cheese; cover and let stand until melted, about 5 minutes. Stir before serving. **Yield:** 3 servings.

Nutrition Facts: 1 cup equals 151 calories, 3 g fat (0 saturated fat), 23 mg cholesterol, 788 mg sodium, 14 g carbohydrate, 0 fiber, 17 g protein. **Diabetic Exchanges:** 1 meat, 1 vegetable, 1/2 fat-free milk.

Tortilla Soup

Pat Cox • Bogata, Texas

Corn tortillas give this soup flavor and texture. It's a fast-growing favorite in the Southeast. I especially like this recipe because it can be made quickly and easily, and it can serve as an appetizer or a main dish.

- 1 medium tomato, quartered
- 1 can (14-1/2 ounces) whole peeled tomatoes with liquid
- 1 small onion, quartered
- 1 garlic clove
- 2 cans (10-1/2 ounces *each*) condensed chicken broth, undiluted
- 1/2 teaspoon chili powder
- 1/2 teaspoon salt
- 1/4 teaspoon pepper
- 1/4 teaspoon ground coriander
- 1/4 teaspoon ground cumin
- 1 tablespoon minced fresh cilantro
- 6 corn tortillas (6 inches)
- 1/4 cup vegetable oil

Sour cream

Shredded cheddar *or* Monterey Jack cheese

Tortilla Soup

Place tomatoes, onion and garlic in a blender or food processor; blend until smooth. Transfer to a large saucepan. Add the chicken broth and seasonings; bring to a boil. Reduce heat and simmer for 3 minutes.

Cut tortillas into 1/4-in. strips; fry in hot oil until crisp and brown. Drain. Ladle soup into bowls; top with tortilla strips, sour cream and cheese. **Yield:** about 4 servings.

Beefy Mushroom Soup

Ginger Ellsworth • Caldwell, Idaho

Here's a tasty way to use leftover roast or steak and get a comforting supper on the table in about a half hour. The warm, savory taste of this mushroom soup is guaranteed to be a hit.

✓ **Uses less fat, sugar or salt. Includes Nutrition Facts or Diabetic Exchanges.**

- 1 medium onion, chopped
- 1/2 cup sliced fresh mushrooms
- 2 tablespoons butter
- 2 tablespoons all-purpose flour
- 2 cups reduced-sodium beef broth
- 2/3 cup cubed cooked lean roast beef
- 1/2 teaspoon garlic powder
- 1/4 teaspoon paprika
- 1/8 teaspoon salt
- 1/4 teaspoon pepper

Dash hot pepper sauce

- 1/4 cup shredded part-skim mozzarella cheese, optional

In a large saucepan, saute the onion and mushrooms in butter until onion is tender; remove with a slotted spoon and set aside. In a bowl, whisk the flour and broth until smooth; add to the pan. Bring to a boil; cook and stir for 1-2 minutes or until thickened.

Add the roast beef, garlic powder, paprika, salt, pepper, hot pepper sauce and onion mixture; cook and stir until heated through. Garnish with cheese if desired. **Yield:** 3 cups.

Nutrition Facts: 1 cup (prepared with reduced-fat butter) equals 164 calories, 8 g fat (4 g saturated fat), 48 mg cholesterol, 572 mg sodium, 11 g carbohydrate, 2 g fiber, 14 g protein.

Chilled Strawberry Soup

Alice Butcher • Penticon, British Columbia

After a day outdoors in the heat, we find that there's nothing more refreshing than a bowl of this chilled, three-ingredient soup.

✓ **Uses less fat, sugar or salt. Includes Nutrition Facts or Diabetic Exchanges.**

- 1 pint fresh strawberries, hulled
- 2 tablespoons sugar
- 1/3 cup white wine *or* white grape juice

In a food processor or blender, combine all of the ingredients; cover and process for 30 seconds or until smooth. Pour into a bowl. Refrigerate until chilled. **Yield:** 2 servings.

Nutrition Facts: 3/4 cup equals 109 calories, trace fat (trace saturated fat), 0 cholesterol, 3 mg sodium, 21g carbohydrate, 3 g fiber, 1 g protein. **Diabetic Exchange:** 1-1/2 fruit.

Chilled Strawberry Soup

Clam Chowder For One

Donna Smith • Fairport, New York

Perfect for one-person households, this comforting chowder is sure to chase the chills.

- 1/2 cup cubed peeled potato
- 1/4 cup chopped onion
- 1/8 teaspoon salt

Pinch pepper

- 1/2 cup water
- 1 can (6-1/2 ounces) chopped clams, drained
- 2/3 cup milk
- 1 tablespoon butter
- 1 bacon strip, cooked and crumbled

Chopped fresh parsley, optional

In a small saucepan, cook potato, onion, salt and pepper in water until vegetables are tender (do not drain). Add clams, milk, butter and bacon; heat through (do not boil). Sprinkle with parsley if desired. **Yield:** 1 serving.

Clam Chowder For One

Pretty Pepper Soup

Bessie Hulett • Shively, Kentucky

I like to create new dishes for my husband and me. I'd rather fuss over a meal and set a fancy table than go out to eat. I often increase the recipe and serve this soup for parties.

- 1 bacon strip
- 1 large sweet red pepper, chopped
- 1/4 cup chopped onion
- 2 garlic cloves, minced
- 1 tablespoon tomato paste
- 1/8 teaspoon paprika
- 3 to 4 drops hot pepper sauce

Dash cayenne pepper

- 1 cup chicken broth, *divided*
- 1 tablespoon butter
- 1 tablespoon all-purpose flour
- 1/2 cup heavy whipping cream
- 1/4 teaspoon salt

Chives and additional chopped red pepper, optional

In a skillet, cook bacon until crisp. Remove to paper towel to drain. To the drippings, add red pepper, onion and garlic; saute until onion is tender, about 4 minutes. Stir in the tomato paste, paprika, hot pepper sauce and cayenne until well blended. Add 1/4 cup broth. Reduce heat; simmer, uncovered, for 5 minutes. Remove from the heat; cool for 10 minutes.

Puree in a blender or food processor; set aside. In a saucepan over low heat, melt butter. Stir in flour; cook and stir for 2 minutes. Gradually add remaining broth; bring to a boil over medium heat. Cook and stir for 2 minutes; reduce heat to low. Gradually stir in cream and salt. Add puree; heat through. Crumble bacon over top. Garnish with chives and red pepper if desired. Serve immediately. **Yield:** 2 servings.

Baked Potato Soup

Linda Mumm • Davenport, Iowa

A neighbor brought over her children's cookbook to show us, and I discovered this recipe for our favorite soup in it! Not only is it delicious, it's easy to prepare.

2	medium potatoes, baked and cooled
1	can (14-1/2 ounces) chicken broth
2	tablespoons sour cream
1/8	teaspoon pepper
1/4	cup shredded cheddar cheese
1	tablespoon crumbled cooked bacon *or* bacon bits
1	green onion, sliced

Peel potatoes and cut into 1/2-in. cubes; place half in a blender. Add broth; cover and process until smooth. Pour into a saucepan. Stir in sour cream, pepper and remaining potatoes. Cook over low heat until heated through (do not boil). Garnish with cheese, bacon and onion. **Yield:** 2 servings.

Chicken Vegetable Soup

Ruby Williams • Bogalusa, Louisiana

Every grandmother knows that nothing cures a cold better than homemade soup. I find this recipe fits nicely to accommodate just my great-grandson and me.

1	medium onion, chopped
1	celery rib, chopped
1	garlic clove, minced
2	teaspoons vegetable oil
1-1/2	cups chicken broth
1	cup diced fresh tomatoes
1	cup cubed cooked chicken
1/4	teaspoon dried marjoram
1/4	teaspoon dried thyme
1/8	teaspoon pepper
1	bay leaf

In a saucepan, saute the onion, celery and garlic in oil until tender. Stir in the broth, tomatoes, chicken, marjoram, thyme, pepper and bay leaf. Bring to a boil. Reduce heat; cover and simmer for 30 minutes or until heated through. Discard bay leaf. **Yield:** 2 servings.

Texas Corn Chowder

Mildred Sherrer • Bay City, Texas

This recipe has been a favorite in our family for years. Now that we have an empty nest, I took it upon myself to cut the recipe down to serve two so we can still enjoy it. The jalapeno adds a little zip and color!

1/4	cup chopped onion
1	tablespoon butter
1	tablespoon all-purpose flour
1	cup diced peeled potato
1	cup water
1	chicken bouillon cube
1	cup fresh *or* frozen corn
1	to 2 teaspoons finely chopped jalapeno *or* green chilies
2	cups milk
1/4	teaspoon garlic salt
1/8	teaspoon pepper
Dash paprika	

In a medium saucepan, saute onion in butter until tender. Stir in flour. Add the potato, water and bouillon; bring to a boil. Reduce heat; cover and simmer for 7-10 minutes or until potato is tender. Add corn, jalapeno, milk and seasonings. Cover and simmer for 15 minutes. **Yield:** 2 servings.

Baked Potato Soup

BEEFED-UP ENTREES

Nothing satisfies like an old-fashioned pot roast, barbecued beef ribs or a thick and meaty spaghetti sauce. Now you can enjoy those familiar tastes without having to worry about leftovers. From veal in wine sauce and rich beef stroganoff to saucy stir-fries and colorful casseroles, this chapter offers all the recipes you need to please the meat-and-potato lover in your home.

Beef Burgundy Over
Noodles p. 114

Beef Stir-Fry for One
p. 103

Chuck Wagon Chow
p. 102

Hobo Dinner
p. 112

Barbecued Beef Ribs for Two
p. 96

Barbecued Beef Ribs for Two

Margery Bryan • Royal City, Washington

I've shared this recipe with many friends who also cook for two. We all agree that small recipes are hard to find! This dish remains one of my favorites since it takes little effort to prepare and is so tasty.

2   pounds beef back ribs
1/2 cup ketchup
2   tablespoons finely chopped onion
2   garlic cloves, minced
2   tablespoons cider vinegar
1   tablespoon brown sugar
1/2 teaspoon chili powder
1/2 teaspoon Worcestershire sauce
1/8 teaspoon garlic powder
Dash hot pepper sauce

Cut ribs into serving-size pieces; place in a large kettle and cover with water. Simmer, uncovered, for 50-60 minutes or until tender. Meanwhile, combine the remaining ingredients in a small saucepan. Simmer, uncovered, for 10 minutes.

Drain ribs; place in a greased shallow 2-qt. baking dish. Cover with sauce. Bake, uncovered, at 350° for 50-60 minutes. **Yield:** 2 servings.

French Veal Chops

French Veal Chops

Betty Biehl • Mertztown, Pennsylvania

Perfectly portioned for two, here's an easy entree you'll turn to regularly. Try it the next time you'd like to prepare a meal that's a bit special.

2   veal chops (1 inch thick)
1/2 teaspoon salt
Dash pepper
1   tablespoon vegetable oil
1/2 cup chopped onion
2   tablespoons butter, *divided*
1/4 cup chicken broth
1/3 cup dry bread crumbs
2   tablespoons grated Parmesan cheese

Sprinkle veal chops with salt and pepper. In a skillet, brown chops on both sides in oil. Sprinkle onion into a greased shallow baking dish; dot with 1 tablespoon butter. Top with chops; drizzle with broth. Melt remaining butter; toss with bread crumbs and cheese. Sprinkle over top.

Bake, uncovered, at 350° for 30-35 minutes or until meat is no longer pink and a meat thermometer reads 160°. **Yield:** 2 servings.

Savory Braised Beef

Savory Braised Beef

Eva Knight • Nashua, New Hampshire

*For the first time in 23 years, I'm cooking for two. It's quite an adjustment, but
I'm getting adept at making the changes. My husband and I like this delicious dish.
With its meat, potatoes and other vegetables, it's a great meal.*

1/2	pound boneless beef chuck roast
3/4	cup water
1	small apple, thinly sliced
1	small onion, thinly sliced
1/4	teaspoon salt, optional
1/4	teaspoon pepper
4	small new potatoes, halved
2	cabbage wedges (about 2 inches thick)
1	can (14-1/2 ounces) stewed tomatoes
1-1/2	teaspoons cornstarch
1-1/2	teaspoons water

Trim fat from meat and cut into 1-in. cubes; brown in a skillet coated with nonstick cooking spray. Add water, apple, onion, salt if desired and pepper. Cover and simmer for 1-1/4 hours.

Add potatoes and cabbage; cover and simmer for 35 minutes or until vegetables are tender. Stir in tomatoes; cover and simmer for 10 minutes. Blend cornstarch and water; stir into skillet. Bring to a boil; cook and stir for 2 minutes. **Yield:** 2 servings.

Traditional Stuffed Peppers

Karen Gentry • Somerset, Kentucky

My husband loves these stuffed peppers because they're so filling. I like how quick they are to prepare and the fact that leftovers don't dominate my refrigerator days later. The peppers are delightful when deli coleslaw is served on the side.

2	large green peppers
1/2	pound ground beef
1/4	cup chopped onion
1	can (15 ounces) tomato sauce, *divided*
1	cup cooked rice
1/8	teaspoon salt
1/8	teaspoon garlic powder
1/8	teaspoon pepper

Cut tops off peppers and remove seeds. Place peppers in a large saucepan and cover with water. Bring to a boil; cook for 3 minutes. Drain peppers and immediately place in ice water; invert on paper towels.

In a small skillet, cook beef and onion over medium heat until meat is no longer pink; drain. Remove from the heat. Stir in 1 cup tomato sauce, rice, salt, garlic powder and pepper. Spoon into the peppers.

Place in an ungreased shallow 2-qt. baking dish. Drizzle with remaining tomato sauce. Cover and bake at 350° for 25-30 minutes or until peppers are tender. **Yield:** 2 servings.

Traditional Stuffed Peppers

Beef with Ramen Noodles

Annette Hemsath • Sutherlin, Oregon

I made up this recipe when I was hungry for Asian food. Everyone who tries it likes it, but each time I make it, I change something slightly. Heat any extras in the microwave or in a skillet the next day for lunch.

- 1 tablespoon cornstarch
- 1 cup beef broth, *divided*
- 1 package (3 ounces) beef ramen noodles
- 1/2 pound boneless beef sirloin steak, cut into thin strips
- 1 tablespoon vegetable oil
- 1 tablespoon soy sauce
- 1 can (14 ounces) whole baby corn, rinsed and drained
- 1 cup fresh broccoli florets
- 1/2 cup diced sweet red pepper
- 1/2 cup grated carrot
- 2 green onions, cut into 1-inch pieces
- 1/4 cup peanuts

In a small bowl, combine cornstarch and 2 tablespoons broth until smooth; set aside. Set aside seasoning packet from noodles. Cook noodles according to package directions.

Beef with Ramen Noodles

In a skillet, stir-fry beef in oil. Add soy sauce; cook for 3-4 minutes or until liquid has evaporated. Drain noodles; add to beef. Stir in the corn, broccoli, red pepper, carrot, onions and remaining broth. Sprinkle contents of seasoning packet over all. Cook for 4-6 minutes or until vegetables are crisp-tender. Stir reserved cornstarch mixture and add to skillet. Bring to a boil; cook and stir for 2 minutes or until thickened. Sprinkle with peanuts. **Yield:** 2 servings.

Braised Short Ribs

Maureen DeGarmo • Martinez, California

Basil, thyme and rosemary combine with Dijon mustard and red wine vinegar for a sensational marinade that's ideal over short ribs. Baked in the oven, they are always so tender.

- 6 tablespoons water
- 6 tablespoons olive oil, *divided*
- 4 teaspoons Dijon mustard
- 4 teaspoons red wine vinegar
- 4 teaspoons dried basil
- 4 teaspoons dried thyme
- 1 tablespoon dried rosemary, crushed
- 1/4 teaspoon pepper
- 6 to 8 boneless beef short ribs (about 1-1/2 pounds)
- 1 can (8 ounces) tomato sauce

In a small bowl, combine water, 2 tablespoons oil, mustard, vinegar and seasonings; mix well. Place ribs in a large resealable plastic bag or shallow glass container. Set aside half of marinade. Pour remaining marinade over ribs; turn to coat. Cover and refrigerate for several hours.

Drain, discarding marinade. In a skillet, brown the ribs in remaining oil. Transfer ribs to a greased shallow 1-qt. baking dish.

Combine tomato sauce and reserved marinade; pour over ribs. Cover and bake at 350° for 1-1/2 hours or until meat is tender. **Yield:** 2 servings.

Corn Chip Beef Bake

Corn Chip Beef Bake

Barbara Bernard • Holyoke, Massachusetts

*After my children left home, I found it difficult to whittle down meals for two,
but I eventually succeeded, and this became one of our preferred dishes.
You can easily freeze the extra portion if you're cooking for one.*

1/2	pound lean ground beef
1/3	cup finely chopped onion
1/3	cup thinly sliced celery
1/3	cup finely chopped green pepper
1/4	teaspoon minced garlic
1	cup cooked brown rice
1	medium tomato, chopped
1	teaspoon lemon juice
1/4	teaspoon salt
1/4	teaspoon hot pepper sauce
1/4	cup mayonnaise
1/2	to 1 cup corn chips, crushed

In a large skillet, cook the beef, onion, celery, green pepper and garlic over medium heat until meat is no longer pink; drain. Stir in the rice, tomato, lemon juice, salt and hot pepper sauce; heat through. Stir in mayonnaise.

Spoon into two 15-oz. baking dishes coated with nonstick cooking spray. Sprinkle with crushed corn chips. Bake, uncovered, at 350° for 13-15 minutes or until heated through. **Yield:** 2 servings.

Veal Scallopini

Karen Bridges • Downers Grove, Illinois

*My husband and I like this fabulous veal dish on birthdays and other special occasions.
The mushroom and wine sauce make it particularly memorable.*

2	tablespoons all-purpose flour
1/8	teaspoon salt
1/8	teaspoon pepper
1	egg
1/2	to 3/4 pound veal cutlets *or* boneless skinless chicken breasts, flattened to 1/4-inch thickness
2	tablespoons olive oil
4	ounces fresh mushrooms, halved
1	cup chicken broth
2	tablespoons Marsala wine

Hot cooked spaghetti

In a shallow bowl, combine the flour, salt, and pepper. In another shallow bowl, lightly beat the egg. Pound veal to 1-in. thickness. Dip in egg, then coat with flour mixture.

In a large skillet, brown veal in oil on both sides. Stir in the mushrooms, broth and wine. Bring to a boil. Reduce heat; simmer, uncovered, for 5-10 minutes or until mushrooms are tender. Serve over spaghetti. **Yield:** 2 servings.

SECRET SHARED

"The secret to successfully reheating frozen foods is in the liquid added," shares Jane Scanlon of Rochester, Minnesota. "I add beef broth to meaty foods, chicken broth to poultry dishes and tomato juice to lasagna."

Spaghetti 'n' Meat Sauce

Carolyn Ozment • Gaylesville, Alabama

This basic recipe has been a mainstay in our family for more than 40 years. I enjoy the small amount of sauce it makes, but I often double or triple the recipe when company is coming. The results are always delicious.

1/2   **pound ground beef**
1/4   **cup chopped onion**
  1   **can (8 ounces) tomato sauce**
  1   **medium tomato, seeded and chopped**
  1   **teaspoon Worcestershire sauce**
1/2   **to 1 teaspoon salt**
1/2   **teaspoon Italian seasoning**
1/4   **teaspoon pepper**
Hot cooked spaghetti

In a skillet, cook beef and onion over medium heat until meat is no longer pink; drain. Add the tomato sauce, tomato, Worcestershire sauce, salt, Italian seasoning and pepper. Bring to a boil. Reduce heat; cover and simmer for 10 minutes or until heated through. Serve over spaghetti. **Yield:** 2 servings.

Spaghetti 'n' Meat Sauce

Chuck Wagon Chow

Dorothy Cowan • Ferndale, California

Try serving this mild, chili-like dish with tortilla chips or flour tortillas. Since it cooks up in a single pot, it's perfect for camping, too.

✓ Uses less fat, sugar or salt. Includes Nutrition Facts or Diabetic Exchanges.

1/3   **pound lean ground beef**
  1   **small onion, chopped**
1/4   **cup chopped green pepper**
  1   **garlic clove, minced**
  1   **can (7 ounces) whole kernel corn, drained**
3/4   **cup kidney beans, rinsed and drained**
1/2   **cup tomato sauce**
  1   **tablespoon chili powder**
1/8   **teaspoon pepper**

In a large saucepan, cook the beef, onion, green pepper and garlic over medium heat until meat is no longer pink; drain. Add the corn, beans, tomato sauce, chili powder and pepper; cover and cook 5-10 minutes longer or until heated through. **Yield:** 2 servings.

Nutrition Facts: 1-1/2 cups equals 300 calories, 7 g fat (3 g saturated fat), 46 mg cholesterol, 509 mg sodium, 38 g carbohydrate, 9 g fiber, 24 g protein.
Diabetic Exchanges: 2-1/2 lean meat, 2 starch, 1 vegetable.

Beef Stir-Fry for One

Joelle Silva • Fair Oaks, California

With tender beef, vegetables and a hint of citrus, this succulent stir-fry is a special meal just for one.

1   teaspoon beef bouillon granules
1/4 cup boiling water
2   teaspoons cornstarch
1   teaspoon sugar
1/4 cup cold water
1   tablespoon cider vinegar
1/4 to 1/2 pound boneless beef sirloin steak, cut into 2-inch strips
1   to 2 tablespoons vegetable oil
2   cups frozen broccoli stir-fry vegetable blend, thawed
1   green onion, sliced
1   garlic clove, minced
1   teaspoon grated orange peel
Hot cooked rice

In a small bowl, dissolve bouillon in boiling water. In another bowl, combine cornstarch and sugar; gradually stir in cold water, vinegar and bouillon until smooth; set aside.

In a skillet, stir-fry beef in oil until no longer pink. Remove and set aside. Add vegetables, onion and garlic to skillet; stir-fry until crisp-tender.

Stir the bouillon mixture and add to the pan. Bring to a boil; cook and stir for 1-2 minutes or until thickened.

Return beef to pan; cook until vegetables are tender and beef is heated through. Stir in orange peel. Serve over rice. **Yield:** 1 serving.

Double-Shell Tacos

Taste of Home Test Kitchen • Greendale, Wisconsin

Two-shell tacos are twice the fun! A warm pita spread with refried beans enfolds a crispy taco shell filled with savory ground beef and tempting toppings for this casual surprise.

1/2 pound ground beef
2   tablespoons taco seasoning
1/3 cup water
1/2 cup refried beans
2   whole gyro-style pitas (6 inches)
2   taco shells
Toppings: chopped green onions, chopped tomatoes, sliced ripe olives, shredded cheddar cheese, sour cream *and/or* shredded lettuce, optional

In a large skillet, cook beef over medium heat until no longer pink; drain. Stir in taco seasoning and water. Bring to a boil. Reduce heat; simmer, uncovered, for 3-4 minutes or until thickened.

Meanwhile, spread 1/4 cup refried beans over one side of each pita. Place on a microwave-safe plate; heat, uncovered, on high for 15-20 seconds or until warmed. Immediately wrap each pita around a taco shell. Fill with beef mixture. Serve with toppings of your choice. **Yield:** 2 servings.

Double-Shell Tacos

Beef Steaks with Blue Cheese

Beef Steaks with Blue Cheese

Gloria Nerone • Mentor, Ohio

My guests often ask for this winning recipe and are almost always surprised at how simple it is to put together.

2   beef tenderloin steaks (1-1/2 inches thick)
2   ounces blue cheese, crumbled
2   tablespoons butter, softened
2   slices white bread, crusts removed and cut into cubes
1   tablespoon olive oil
2   tablespoons grated Parmesan cheese

Place meat on broiler pan. Broil 4-6 in. from the heat for 5-8 minutes on each side or until meat is browned and cooked to desired doneness (for medium-rare, a meat thermometer should read 145°; medium, 160°; well-done, 170°).

Meanwhile, in a bowl, combine the blue cheese and butter; set aside. In a skillet, saute bread cubes in oil until golden brown. Sprinkle with Parmesan cheese. Top steaks with blue cheese mixture and sprinkle with croutons; broil 1 minute longer or until cheese is slightly melted. **Yield:** 2 servings.

Beef Patties with Gravy

Sharon Manus • Smyrna, Tennessee

I like to season beef patties with onion, fresh mushrooms and golden mushroom soup for this tasty main course. It's a quick and hearty meal when served over mashed potatoes and alongside a vegetable medley.

1   egg
1/2   cup soft bread crumbs
1   tablespoon finely chopped onion
1/2   pound lean ground beef
1   can (10-3/4 ounces) condensed golden mushroom soup, undiluted
2/3   cup water
1/2   cup sliced fresh mushrooms
Hot cooked noodles, rice *or* mashed potatoes

In a bowl, combine the egg, bread crumbs and onion. Crumble beef over mixture and mix well. Shape into two patties.

In a skillet, cook patties until browned on both sides. In a bowl, combine the soup, water and mushrooms; pour over patties. Bring to a boil. Reduce heat; cover and simmer until meat is no longer pink. Serve over noodles, rice or potatoes. **Yield:** 2 servings.

Hearty Skillet Stew

Hearty Skillet Stew

Karlene Endicott • Greenwood, California

A sweet sauce enhances the beef and vegetables in this comforting stew. A neighbor gave me the recipe dozens of years ago, and my husband and I still prepare it regularly.

✓ **Uses less fat, sugar or salt. Includes Nutrition Facts or Diabetic Exchanges.**

- 1/2 **pound boneless beef top round steak, cut into 1/2-inch cubes**
- 1/3 **cup chopped onion**
- 2 **cups chopped cabbage**
- 2 **medium carrots, chopped**
- 1 **medium potato, cut into 1/2-inch chunks**
- 3/4 **cup water**
- 1/3 **cup reduced-sodium soy sauce**
- 2 **to 3 tablespoons sugar**
- 1/2 **teaspoon cornstarch**
- 1 **teaspoon cold water**

In a large nonstick skillet coated with nonstick cooking spray, brown steak with onion. Stir in the cabbage, carrots, potato, water, soy sauce and sugar; bring to a boil. Reduce heat; cover and simmer for 25 minutes or until carrots and potato are tender.

In a small bowl, combine cornstarch and cold water until smooth; stir into beef mixture. Bring to a boil; cook and stir for 1-2 minutes or until thickened. **Yield:** 2 servings.

Nutrition Facts: 1-1/2 cups equals 371 calories, 4 g fat (1 g saturated fat), 64 mg cholesterol, 1,689 mg sodium, 51 g carbohydrate, 6 g fiber, 32 g protein.

Marinated Sirloin Steaks

Sarah Vasques • Milford, New Hampshire

Asian influences meet Mediterranean flavor in these grilled steaks. The blend of honey and soy sauce really works well with the olive oil and balsamic vinegar. The marinade is also great when grilling New York strip steaks.

✓ Uses less fat, sugar or salt. Includes Nutrition Facts or Diabetic Exchanges.

- 1/4 cup honey
- 3 tablespoons reduced-sodium soy sauce
- 2 tablespoons olive oil
- 1 tablespoon balsamic vinegar
- 2 garlic cloves, peeled
- 1/4 teaspoon coarsely ground pepper
- 2 boneless beef sirloin steaks (4 ounces each)
- 3 green onions, sliced

In a blender, combine the honey, soy sauce, oil, vinegar, garlic and pepper; cover and process until blended. Pour 1/3 cup marinade into a large resealable plastic bag; add steaks and onions. Seal bag and turn to coat; refrigerate for at least 1-2 hours. Cover and refrigerate remaining marinade for basting.

Coat grill rack with nonstick cooking spray before starting the grill. Drain and discard marinade. Grill steaks, covered, over medium-hot heat for 4-5 minutes on each side or until meat reaches desired doneness (for medium-rare, a meat thermometer should read 145°; medium, 160°; well-done, 170°), basting occasionally with reserved marinade. **Yield:** 2 servings.

Nutrition Facts: 1 steak equals 287 calories, 12 g fat (3 g saturated fat), 63 mg cholesterol, 506 mg sodium, 21 g carbohydrate, 1 g fiber, 23 g protein. **Diabetic Exchanges:** 3 lean meat, 1-1/2 fruit, 1 fat.

Meatballs with Vegetable Sauce

Dorothy Stegall • Appleton, Wisconsin

This is such an easy way to make meatballs without all the mess of frying and turning each one. Best of all, they can be made ahead and frozen, and then added to the tangy, vegetable-rich sauce. Serve them over noodles or rice.

- 1 egg yolk, lightly beaten
- 1 tablespoon milk
- 3 tablespoons soft bread crumbs
- 2 tablespoons finely chopped onion
- 1/4 teaspoon salt
- 1/2 pound ground beef

SAUCE:
- 1/4 cup sliced fresh mushrooms
- 1/4 cup chopped celery
- 3 tablespoons chopped onion
- 3 tablespoons chopped green pepper
- 1 teaspoon butter
- 1/2 cup tomato sauce
- 2 tablespoons brown sugar
- 2 tablespoons beef broth
- 4 teaspoons lemon juice
- 1/8 teaspoon garlic powder

Hot cooked noodles

In a bowl, combine the first five ingredients. Crumble beef over mixture and mix well. Shape into 1-in. balls. Place 1 in. apart on a greased baking pan. Bake, uncovered, at 425° for 10-12 minutes or until no longer pink. Drain on paper towels.

Meanwhile, in a saucepan, saute the mushrooms, celery, onion and green pepper in butter. Add the tomato sauce, brown sugar, broth, lemon juice and garlic powder. Bring to a boil. Reduce heat; add the meatballs. Cover and simmer for 15 minutes or until heated through. Serve over noodles. **Yield:** 2 servings.

Marinated Sirloin Steaks

Pepper Steak

Pepper Steak

Mrs. Henry Sepanks • Atlanta, New York

I came across a terrific steak recipe more than 40 years ago as a newlywed and it eventually became a standby. I still make the main dish for my husband and me in this pared-down version. Our daughters make it for their families as well.

1/2	pound beef round steak (3/4 inch thick), trimmed
1	tablespoon vegetable oil
1/4	cup chopped onion
1	garlic clove, minced
1	beef bouillon cube
3/4	cup boiling water
1/8	teaspoon pepper
1	can (14-1/2 ounces) stewed tomatoes
1	medium green pepper, cut into rings
1/4	cup cold water
2	tablespoons cornstarch
2	tablespoons soy sauce

Hot cooked noodles, optional

Cut meat into 2-in. x 1-in. strips; brown in a skillet in oil for 10 minutes. Add onion and garlic; cook for 3-4 minutes. Dissolve bouillon in boiling water; pour into skillet. Sprinkle meat with pepper. Cover and simmer for 35-40 minutes or until meat is tender.

Add tomatoes and green pepper; cover and simmer for 10 minutes. Combine cold water, cornstarch and soy sauce; stir into broth. Bring to a boil; cook and stir for 2 minutes. Serve over noodles if desired. **Yield:** 2 servings.

Oriental Skillet Supper

Donna Shroyer • Titonka, Iowa

Here is a colorful combination of cube steak, vegetables and rice that makes a quick and simple meal for one. It's a tasty one-dish supper.

1/4 pound beef cube steaks, cut into strips
2 teaspoons vegetable oil
1/4 cup julienned green pepper
2 tablespoons chopped celery
2 teaspoons cornstarch
1/4 cup water
4 teaspoons soy sauce
1/2 teaspoon sugar
1/8 teaspoon salt
1 small tomato, cut into wedges
Hot cooked rice

In a small skillet, stir-fry the steak in oil for 4 minutes or until no longer pink. Remove steak and keep warm. Stir-fry green pepper and celery until crisp-tender.

Combine cornstarch, water, soy sauce, sugar and salt until smooth; add to the skillet. Bring to a boil. Cook and stir for 1 minute or until thickened. Add steak and tomato to skillet; heat through. Serve over rice. **Yield:** 1 serving.

Surf 'n' Turf Dinner

Colleen Gonring • Brookfield, Wisconsin

Beef and seafood make a tantalizing twosome in this classic dinner sized right for a couple.

2 teaspoons finely chopped onion
1 garlic clove, minced
1 tablespoon olive oil, *divided*
1 tablespoon butter, *divided*
2 tablespoons beef broth
8 uncooked medium shrimp (about 1/4 pound), peeled and deveined
2 teaspoons minced fresh parsley
2 beef tenderloin steaks (6 ounces and 1-1/2 to 2 inches thick *each*)

In a small skillet, saute the onion and garlic in 1-1/2 teaspoons oil and 1-1/2 teaspoons butter until tender. Add broth; cook and stir for 1 minute. Add the shrimp; cook and stir until shrimp turn pink, about 3-5 minutes. Stir in parsley. Cut a pocket in each steak; place three shrimp in each pocket. Cover remaining shrimp and broth mixture; keep warm.

In a large skillet, heat remaining oil and butter over medium-high heat. Add steaks; cook until meat reaches desired doneness (about 10-13 minutes for medium), turning once. Top with reserved shrimp and broth mixture. **Yield:** 2 servings.

Surf 'n' Turf Dinner

Vegetable Meat Loaf

Vegetable Meat Loaf

Judi Brinegar • Liberty, North Carolina

Finely chopped onion, green pepper and celery are mixed with shredded carrot and combined with ground beef in this unique loaf. Seasoned with a hint of garlic and topped with chili sauce, it's a nice main course with baked potatoes on the side.

1/2	pound ground beef
1	slice bread, torn into small pieces
1	egg, beaten
1/4	cup shredded carrot
2	tablespoons finely chopped onion
2	tablespoons finely chopped green pepper
2	tablespoons finely chopped celery
1/2	teaspoon salt

Dash *each* pepper and garlic powder

5	tablespoons chili sauce *or* ketchup, *divided*

In a bowl, combine ground beef, bread, egg, carrot, onion, green pepper, celery, seasonings and 2 tablespoons chili sauce or ketchup.

Form into a loaf in an ungreased 5-3/4-in. x 3-in. x 2-in. loaf pan. Spoon remaining chili sauce or ketchup over loaf. Bake, uncovered, at 350° for 45-50 minutes or until meat is no longer pink and a meat thermometer reads 160°. **Yield:** 2 servings.

Veal Shank Fricassee

Jean Wright • Clarkston, Washington

This recipe was in a cookbook my mother gave me in 1944. Inside the cover she wrote, "When and if Jean ever gets married." Well, this recipe and many others from the book have graced my dinner table for over 55 years!

2	tablespoons all-purpose flour
2	teaspoons salt
1/2	teaspoon dried thyme
1/2	teaspoon dried parsley flakes
1/8	teaspoon pepper
1/8	teaspoon cayenne pepper
2	veal shanks (about 1 pound)
1	tablespoon vegetable oil
1-1/2	cups water *divided*
1	medium onion, chopped
1	celery rib, chopped
1	bay leaf
4	medium carrots, cut into 1-inch slices
2	medium potatoes, peeled and cut into 1-inch cubes
2	tablespoons cornstarch

In a shallow dish, combine the flour and seasonings. Add veal shanks; turn to coat. In a Dutch oven or large skillet, brown veal in oil over medium heat. Pour 1-1/4 cups water into pan; add the onion, celery and bay leaf. Bring to a boil over medium heat. Reduce heat; cover and simmer for 1 hour.

Add carrots and potatoes; cover and cook 30 minutes longer or until meat and vegetables are tender. Remove meat and vegetables to a serving platter and keep warm. Pour drippings and loosened browned bits into a measuring cup. Skim fat and discard bay leaf.

In a saucepan, combine cornstarch and the remaining water until smooth. Gradually stir in the drippings. Bring to a boil; cook and stir for 2 minutes or until thickened. Serve with meat and vegetables. **Yield:** 2 servings.

Hobo Dinner

Pat Walter • Pine Island, Minnesota

In this recipe, the meat and vegetables cook together in a piece of foil. This single-serving supper is a favorite. I especially like the fact that there is hardly any cleanup.

✓ **Uses less fat, sugar or salt. Includes Nutrition Facts or Diabetic Exchanges.**

1/4	pound ground beef
1	potato, sliced
1	carrot, sliced
2	tablespoons chopped onion

Salt and pepper, optional

Shape beef into a patty; place in the center of a piece of heavy-duty foil. Top with potato, carrot and onion. Sprinkle with salt and pepper if desired. Fold foil over and seal well; place on a baking sheet. Bake at 350° for 45 minutes. Open foil carefully. **Yield:** 1 serving.

Nutrition Facts: 1 serving (prepared with lean ground beef and calculated without added salt) equals 374 calories, 9 g fat (4 saturated fat), 69 mg cholesterol, 84 mg sodium, 46 g carbohydrate, 6 fiber, 27 g protein.

Editor's Note: Dinner may also be grilled, covered, over medium heat for 45-60 minutes or until potato is tender.

Reuben Meat Loaf

Denise Wahl • Lockport, Illinois

If you're a fan of Reuben sandwiches, you'll love this satisfying rolled loaf made with rye bread crumbs, sauerkraut, corned beef and Swiss cheese. Served with potato dumplings, it's a great meal.

1	egg, beaten
2	tablespoons chopped onion
2	tablespoons milk
1/3	pound lean ground beef
1-1/4	cups soft rye bread crumbs
2	tablespoons Dijon mustard
1/2	cup sauerkraut, rinsed and well drained
8	slices deli corned beef (about 2 ounces), *divided*
3/4	cup shredded Swiss cheese, *divided*

Reuben Meat Loaf

In a small bowl, combine the egg, onion and milk. Crumble beef over mixture and mix well. Add bread crumbs; mix gently. On a piece of heavy-duty foil, pat beef mixture into an 8-in. x 6-in. rectangle.

Spread mustard over loaf to within 1 in. of edges. Layer with sauerkraut, six slices of corned beef and 1/2 cup Swiss cheese. Roll up jelly-roll style, starting with a short side and peeling foil away while rolling. Seal seam and ends.

Place meat loaf seam side down in a shallow 1-qt. baking dish coated with nonstick cooking spray. Bake, uncovered, at 350° for 25 minutes. Top with remaining corned beef and cheese. Bake 5 minutes longer or until no longer pink and a meat thermometer reads 160°. Using two large spatulas, carefully transfer meat loaf to a serving platter. **Yield:** 2 servings.

Skillet Steak Supper

Skillet Steak Supper

Sandra Fisher • Kent, Washington

With all of the ingredients cooked in one skillet, this steak dish couldn't be quicker to prepare...or to clean! The wine and mushroom sauce makes it seem special.

2   boneless beef sirloin steaks (6 ounces *each*)
1/2 teaspoon salt, *divided*
1/2 teaspoon pepper, *divided*
1   tablespoon olive oil
2   tablespoons white wine *or* chicken broth
1/2 pound fresh mushrooms, sliced
3   tablespoons chopped green onions
1   to 2 tablespoons butter
1   tablespoon Worcestershire sauce
1   teaspoon Dijon mustard

Sprinkle steaks with 1/4 teaspoon salt and 1/4 teaspoon pepper. In a large skillet, cook steaks in oil over medium-high heat for 4-5 minutes on each side or until meat reaches desired doneness (for medium-rare, a meat thermometer should read 145°; medium, 160°; well-done, 170°). Remove and keep warm.

Add wine or broth to skillet. Stir in the mushrooms, onions, butter, Worcestershire sauce, mustard and remaining salt and pepper. Bring to a boil; cook and stir for 4-5 minutes or until mushrooms are tender. Serve over steaks. **Yield:** 2 servings.

Taco Plate for Two

Sue Ross • Casa Grande, Arizona

This savory combination of beef, onion, green chilies and taco sauce is spooned over tortilla chips for a casual dinner or hearty late-night snack.

Taco Plate for Two

1/2   pound ground beef
1/2   cup chopped onion
1/3   cup taco sauce
1/4   cup chopped green chilies
1/4   teaspoon salt
  1   cup broken tortilla chips
1/2   cup shredded cheddar cheese

In a skillet, cook beef and onion over medium heat until meat is no longer pink; drain. Stir in the taco sauce, chilies and salt. Cover and cook over medium-low heat for 6-8 minutes or until heated though. Spoon over chips; sprinkle with cheese. **Yield:** 2 servings.

Beef Burgundy Over Noodles

Margaret Welder • Madrid, Iowa

I received this delightful recipe from my sister-in-law years ago. Whenever I serve it to guests, they always request the recipe. The tender beef, mushrooms and flavorful sauce are delicious with noodles.

✓ Uses less fat, sugar or salt. Includes Nutrition Facts or Diabetic Exchanges.

1/2   pound boneless sirloin steak, cut into 1/4-inch strips
  2   tablespoons diced onion
  2   teaspoons butter
1-1/2   cups quartered fresh mushrooms
3/4   cup dry red wine *or* beef broth
1/4   cup plus 2 tablespoons water, *divided*
  3   tablespoons minced fresh parsley, *divided*
  1   bay leaf
  1   whole clove
1/4   teaspoon salt
1/8   teaspoon pepper
  1   tablespoon all-purpose flour
1/2   teaspoon browning sauce, optional
1-1/2   cups hot cooked egg noodles

In a Dutch oven or nonstick skillet, brown beef and onion in butter over medium heat. Add the mushrooms, wine or broth, 1/4 cup water, 2 tablespoons parsley, bay leaf, clove, salt and pepper. Bring to a boil. Reduce heat; cover and simmer for 1 hour or until beef is tender.

Combine flour and remaining water until smooth; stir into beef mixture. Bring to a boil; cook and stir for 2 minutes or until thickened. Discard bay leaf and clove. Stir in browning sauce if desired. Serve over noodles. Sprinkle with remaining parsley. **Yield:** 2 servings.

Nutrition Facts: 1-1/2 cups (calculated without noodles) equals 410 calories, 12 g fat (5 g saturated fat), 125 mg cholesterol, 403 mg sodium, 37 g carbohydrate, 2 g fiber, 33 g protein. **Diabetic Exchanges:** 3 lean meat, 2 starch, 1 vegetable, 1/2 fat.

Flank Steak Stir-Fry

Taste of Home Test Kitchen • Greendale, Wisconsin

A combination of broccoli, mushrooms, carrot and ginger nearly steal the show from the juicy strips of steak found in this fast dinner solution.

2 teaspoons cornstarch
1/3 cup beef broth
1 tablespoon soy sauce
1/8 teaspoon pepper
1/2 pound beef flank steak, cut into 1/4-inch strips
3/4 cup fresh *or* frozen broccoli florets
1/2 cup sliced fresh mushrooms
1/4 cup julienned sweet red pepper
1/4 cup julienned carrot
1/8 teaspoon ground ginger
1 tablespoon vegetable oil
Hot cooked rice

In a small bowl, combine the cornstarch, broth, soy sauce and pepper until smooth; set aside.

In a skillet, stir-fry the beef, broccoli, mushrooms, red pepper, carrot and ginger in oil until meat is no longer pink and vegetables are crisp-tender.

Stir broth mixture; add to the skillet. Bring to a boil; cook and stir for 2 minutes or until thickened. Serve over rice. **Yield:** 2 servings.

Potato Pizza

Peggy Key • Grant, Alabama

Looking for a change-of-pace pizza? Consider a "crust" of sliced potato topped with a saucy ground beef mixture and grated cheese. I've won two honors with this recipe.

1 large potato, peeled and thinly sliced
1 tablespoon water
1/3 pound lean ground beef
1/3 cup condensed cheddar cheese soup, undiluted
1/4 cup milk
1/2 cup pizza sauce
1/3 cup shredded part-skim mozzarella cheese
1/3 cup shredded cheddar cheese

Potato Pizza

Place the potato slices in a small microwave-safe dish; add water. Cover and microwave on high for 10 minutes or until tender; drain. Layer potato slices evenly on a 7-1/2-in. pizza pan coated with nonstick cooking spray; set aside.

In a skillet, cook beef over medium heat until no longer pink; drain. Stir in soup and milk. Pour over potatoes. Top with pizza sauce and cheeses. Bake at 400° for 15-20 minutes or until heated through and cheese is melted. **Yield:** 2 servings.

Editor's Note: This recipe was tested in a 1,100-watt microwave.

Hamburger Mac Skillet

Barbara Kemmer • Rohnert Park, California

This recipe makes just the right amount for my husband and me. A touch of Worcestershire sauce adds a distinctive taste, and I like that it all comes together in one pan.

1/2	pound ground beef
1/4	cup chopped onion
1/4	cup chopped green pepper
1	garlic clove, minced
1	can (11-1/2 ounces) tomato juice
1/2	cup uncooked elbow macaroni
1	teaspoon Worcestershire sauce
3/4	teaspoon salt
1/8	teaspoon pepper

In a skillet, cook the beef, onion, green pepper and garlic over medium heat until meat is no longer pink; drain. Add the tomato juice, macaroni, Worcestershire sauce, salt and pepper; bring to a boil. Reduce heat; cover and simmer for 20 minutes or until macaroni is tender. **Yield:** 2 servings.

Sesame Sirloin Steak

Paulette Barnett • Guelph, Ontario

The first time I tried these grilled steaks was years ago when we went to my in-laws for a Mother's Day dinner. We've made a few adjustments to the recipe, only improving on the super taste.

1/4	cup soy sauce
2	tablespoons sesame seeds, toasted
2	garlic cloves, minced
2	tablespoons olive oil
2	tablespoons brown sugar
1/4	teaspoon pepper
Dash to 1/8	teaspoon hot pepper sauce
3/4	pound boneless beef sirloin steak (about 3/4 inch thick)

In a large resealable plastic bag, combine the soy sauce, sesame seeds, garlic, oil, brown sugar, pepper and hot pepper sauce. Pierce steak on both sides with a fork; place in the bag. Seal and turn to coat; refrigerate for 8 hours or overnight.

Drain and discard marinade. Grill the steak, covered, over medium heat for 7-9 minutes on each side or until meat reaches desired doneness (for medium-rare, a meat thermometer should read 145°; medium, 160°; well-done, 170°). **Yield:** 2 servings.

Beef and Rice for Two

Emma Magielda • Amsterdam, New York

Many casseroles make enough to feed a crowd, but this easy recipe is perfectly portioned for two people. It's a great find that I hope you enjoy.

2/3	cup uncooked long grain rice
1	tablespoon vegetable oil
2	cups water
2	teaspoons beef bouillon granules
2	celery ribs, thinly sliced
1	small green pepper, chopped
1	small onion, chopped
2	teaspoons soy sauce
1-1/2	cups cubed cooked beef

In a large saucepan over medium heat, saute rice in oil until golden brown. Add the water, bouillon, celery, green pepper, onion and soy sauce. Bring to a boil. Reduce heat; cover and simmer for 15 minutes.

Stir in the beef. Cover and simmer for 5-10 minutes or until rice and vegetables are tender. **Yield:** 2 servings.

Hamburger Mac Skillet

Lasagna Roll-Ups

Virginia Foley • Manchester, New Hampshire

*Lasagna was considered company fare because most recipes make too much.
Then I saw a dish that rolled lasagna noodles into individual servings,
and I adapted it to my original recipe.*

1/4 to 1/3 pound ground beef
2 tablespoons chopped onion
1 garlic clove, minced
1 can (16 ounces) crushed tomatoes
1/2 teaspoon salt
1/2 teaspoon dried oregano
Dash cayenne pepper
1-1/4 cups small-curd cottage cheese, drained
1/4 cup grated Parmesan cheese
1 egg, lightly beaten
1 tablespoon minced fresh parsley
   or 1 teaspoon dried parsley flakes
1/4 teaspoon onion powder
6 lasagna noodles, cooked and drained
1/2 cup shredded part-skim mozzarella cheese

In a skillet, cook beef, onion and garlic over medium heat until meat is no longer pink; drain. Add tomatoes, salt, oregano and cayenne; simmer for 10 minutes.

Spoon half of the meat sauce into a greased 9-in. square baking dish. Combine cottage cheese, Parmesan cheese, egg, parsley and onion powder; spread 1/4 cupful on each noodle.

Carefully roll up and place seam side down over meat sauce. Top with remaining meat sauce. Sprinkle with mozzarella cheese.

Cover and bake at 375° for 30-35 minutes or until heated through. Let stand 10 minutes before serving. **Yield:** 2 servings.

Herbed London Broil

Sharon Patnoe • Elkins, Arkansas

I received this recipe from my stepfather. It's good whether you grill or broil the meat, and I've never met a person who didn't enjoy the tender beef as much as we do.

1/4 cup chopped onion
1/4 cup lemon juice
  2 tablespoons vegetable oil
1/4 teaspoon *each* celery seed, salt, dried thyme and oregano
1/4 teaspoon dried rosemary, crushed
  1 garlic clove, minced
Dash pepper
  1 beef flank steak (1/2 to 3/4 pound)

In a large resealable bag, combine the onion, lemon juice, oil and seasonings; add steak. Seal bag and turn to coat; refrigerate for several hours or overnight, turning once.

Drain and discard marinade. Grill steak, uncovered, over medium heat for 6-7 minutes on each side or until meat reaches desired doneness (for medium-rare, a meat thermometer should read 145°; medium, 160°; well-done, 170°). Slice thinly across the grain. **Yield:** 2 servings.

Asparagus Veal Cordon Bleu

Jeanne Molloy • Feeding Hills, Massachusetts

I try to make varied meals for two that are both appetizing and interesting. I sometimes double this recipe so we can have the leftovers for lunch the next day because they reheat so well in the microwave.

  8 fresh asparagus spears, trimmed
  2 tablespoons water
  2 veal cutlets (6 ounces *each*)
1/4 teaspoon salt
1/8 teaspoon pepper
  2 garlic cloves, minced
  1 tablespoon olive oil
  4 large fresh mushrooms, sliced
  2 thin slices prosciutto *or* deli ham
1/2 cup shredded Italian cheese blend

Asparagus Veal Cordon Bleu

Place asparagus and water in an 11-in. x 7-in. x 2-in. microwave-safe dish. Cover and microwave on high for 2-3 minutes or until crisp-tender; drain and set aside.

Flatten veal to 1/4-in. thickness; sprinkle with salt and pepper. In a small skillet, saute garlic in oil. Add veal; brown for 2-3 minutes on each side.

Transfer to an ungreased 11-in. x 7-in. x 2-in. baking dish. In the pan drippings, saute mushrooms until tender; spoon over veal. Top each with four asparagus spears and a slice of prosciutto. Sprinkle with cheese. Bake, uncovered, at 350° for 5-10 minutes or until juices run clear. **Yield:** 2 servings.

Barley Burger Stew

Judy McCarthy • Derby, Kansas

I found this hearty stew recipe in a cookbook I purchased at a flea market. The blend of beef and barley really hits the spot on cool days.

Barley Burger Stew

1/2	pound ground beef
1	small onion, chopped
1/4	cup chopped celery
2-1/4	cups tomato juice
1/2	cup water
1/4	cup medium pearl barley
1	to 1-1/2 teaspoons chili powder
1/2	teaspoon salt
1/4	teaspoon pepper

In a saucepan over medium heat, cook beef, onion and celery until meat is no longer pink; drain. Stir in tomato juice, water, barley, chili powder, salt and pepper. Bring to a boil. Reduce heat; cover and simmer for 50-60 minutes or until barley is tender. **Yield:** 2 servings.

Old-Fashioned Swiss Steak

Vera Kleiber • Raleigh, North Carolina

My husband and I have enjoyed this recipe for years. The comforting sauce is wonderful, and the dish always brings back memories.

✓ Uses less fat, sugar or salt. Includes Nutrition Facts or Diabetic Exchanges.

3/4	pound boneless beef top round steak
1/4	to 1/2 teaspoon salt
1/8	teaspoon pepper
1	tablespoon all-purpose flour
1	tablespoon canola oil
1	medium onion, chopped
1	can (5-1/2 ounces) tomato juice
1/2	cup diced canned tomatoes
2	teaspoons lemon juice
2	teaspoons Worcestershire sauce
1	to 2 teaspoons brown sugar
1/2	teaspoon prepared mustard

Cut steak into two pieces; sprinkle with salt and pepper. Using a mallet, pound flour into the meat. In a large skillet, brown meat in oil on both sides. Transfer to a shallow 1-qt. baking dish coated with nonstick cooking spray.

In the same skillet, saute onion in drippings until tender. Stir in the remaining ingredients. Pour over meat. Cover and bake at 350° for 1-1/2 hours or until tender. **Yield:** 2 servings.

Nutrition Facts: 1 serving (prepared with 1/4 teaspoon salt and reduced-sodium tomato juice) equals 361 calories, 12 g fat (2 g saturated fat), 96 mg cholesterol, 541 mg sodium, 20 g carbohydrate, 3 g fiber, 41 g protein.

Peppered Beef in Garlic Sauce

Jennifer Woelfel • Milwaukee, Wisconsin

Onion, garlic and red wine are combined with beef broth in a pleasant sauce that's similar to au jus in this sirloin steak entree. It's a special dish for two.

✓ Uses less fat, sugar or salt. Includes Nutrition Facts or Diabetic Exchanges.

Coarsely ground pepper
- 1/4 teaspoon salt
- 2 boneless beef sirloin steaks (5 ounces *each*)
- 3/4 cup beef broth
- 3/4 cup dry red wine *or* additional beef broth
- 1 small red onion, quartered and thinly sliced
- 2 garlic cloves, minced
- 1/2 teaspoon sugar
- 1/4 teaspoon dried marjoram

Dash hot pepper sauce

Sprinkle pepper and salt over steaks and press into both sides. In a nonstick skillet coated with nonstick cooking spray, brown steaks on both sides over medium-high heat. Remove and keep warm.

In the same skillet, combine the remaining ingredients. Bring to a boil; cover and cook for 2 minutes. Uncover; cook 5-6 minutes longer or until meat is cooked to desired doneness (for medium-rare, a meat thermometer should read 145°; medium, 160°; well-done, 170°). **Yield:** 2 servings.

Nutrition Facts: 1 steak with 1/4 cup sauce equals 304 calories, 9 g fat (3 g saturated fat), 85 mg cholesterol, 1,109 mg sodium, 7 g carbohydrate, 1 g fiber, 34 g protein. **Diabetic Exchanges:** 4-1/2 lean meat, 1 fat.

Pot Roast for Two

Judy Armstrong • Norwell, Massachusetts

A satisfying pot roast dinner doesn't have to feed an army, and this recipe proves it. I love the bold combination of spices in this full-flavored, meal-in-one dish.

- 2 beef eye of round steaks
- 2 small carrots, cut into 3/4-inch chunks
- 2 small potatoes, peeled and cut into 1/2-inch slices
- 1 celery rib, coarsely chopped
- 1 small onion, sliced
- 1 can (14-1/2 ounces) diced tomatoes, undrained
- 1/4 cup beef broth
- 2 garlic cloves, thinly sliced
- 2 teaspoons onion soup mix
- 1 teaspoon salt
- 1/2 teaspoon Italian seasoning
- 1/4 teaspoon pepper
- 1/8 teaspoon aniseed
- 1/8 teaspoon *each* ground cinnamon, ginger and nutmeg

Dash ground cloves

Place steaks in an ungreased 2-1/2-qt. baking dish. Top with carrots, potatoes, celery and onion. Combine the tomatoes, broth, garlic, soup mix and seasonings; pour over vegetables. Cover and bake at 350° for 1-1/2 to 1-3/4 hours or until meat and vegetables are tender. **Yield:** 2 servings.

Pot Roast for Two

POULTRY FOR A PAIR

Not only are chicken and turkey dishes loaded with heartwarming flavor and down-home appeal, but they usually cook up without much effort and please a variety of palates. Turn to this chapter the next time you need a moist, tender poultry specialty that won't take up all of your time or fill up your fridge with leftovers.

Chicken Fajitas
p. 142

Sesame Chicken Stir-Fry
p. 143

Turkey-Stuffed Peppers
p. 136

Chicken Red Pepper Saute
p. 148

Bacon-Wrapped Chicken
p. 137

Cajun Chicken Pasta

Cajun Chicken Pasta

LaDonna Reed • Ponca City, Oklahoma

A rich, creamy sauce tops this satisfying chicken and pasta dish. You can adjust the "heat level" by increasing or decreasing the amount of Cajun spice you use.

2   ounces uncooked fettuccine
2   boneless skinless chicken breast halves (5 ounces *each*), cut into 1-inch pieces
1   to 2 teaspoons Cajun seasoning
4   teaspoons olive oil, *divided*
1   cup sliced fresh mushrooms
1/2   cup thinly sliced green onions
1/2   medium green pepper, chopped
2   teaspoons minced garlic
1   tablespoon cornstarch
1   cup half-and-half cream
1/4   teaspoon salt, optional
1/4   teaspoon pepper
2   tablespoons grated Parmesan cheese

Cook fettuccine according to package directions. Meanwhile, sprinkle chicken with Cajun seasoning. In a large skillet, cook chicken in 2 teaspoons oil over medium heat until no longer pink. Remove with a slotted spoon and keep warm. Add remaining oil to the drippings; saute the mushrooms, onions, green pepper and garlic until crisp-tender.

Combine cornstarch and cream until smooth; stir into vegetable mixture. Bring to a boil over medium heat; cook and stir for 1 minute or until thickened. Add salt if desired and pepper. Return chicken to the pan.

Drain fettuccine and add to pan; toss gently. Cook for 1-2 minutes or until heated through. Sprinkle with Parmesan cheese. **Yield:** 2 servings.

Tarragon Turkey Patties

Lois Kinneberg • Phoenix, Arizona

These ground turkey patties are excellent with a green vegetable side dish for a no-fuss supper for two. We particularly like the tarragon-mustard sauce.

✓ **Uses less fat, sugar or salt. Includes Nutrition Facts or Diabetic Exchanges.**

1/2	cup crushed corn bread stuffing
1/4	cup egg substitute
2	tablespoons minced fresh tarragon *or 2 teaspoons dried tarragon*
1/4	teaspoon pepper
1/2	pound lean ground turkey
1	cup reduced-sodium chicken broth
2	tablespoons minced fresh tarragon *or 2 teaspoons dried tarragon*
1-1/2	teaspoons Dijon mustard

In a bowl, combine the stuffing, egg substitute, tarragon and pepper. Crumble turkey over mixture and mix well. Shape into four patties.

In a nonstick skillet coat with nonstick cooking spray, cook patties over medium heat for 4 minutes on each side or until juices run clear and a meat thermometer reads 165°. Remove and keep warm.

For sauce, add the broth, tarragon and mustard to the skillet; bring to a boil. Reduce heat; simmer, uncovered, for 5 minutes or until reduced by three-fourths. Serve with turkey patties. **Yield:** 2 servings.

Nutrition Facts: 2 patties with 2 tablespoons sauce equals 259 calories, 10 g fat (3 g saturated fat), 90 mg cholesterol, 830 mg sodium, 13 g carbohydrate, 1 g fiber, 27 g protein. **Diabetic Exchanges:** 3 lean meat, 1 starch.

Cheese-Stuffed Hawaiian Pizza

Mary Roberts-Rathje • Swisher, Iowa

This is such a quick, tasty idea. I rely on purchased flour tortillas to form the crust for an easy, five-ingredient pizza. It only takes about half an hour from start to stomach!

2	flour tortillas (10 inches)
1-1/2	cups (6 ounces) shredded part-skim mozzarella cheese, *divided*
1/4	cup pizza sauce
1/2	cup pineapple tidbits, drained
3/4	cup diced fully cooked chicken

Place one tortilla on a baking sheet coated with nonstick cooking spray. Sprinkle with 1 cup cheese. Top with second tortilla; spread with pizza sauce. Sprinkle with pineapple, chicken and remaining cheese. Bake at 375° for 15 minutes or until tortillas are crisp and cheese is melted. **Yield:** 2 servings.

Cheese-Stuffed Hawaiian Pizza

Marinated Turkey for Two

Rachel Wellborne • Jacksonville, North Carolina

For years, I've been exchanging recipes by correspondence with other family cooks. A dear friend in North Carolina shared this one. What's best about this recipe is that it allows you to enjoy down-home turkey flavor without preparing a whole bird.

2   **turkey breast tenderloins (about 1 pound *each*)**
1-1/2   **cups pineapple juice**
1/3   **cup sugar**
3/4   **teaspoon salt**
1/8   **teaspoon pepper**
1/8   **teaspoon ground ginger**
Dash ground cloves
Dash garlic powder

Place the turkey in a shallow glass dish. Combine remaining ingredients; mix well. Set aside 1/3 cup; cover and refrigerate. Pour the remaining marinade over turkey. Cover and refrigerate 4 hours or overnight.

Drain and discard marinade. Place turkey in an ungreased 11-in. x 7-in. x 2-in. baking dish. Pour reserved marinade over turkey. Cover and bake at 350° for 30 minutes. Uncover and bake 20-30 minutes longer or until no longer pink, basting twice. Slice and serve immediately. **Yield:** 2 servings.

Lemon Chicken 'n' Rice

Gerry Smailes • Edmonton, Alberta

This barley and rice medley combines a flavorful lemon-and-dill sauce with tender chicken. Serve it with green beans and you'll have a savory meal for two on the table in under an hour.

✓ Uses less fat, sugar or salt. Includes Nutrition Facts or Diabetic Exchanges.

1/4   **cup uncooked long grain rice**
1/4   **cup medium pearl barley**
1   **tablespoon butter**
1-2/3   **cups chicken broth, *divided***
2/3   **cup water**
3   **to 4 medium fresh mushrooms, sliced**
2   **tablespoons chopped green onion**
2   **boneless skinless chicken breast halves (6 ounces *each*)**
2   **teaspoons canola oil**
1/3   **cup white wine *or* additional chicken broth**
2   **teaspoons cornstarch**
1/2   **cup evaporated milk**
1   **teaspoon grated lemon peel**
1/2   **teaspoon dill weed**
1/8   **teaspoon salt**
1/8   **teaspoon pepper**

In a small saucepan, saute rice and barley in butter for 4-5 minutes or until lightly browned. Add 1 cup broth, water, mushrooms and onion; bring to a boil. Reduce heat; cover and simmer for 20-22 minutes or until tender.

Meanwhile, flatten chicken to 1/2-in. thickness. In a large skillet, brown chicken in oil on both sides. Add 1/3 cup broth and wine or additional broth. Simmer, uncovered, for 10 minutes, turning once. Remove chicken and keep warm.

Combine cornstarch and milk until smooth; stir into pan juices. Stir in the lemon peel, dill, salt, pepper and remaining broth. Bring to a boil; cook and stir for 2 minutes or until thickened. Let rice mixture stand for 5 minutes, then fluff with a fork. Serve chicken over rice. Top with dill sauce. **Yield:** 2 servings.

Nutrition Facts: 1 chicken breast half with 1/3 cup sauce and 3/4 cup rice mixture (prepared with reduced-fat butter, reduced-sodium broth and fat-free evaporated milk) equals 531 calories, 12 g fat (4 g saturated fat), 107 mg cholesterol, 863 mg sodium, 51 g carbohydrate, 5 g fiber, 47 g protein.

Rosemary Chicken

Luke Armstead • Oregon City, Oregon

This is a terrific recipe for anyone who cooks for one or two people. Plus, it can easily be doubled to feed more. It is perfect for fast-paced weekdays and makes a complete meal when served with buttered beans and rolls.

✓ **Uses less fat, sugar or salt. Includes Nutrition Facts or Diabetic Exchanges.**

Rosemary Chicken

> 2 boneless skinless chicken breast halves (4 ounces *each*)
> 2 teaspoons canola oil
> 1 tablespoon lemon juice
> 1 teaspoon dried rosemary, crushed
> 1/2 teaspoon dried oregano
> 1/4 teaspoon pepper

Flatten chicken to 1/4-in. thickness. In a nonstick skillet, cook chicken in oil over medium-high heat for 3-4 minutes on each side or until juices run clear. Sprinkle with lemon juice, rosemary, oregano and pepper. **Yield:** 2 servings.

Nutrition Facts: One serving equals 172 calories, 6 g fat (1 g saturated fat), 66 mg cholesterol, 74 mg sodium, 1 g carbohydrate, 1 g fiber, 26 g protein.
Diabetic Exchanges: 3-1/2 very lean meat, 1 fat.

Veggie Turkey Roll-Ups

Gertrude Peischl • Allentown, Pennsylvania

Slices of turkey are rolled around an assortment of vegetables in my favorite two-serving supper. A sauce of lemon juice, white wine and basil makes a tasty addition.

> 1/4 cup *each* julienned sweet red pepper, carrot, yellow summer squash and zucchini
> 4 uncooked turkey breast slices
> 2 tablespoons all-purpose flour
> 1/8 teaspoon paprika
> 1 tablespoon vegetable oil
> 1/4 cup water
> 3 tablespoons lemon juice
> 4-1/2 teaspoons white wine *or* additional water
> 2-1/4 teaspoons chicken bouillon granules
> 1/2 teaspoon dried basil

Combine the red pepper, carrot, summer squash and zucchini; spoon down the center of each turkey slice. Roll up and secure ends with toothpicks.

In a shallow bowl, combine flour and paprika; roll turkey in mixture until coated. In a skillet over medium heat, cook roll-ups in oil until golden brown.

In a bowl, combine the remaining ingredients; pour over turkey. Cover and simmer for 3 minutes or until meat juices run clear and the vegetables are crisp-tender. Discard toothpicks from roll-ups; serve with the pan drippings. **Yield:** 2 servings.

Orange-Honey Cashew Chicken

Orange-Honey Cashew Chicken

Raymonde Bourgeois • Swastika, Ontario

This sweet, honey-citrus sauce turns ordinary poultry into something special. I like to serve it with rice.

1-1/4 cups orange juice, *divided*
1 tablespoon lemon juice
1/4 teaspoon salt
Dash pepper
2 boneless skinless chicken breast halves (about 5 ounces *each*)
1 to 2 teaspoons olive oil
1/3 cup chopped onion
1/4 cup honey
1 teaspoon minced fresh parsley
Hot cooked rice
1 tablespoon cornstarch
2 tablespoons water
3 tablespoons chopped salted cashews

In a resealable bag, combine 1/2 cup orange juice, lemon juice, salt and pepper; add chicken. Seal bag and turn to coat; refrigerate for 4-8 hours or overnight.

Drain and discard marinade. In a skillet, cook chicken in oil for 2-3 minutes on each side or until browned. Remove and keep warm. In the drippings, saute onion until tender. Combine the honey, parsley and remaining orange juice; stir into skillet. Bring to a boil.

Return chicken to the pan. Reduce heat; cover and simmer for 8-10 minutes or until chicken juices run clear. Place chicken over rice. Combine cornstarch and water until smooth; stir into cooking juices. Bring to a boil; cook and stir for 1-2 minutes or until thickened. Pour over chicken. Sprinkle with cashews. **Yield:** 2 servings.

Alfredo Chicken Lasagna

Bridgette Monaghan • Masonville, Iowa

This easy recipe is elegant enough to double and prepare for company. I've served it often, and everyone comments on its rich flavor. I love the fact that it can be made ahead of time.

6 ounces boneless skinless chicken breast, cut into bite-size pieces
1 cup sliced fresh mushrooms
2 tablespoons chopped onion
1 garlic clove, minced
1 tablespoon olive oil
1 tablespoon all-purpose flour
1 cup Alfredo sauce
3/4 cup 2% cottage cheese
1/4 cup plus 2 tablespoons shredded Parmesan cheese, *divided*
1 egg, lightly beaten
1/2 teaspoon Italian seasoning
1/2 teaspoon dried parsley flakes
4 lasagna noodles, cooked and drained
1-1/2 cups (6 ounces) shredded part-skim mozzarella cheese

In a large skillet, saute the chicken, mushrooms, onion and garlic in oil until chicken is no longer pink. Stir in flour until blended; stir in Alfredo sauce. Bring to a boil. Reduce heat; simmer, uncovered, for 5 minutes. In a small bowl, combine the cottage cheese, 1/4 cup Parmesan cheese, egg, Italian seasoning and parsley.

Spread 1/2 cup Alfredo mixture in an 8-in. x 4-in. x 2-in. loaf dish coated with nonstick cooking spray. Layer with two noodles (trimmed to fit pan), half of the cottage cheese mixture, 3/4 cup Alfredo mixture and 3/4 cup mozzarella cheese. Sprinkle with remaining Parmesan cheese. Repeat the layers.

Cover and bake at 350° for 30 minutes. Uncover; bake 10 minutes longer or until bubbly. Let stand for 10 minutes before cutting. **Yield:** 3 servings.

Teriyaki Chicken Breast

Becky Bolte • Jewell, Kansas

Seasoned rice makes a nice addition to teriyaki chicken in this dinner. The fantastic marinade is a breeze to whip up, and the meat only needs to sit in it for an hour or so. Try using the recipe for a grilled chicken kabob as well.

- 2 tablespoons chicken broth
- 1 tablespoon soy sauce
- 2 teaspoons sugar
- 1 teaspoon vegetable oil
- 1 garlic clove, minced

Pinch ground ginger

- 1 boneless skinless chicken breast half

Additional chicken broth

- 1/2 cup uncooked instant rice
- 2 tablespoons frozen peas

In a small resealable bag or shallow glass container, combine the first six ingredients. Add chicken; seal bag or cover container. Refrigerate for 1 hour.

Remove chicken from marinade and set marinade aside. Broil the chicken for 12 minutes or until juices run clear, turning once.

Meanwhile, add broth to marinade to measure 2/3 cup. Pour into a small saucepan; bring to a rolling boil. Boil for 5 minutes. Add rice and peas; cover and let stand for 5 minutes. Serve with chicken. **Yield:** 1 serving.

Chicken Bundles for Two

Chicken Bundles For Two

Cheryl Landis • Honey Brook, Pennsylvania

For a picture-perfect dinner for two...without a lot of work...season chicken breasts and vegetables with sage and dill, then wrap everything in foil, so the whole meal can be grilled at once.

- 2 boneless skinless chicken breast halves
- 2 medium red potatoes, quartered and cut into 1/2-inch slices
- 1/4 cup chopped onion
- 1 medium carrot, cut into 1/4-inch slices
- 1 celery rib, cut into 1/4-inch slices
- 1/2 teaspoon rubbed sage

Salt and pepper to taste

Fresh dill sprigs

Divide chicken and vegetables between two pieces of double-layered heavy-duty foil (about 18 in. square). Sprinkle with sage, salt and pepper; top with dill sprigs. Fold foil around the mixture and seal tightly.

Grill, covered, over medium heat for 30 minutes or until the chicken juices run clear and vegetables are tender. **Yield:** 2 servings.

Honey Baked Chicken

Helen Whelan • Jarrettsville, Maryland

After our children left home, I had to learn to cook all over again. I began to economize on food purchases by buying meats in quantity and freezing extras for future menus. My husband especially loves this chicken recipe, which I pared down to fit our lifestyle today.

 2 chicken breast halves (bone-in)
 2 tablespoons butter
1/2 cup honey
1/2 teaspoon salt
 1 tablespoon prepared mustard

Place the chicken in a greased or foil-lined 9-in. square baking pan. Bake, uncovered, at 325° for 30 minutes. Meanwhile, in a small saucepan, combine remaining ingredients; cook and stir over low heat until well blended and heated through. Pour over chicken.

Bake, uncovered, 30-35 minutes longer or until chicken juices run clear. Baste before serving. **Yield:** 2 servings.

Honey Baked Chicken

Turkey Lattice Pie

Taste of Home Test Kitchen • Greendale, Wisconsin

Frozen veggies and refrigerated crescent rolls make this the easiest potpie you've ever assembled. Not only does it serve two, but it's a smart way to use up any cooked turkey sitting in the fridge.

 1 cup water
1/2 cup frozen mixed vegetables
 2 teaspoons chicken bouillon granules
 2 tablespoons plus 1/2 teaspoon cornstarch
 1 cup milk
 1 cup cubed cooked turkey
1/2 cup shredded cheddar cheese
 2 teaspoons minced fresh parsley
1/4 teaspoon salt
1/8 teaspoon pepper
 1 tube (4 ounces) refrigerated crescent rolls

In a saucepan, bring the water, vegetables and bouillon to a boil. Reduce heat; simmer, uncovered, for 3-5 minutes or until vegetables are tender. In a small bowl, combine cornstarch and milk until smooth; add to the vegetable mixture. Bring to a boil; cook and stir for 1-2 minutes or until thickened. Add the turkey, cheese, parsley, salt and pepper. Pour into a greased 8-in. square baking dish.

Unroll crescent roll dough; separate into two rectangles. Seal seams and perforations. Place long sides together to form a square; pinch edges together to seal. Cut into eight strips; make a lattice crust over hot turkey mixture. Bake at 375° for 25-30 minutes or until top is golden brown. **Yield:** 2 servings.

Chicken and Julienned Veggies

Chicken and Julienned Veggies

Lois Crissman • Mansfield, Ohio

Thyme seasons this quick skillet entree. I serve the browned chicken breasts, colorful sliced carrot and zucchini and savory sauce over spaghetti for a pleasing meal.

✓ Uses less fat, sugar or salt. Includes Nutrition Facts or Diabetic Exchanges.

- **2** boneless skinless chicken breast halves (4 ounces *each*)
- **2** teaspoons olive oil
- **1/2** cup plus 2 tablespoons reduced-fat reduced-sodium condensed cream of chicken soup, undiluted
- **1/4** cup fat-free milk
- **1/4** teaspoon dried thyme
- **1/4** teaspoon salt
- **1/8** teaspoon white pepper
- **1** medium carrot, julienned
- **1** cup julienned zucchini

Hot cooked spaghetti, optional

In a nonstick skillet, brown chicken in oil. In a bowl, combine the soup, milk, thyme, salt and pepper until smooth; pour over chicken. Add carrot. Reduce heat; cover and simmer for 5 minutes, stirring occasionally. Add zucchini; cover and simmer 5 minutes longer or until chicken is no longer pink. Serve over spaghetti if desired. **Yield:** 2 servings.

Nutrition Facts: 1 chicken breast half with 2/3 cup vegetable mixture, calculated without spaghetti, equals 261 calories, 9 g fat (2 g saturated fat), 74 mg cholesterol, 955 mg sodium, 13 g carbohydrate, 2 g fiber, 30 g protein. **Diabetic Exchanges:** 3 lean meat, 1 vegetable, 1/2 starch, 1/2 fat.

Italian Turkey Breast

Helen Vail • Glenside, Pennsylvania

We enjoy this Italian-style turkey dish as a delightful change of pace. The dressed-up turkey slices are never dry, and they cook in just minutes.

1   tablespoon all-purpose flour
1/8 teaspoon pepper
2   turkey breast slices (3 ounces *each*)
2   teaspoons olive oil
1   teaspoon margarine
1   can (8 ounces) no-salt-added tomato sauce
1   teaspoon *each* dried oregano, basil and thyme

2   teaspoons shredded part-skim mozzarella cheese
1   teaspoon nonfat Parmesan cheese topping

In a shallow bowl, combine flour and pepper; dredge the turkey slices. In a skillet over medium heat, brown turkey in oil and margarine. Combine tomato sauce, oregano, basil and thyme; pour over turkey. Bring to a boil; reduce heat. Cover and simmer for 3-4 minutes or until meat is no longer pink. Sprinkle with cheeses. **Yield:** 2 servings.

Dijon Chicken

Taste of Home Test Kitchen • Greendale, Wisconsin

Prepared salad dressing and Dijon mustard easily flavor chicken breasts in this no-nonsense, comforting one-dish dinner.

1/3 cup prepared ranch salad dressing
1   tablespoon Dijon mustard
2   boneless skinless chicken breast halves (4 ounces *each*)
2   tablespoons butter
3   tablespoons white wine *or* chicken broth

Hot cooked long grain and wild rice *or* pasta

Fresh parsley, optional

In a small bowl, combine salad dressing and mustard; set aside. In a skillet, cook chicken in butter over medium heat for 8-10 minutes or until juices run clear. Remove and keep warm.

Add wine or broth to skillet; cook over medium heat for 2 minutes, stirring to loosen browned bits from pan. Whisk in mustard mixture; cook and stir until blended and heated through. Serve over chicken and rice or pasta. Garnish with parsley if desired. **Yield:** 2 servings.

Dijon Chicken

Turkey Meatballs in Garlic Sauce

Audrey Thibodeau • Mesa, Arizona

This is a downsized recipe that we enjoy. It makes a satisfying dinner for two, served over hot rice or noodles. I also like to accompany it with baked acorn squash.

2 tablespoons milk
1/2 teaspoon Worcestershire sauce
2 to 3 drops hot pepper sauce
1/2 cup finely crushed butter-flavored crackers (about 10 crackers)
1 tablespoon minced fresh parsley
1/4 teaspoon salt
1/8 teaspoon pepper
1/2 pound lean ground turkey
1 cup V8 juice
1/4 cup chicken broth
2 garlic cloves, minced
Hot cooked rice

In a large bowl, combine the first seven ingredients. Crumble turkey over mixture and mix well. Shape into six meatballs. Place in a greased 9-in. pie plate. Bake, uncovered, at 400° for 10 minutes.

Meanwhile, in a small bowl, combine the V8 juice, broth and garlic. Turn meatballs; spoon sauce over top. Reduce heat to 350°. Bake 20 minutes longer, basting every 5 minutes. Serve over rice. **Yield:** 2 servings.

Citrus Chicken

Wendy Anderson • Santa Rosa, California

I adapted this delightful recipe from a cookbook, and it became one of my husband's favorites. It's proof that a light recipe can still be big on flavor.

✓ Uses less fat, sugar or salt. Includes Nutrition Facts or Diabetic Exchanges.

1 tablespoon cornstarch
1/2 teaspoon ground ginger
1/8 to 1/4 teaspoon cayenne pepper
1/3 cup orange juice
3 tablespoons reduced-sodium soy sauce
2 tablespoons water
2 tablespoons lemon juice
1 tablespoon honey
1 garlic clove, minced
1/2 teaspoon grated orange peel
1/2 teaspoon grated lemon peel
10 ounces boneless skinless chicken breasts, cut into 3/4-inch pieces
1 tablespoon olive oil
Hot cooked pasta, optional
1/4 cup sliced green onions

In a bowl, combine the cornstarch, ginger and cayenne. Stir in the orange juice, soy sauce, water, lemon juice, honey, garlic, orange and lemon peel until smooth; set aside.

In a skillet, saute chicken in oil until no longer pink. Stir cornstarch mixture and add to the pan. Bring to a boil; cook and stir for 1-2 minutes or until thickened. Serve over pasta if desired. Sprinkle with onions. **Yield:** 2 servings.

Nutrition Facts: 1 cup chicken mixture equals 305 calories, 10 g fat (2 g saturated fat), 78 mg cholesterol, 979 mg sodium, 22 g carbohydrate, 1 g fiber, 31 g protein. **Diabetic Exchanges:** 4 lean meat, 1 starch, 1/2 fruit.

Turkey Meatballs in Garlic Sauce

Deviled Chicken Thighs

Bernice Morris • Marshfield, Missouri

When I make this dish, I invite my next-door neighbor over for supper. It's just enough for the two of us. This tasty chicken is tender and juicy, with a bit of crunch from the cashews.

Deviled Chicken Thighs

1 teaspoon butter, softened
1 teaspoon cider vinegar
1 teaspoon prepared mustard
1 teaspoon paprika
Dash pepper
2 boneless skinless chicken thighs (about 4 ounces *each*)
3 tablespoons soft bread crumbs
2 tablespoons chopped cashews

In a bowl, combine the butter, vinegar, mustard, paprika and pepper. Spread over chicken thighs. Place in a greased 11-in. x 7-in. x 2-in. baking dish. Sprinkle with bread crumbs.

Bake, uncovered, at 400° for 15 minutes. Sprinkle with the cashews. Bake 7-12 minutes longer or until chicken juices run clear and topping is golden brown. **Yield:** 2 servings.

Turkey-Stuffed Peppers

Julie Grose • Lompoc, California

Not all stuffed peppers have ground beef and tomato sauce! I rely on ground turkey and a white sauce to give this variation its wonderful, down-home appeal.

2 large green peppers, tops and seeds removed
1/2 pound ground turkey
1 small onion, chopped
1 garlic clove, minced
2 tablespoons butter
1 tablespoon all-purpose flour
1/2 teaspoon salt
1/8 teaspoon pepper
1/2 cup milk
1/2 cup chopped tomato
4 tablespoons shredded cheddar cheese, *divided*

In a large saucepan, cook peppers in boiling water for 3 minutes. Drain and rinse with cold water; set aside.

In a skillet, cook the turkey, onion and garlic over medium heat until meat is no longer pink; drain and set aside. In the same skillet, melt butter. Stir in flour, salt and pepper until smooth. Gradually add milk. Bring to a boil; cook and stir for 1-2 minutes or until thickened. Return turkey mixture to skillet. Stir in tomato and 2 tablespoons cheese; heat through. Spoon into peppers; sprinkle with the remaining cheese.

Place in a greased 1-qt. baking dish. Cover and bake at 350° for 25-30 minutes or until peppers are tender and filling is hot. **Yield:** 2 servings.

Bacon-Wrapped Chicken

LaDonna Reed • Ponca City, Oklahoma

I spread chicken breasts with a creamy filling, roll them up, wrap them in bacon and bake them. For a spicier version, try using sliced jalapeno peppers instead of green chilies.

✓ Uses less fat, sugar or salt. Includes Nutrition Facts or Diabetic Exchanges.

4	bacon strips
2	boneless skinless chicken breast halves (6 ounces *each*)
1/4	teaspoon seasoned salt, optional
1/4	cup canned chopped green chilies
1-1/2	ounces cream cheese, softened
1	garlic clove, minced

In a large skillet, cook bacon over medium heat until partially cooked but not crisp; drain on paper towels. Flatten chicken to 1/4-in. thickness. Sprinkle with seasoned salt if desired.

In a small bowl, combine the chilies, cream cheese and garlic. Spread over one side of each chicken breast. Roll up and tuck ends in. Wrap each with two bacon strips; secure with toothpicks.

Place in an 8-in. square baking dish coated with nonstick cooking spray. Bake, uncovered, at 375° for 30-35 minutes or until chicken juices run clear. Discard toothpicks. **Yield:** 2 servings.

Nutrition Facts: One serving equals 316 calories, 12 g fat (5 g saturated fat), 121 mg cholesterol, 486 mg sodium, 3 g carbohydrate, 1 g fiber, 45 g protein.

Chicken Parmesan

Mary Dennis • Bryan, Ohio

This popular combination of chicken breasts, spaghetti sauce, cheese and mushrooms makes a pretty dish, and it's oh-so flavorful, too.

2	boneless skinless chicken breast halves
2	teaspoons vegetable oil
1-1/2	cups spaghetti sauce
1	can (4 ounces) mushroom stems and pieces, drained
1/2	cup shredded part-skim mozzarella cheese
2	tablespoons grated Parmesan cheese

Hot cooked linguine

In an ovenproof skillet, brown chicken in oil over medium heat. Add spaghetti sauce and mushrooms. Bring to a boil. Reduce heat; cover and simmer for 10-15 minutes or until chicken is no longer pink.

Sprinkle with cheeses. Broil 4-6 in. from the heat for 3-4 minutes or until cheese is melted. Serve over linguine. **Yield:** 2 servings.

Chicken Parmesan

Turkey Meat Loaf

Turkey Meat Loaf

Judy Prante • Portland, Oregon

I like to make just enough food for two servings, but this recipe is easy to double. A friend told me it was the best turkey loaf she'd ever eaten!

4-1/2   **teaspoons water**
1-1/2   **teaspoons teriyaki sauce**
   1   **cup cubed bread**
   1   **egg, beaten**
   2   **tablespoons chopped onion**
   1   **tablespoon chopped green pepper**
   1   **tablespoon shredded part-skim mozzarella cheese**
   1   **tablespoon shredded cheddar cheese**
Dash garlic powder
Dash celery seed
  1/2   **pound ground turkey**
   1   **tablespoon grated Parmesan cheese**

In a bowl, combine the water, teriyaki sauce and bread cubes; let stand for 5 minutes. Add the egg, onion, green pepper, mozzarella and cheddar cheeses, garlic powder and celery seed. Crumble turkey over mixture and mix well.

Pat into an ungreased 5-3/4-in. x 3-in. x 2-in. loaf pan. Sprinkle with Parmesan cheese. Bake, uncovered, at 350° for 1 hour or until a meat thermometer reads 165° drain. **Yield:** 2 servings.

Editor's Note: This recipe can easily be doubled to serve four. Shape meat mixture into a loaf in an 11-in. x 7-in. x 2-in. baking dish. Bake as directed for about 1-1/4 hours or until a meat thermometer reads 165°.

Veggie Chicken Packet

Teresa Stough • Augusta, Georgia

If you ask me, cooking doesn't get much easier than this delicious idea. An aluminum foil "boat" holds a chicken breast, rice, veggies and seasonings for a one-dish delight. Best of all, there's never any leftovers.

- 2 tablespoons uncooked instant rice
- 1 bone-in chicken breast half
- 1/4 cup sliced carrot
- 2 onion slices, separated into rings
- 1/4 cup *each* julienned green and sweet red pepper
- 1 tablespoon water
- 1 tablespoon Worcestershire sauce
- 2 to 3 teaspoons soy sauce
- 1 tablespoon butter

Place rice in the center of a piece of heavy-duty foil (about 14 in. square); top with chicken and vegetables. Combine the water, Worcestershire sauce and soy sauce; pour over vegetables. Dot with butter. Fold foil around the chicken and vegetables and seal tightly.

Place in a baking pan. Bake at 350° for 65-75 minutes or until chicken juices run clear. Open foil carefully to allow steam to escape. **Yield:** 1 serving.

Tangy Glazed Chicken

Barbara Haney • St. Louis, Missouri

This finger-licking citrus sauce offers a hint of sweet apple flavor, making it perfect over bone-in chicken breasts. Serve them with potatoes or rice and a salad if you wish.

- 2 bone-in chicken breast halves
- 1/4 teaspoon salt, optional
- 4-1/2 teaspoons butter
- 1 small onion, thinly sliced
- 1 celery rib, thinly sliced
- 1/2 cup chicken broth
- 1/2 cup apple jelly
- 3 tablespoons orange juice
- 1 tablespoon minced fresh parsley
- 1/4 to 1/2 teaspoon dried thyme

Sprinkle chicken with salt if desired. In a large skillet, melt butter over medium heat; brown chicken on all sides. Remove and keep warm.

In the pan drippings, saute onion and celery until tender. Add the remaining ingredients; cook and stir until jelly is melted. Return chicken to pan. Cook, uncovered, for 30-35 minutes or until meat juices run clear. Remove skin if desired. Top chicken with onion mixture. **Yield:** 2 servings.

Tangy Glazed Chicken

Grilled Chicken Veggie Dinner

Kenneth Dunn Sr. • Bedford, Kentucky

Low in carbs, high in flavor, this chicken specialty was created on the spur of the minute using veggies fresh from our garden. It's delicious by itself or served over buttered noodles. For variety, you might use bone-in chicken breasts instead of thighs or substitute lemon-pepper for the seasoned pepper.

☑ **Uses less fat, sugar or salt. Includes Nutrition Facts or Diabetic Exchanges.**

4	chicken thighs (4 ounces *each*)
1-1/2	teaspoons olive oil
1/2	teaspoon salt, *divided*
1/2	teaspoon seasoned pepper
1/2	*each* medium green, sweet red and yellow pepper, sliced
1	medium onion, halved and sliced
1-1/2	teaspoons Italian seasoning
1/4	teaspoon garlic powder
2	plum tomatoes, cut into wedges

Rub both sides of chicken with oil; sprinkle with 1/4 teaspoon salt and pepper. Place skin side down on grill rack. Grill, covered, over medium heat for 5 minutes. Turn; grill 5-6 minutes longer or until golden brown.

Place chicken on a double thickness of heavy-duty foil (about 18 in. square). Top with peppers, onion, Italian seasoning, garlic powder and the remaining salt. Seal foil tightly.

Grill, covered, over indirect medium heat for 20 minutes. Open foil carefully; add tomatoes. Reseal foil; grill 4-5 minutes longer or until chicken juices run clear and vegetables are tender. **Yield:** 2 servings.

Nutrition Facts: 1 serving (calculated without chicken skin) equals 170 calories, 8 g fat (2 g saturated fat), 38 mg cholesterol, 631 mg sodium, 13 g carbohydrate, 3 g fiber, 13 g protein.

Apricot-Glaze Chicken

Apricot-Glaze Chicken

Retha Kaye Naylor • Frankton, Indiana

My husband knows what's on the supper menu when our boys drive home from college because this entree has become our homecoming tradition. Best of all, it's easy to make for any number of people.

2	boneless skinless chicken breast halves
1/4	cup mayonnaise
1/4	cup apricot preserves
2	tablespoons dried minced onion

Place chicken in a greased 9-in. square baking dish. Combine the mayonnaise, preserves and onion; spoon over chicken. Bake, uncovered, at 350° for 25 minutes or until chicken juices run clear. **Yield:** 2 servings.

Tasty Turkey and Mushrooms

Nancy Zimmerman • Cape May Court House, New Jersey

Fresh mushrooms star in this yummy recipe for turkey. It takes just minimal preparation and makes a great main dish.

☑ Uses less fat, sugar or salt. Includes Nutrition Facts or Diabetic Exchanges.

1	garlic clove, minced
1	tablespoon butter
1/2	pound boneless skinless turkey breast, cut into 2-inch strips
3/4	cup reduced-sodium beef broth
1	tablespoon tomato paste
2	cups sliced fresh mushrooms
1/8	teaspoon salt

In a large nonstick skillet, saute garlic in butter until tender. Add turkey; cook until juices run clear. Remove and keep warm. Add the broth, tomato paste, mushrooms and salt to skillet; cook for 3-5 minutes or until mushrooms are tender, stirring occasionally. Return turkey to the pan and heat through. **Yield:** 2 servings.

Nutrition Facts: 1 cup equals 209 calories, 7 g fat (4 g saturated fat), 88 mg cholesterol, 435 mg sodium, 5 g carbohydrate, 1 g fiber, 31 g protein. **Diabetic Exchanges:** 4 lean meat, 1 vegetable, 1 fat.

Tasty Turkey and Mushrooms

Oven-Barbecued Chicken

Agnes Golian • Garfield Heights, Ohio

On a lazy sunny summer day, this chicken is the best ever. We enjoy it with baked beans and watermelon. Try the zesty barbecue sauce on other meats, too.

2	chicken leg quarters
1	tablespoon canola oil
1/4	cup ketchup
2	tablespoons Worcestershire sauce
1	tablespoon sugar
1	tablespoon cider vinegar
1	tablespoon steak sauce

Dash hot pepper sauce

In a large nonstick skillet, brown chicken in oil. Transfer to an 8-in. square baking dish coated with nonstick cooking spray.

In a bowl, combine the ketchup, Worcestershire sauce, sugar, vinegar, steak sauce and hot pepper sauce; pour over chicken.

Bake, uncovered, at 350° for 55-60 minutes or until chicken juices run clear, basting every 15 minutes with sauce. **Yield:** 2 servings.

Chicken Fajitas

Kathleen Smith • Pittsburgh, Pennsylvania

This is the best fajita recipe I've ever used. It sounds complicated, but it really isn't. The servings are hearty, but this dish is so good that my husband and I never have a problem finishing it!

✓ Uses less fat, sugar or salt. Includes Nutrition Facts or Diabetic Exchanges.

- 1/4 cup lime juice
- 1 tablespoon reduced-sodium soy sauce
- 2 teaspoons canola oil
- 1 garlic clove, minced
- 1/2 teaspoon salt
- 1/2 teaspoon chili powder
- 1/2 teaspoon cayenne pepper
- 1/2 teaspoon Liquid Smoke, optional
- 1/4 teaspoon pepper
- 2 boneless skinless chicken breast halves (4 ounces *each*)

FILLING:
- 1 medium onion, julienned
- 1/2 small sweet red *or* green pepper, julienned
- 2 teaspoons canola oil
- 1/2 teaspoon lime juice
- 1 teaspoon reduced-sodium soy sauce
- 4 fat-free tortillas (6 inches), warmed

Salsa and sour cream, optional

In a large resealable plastic bag, combine the first nine ingredients; add chicken. Seal bag and turn to coat; refrigerate for at least 2 hours.

Coat grill rack with nonstick cooking spray before starting the grill. Drain and discard marinade. Grill chicken, covered, over medium heat for 4-6 minutes on each side or until juices run clear. Set aside and keep warm.

In a large nonstick skillet, saute the onion and red pepper in oil for 5 minutes. Combine the lime juice and soy sauce; pour into skillet. Cook for 2 minutes or until vegetables are tender. Cut chicken into thin slices; place on tortillas. Top with vegetable mixture and roll up. Serve with salsa and sour cream if desired. **Yield:** 4 fajitas.

Nutrition Facts: 2 fajitas (calculated without salsa and sour cream) equals 246 calories, 8 g fat (1 g saturated fat), 66 mg cholesterol, 628 mg sodium, 15 g carbohydrate, 3 g fiber, 29 g protein. **Diabetic Exchanges:** 3 very lean meat, 1 starch, 1 fat.

Garlic Chicken on Rice

Becky Bolte • Jewell, Kansas

This 1-hour marinade is perfect for someone who lives alone and doesn't want to spend a lot of time in the kitchen. Soy sauce, honey and ground ginger give the skillet dish a tasty flair.

- 1/4 cup chopped onion
- 2 garlic cloves, minced
- 1/4 cup lemon juice
- 2 tablespoons soy sauce
- 1 tablespoon honey
- 2 teaspoons ground ginger
- 1 chicken breast half, skinned, boned and cut into strips
- 1/2 cup chicken broth
- 1/2 cup uncooked instant rice
- 1 tablespoon chopped fresh parsley
- 1/2 teaspoon grated orange peel

In a small bowl, combine onion, garlic, lemon juice, soy sauce, honey and ginger. Add chicken; cover and refrigerate for at least 1 hour.

In a small saucepan, bring chicken broth to a boil. Remove from the heat; stir in rice, parsley and orange peel. Cover and let stand for 5 minutes. Meanwhile, cook the chicken and marinade in a hot skillet until no longer pink. Serve over rice. **Yield:** 1 serving.

Pepper Jack Stuffed Chicken

Taste of Home Test Kitchen • Greendale, Wisconsin

Spicy cheese and Mexican seasoning give plenty of zip to these tender chicken rolls. Round out the meal with rice pilaf and pineapple tidbits. Or microwave frozen broccoli and serve peppermint ice cream for dessert.

- 2 ounces pepper Jack cheese
- 2 boneless skinless chicken breast halves
- 1 teaspoon Mexican *or* taco seasoning
- 1 tablespoon vegetable oil

Cut cheese into two 2-1/4-in. x 1-in. x 3/4-in. strips. Flatten chicken to 1/4-in. thickness. Place a strip of cheese down the center of each chicken breast half; fold chicken over cheese and secure with toothpicks. Rub Mexican seasoning over chicken.

In a large skillet, brown chicken in oil on all sides. Transfer to a greased 8-in. square baking dish. Bake, uncovered, at 350° for 25-30 minutes or until chicken juices run clear. Discard toothpicks. **Yield:** 2 servings.

Pepper Jack Stuffed Chicken

Sesame Chicken Stir-Fry

Michelle McWilliams • Fort Lupton, Colorado

When we were first married, my husband frequently had to work late. This eye-catching stir-fry was a satisfying alternative to a big dinner for me.

- 1 boneless skinless chicken breast half, cut into thin strips
- 2 teaspoons vegetable oil
- 7 snow peas
- 1 cup fresh broccoli florets
- 1/3 cup julienned sweet red pepper
- 3 medium fresh mushrooms, sliced
- 3/4 cup chopped onion
- 1 tablespoon cornstarch
- 1 teaspoon sugar
- 1/2 cup cold water
- 3 to 4 tablespoons soy sauce

Hot cooked rice
- 1 teaspoon sesame seeds, toasted

In a skillet or wok, stir-fry chicken in oil for 6-8 minutes or until juices run clear. Remove chicken and set aside. In the same skillet, stir-fry peas, broccoli and red pepper for 2-3 minutes. Add mushrooms and onion; stir-fry for 3-4 minutes.

Combine cornstarch and sugar; stir in water and soy sauce until smooth. Add to the pan. Bring to a boil; cook and stir for 1-2 minutes or until thickened. Return chicken to the pan; cook until mixture is heated through and vegetables are tender. Serve over rice. Sprinkle with sesame seeds. **Yield:** 1 serving.

Mini Turkey Loaf

Mini Turkey Loaf

Vikki Metz • Tavares, Florida

Onion, green pepper and apple juice flavor this moist ground turkey loaf. Drizzled with pan gravy, it makes a satisfying main course for Sunday dinner or busy weeknights.

☑ **Uses less fat, sugar or salt. Includes Nutrition Facts or Diabetic Exchanges.**

- 1/4 cup chopped onion
- 1/4 cup chopped green pepper
- 1/4 cup chopped fresh mushrooms
- 1 teaspoon olive oil
- 1 cup unsweetened apple juice, *divided*
- 1/2 teaspoon garlic powder
- 1/2 teaspoon onion powder
- 1/4 teaspoon salt
- 1/8 teaspoon pepper
- 1/2 pound ground turkey
- 2 tablespoons cornstarch
- 3 tablespoons cold water
- 1 teaspoon soy sauce

In a small skillet, saute the onion, green pepper and mushrooms in oil until tender. Remove from the heat; cool.

In a large bowl, combine the vegetables, 2 tablespoons apple juice, garlic powder, onion powder, salt and pepper. Crumble turkey over mixture and mix well.

Shape into a loaf in an 11-in. x 7-in. x 2-in. baking dish coated with nonstick cooking spray. Bake at 350° for 40-45 minutes or until meat is no longer pink and a meat thermometer reads 165°.

In a small saucepan, bring remaining apple juice to a boil. In a small bowl, combine the cornstarch, water and soy sauce until smooth. Gradually whisk into apple juice. Bring to a boil; cook and stir for 2 minutes or until thickened. Serve with turkey loaf. **Yield:** 2 servings.

Nutrition Facts: One serving (prepared with ground turkey breast and reduced-sodium soy sauce) equals 296 calories, 12 g fat (3 g saturated fat), 90 mg cholesterol, 507 mg sodium, 26 g carbohydrate, 1 g fiber, 21 g protein. **Diabetic Exchanges:** 2 lean meat, 1-1/2 starch, 1-1/2 fat.

Mandarin Orange Chicken

Gloria Warczak • Cedarburg, Wisconsin

French salad dressing, soy sauce, garlic and ginger do a wonderful job of punching up the flavor in this main course. The chicken leg quarters make a nice change of pace and the mandarin oranges offer a sunny burst of citrus.

- 2 chicken leg quarters
- 1/2 cup French salad dressing
- 2 tablespoons reduced-sodium soy sauce
- 1/2 teaspoon chicken bouillon granules
- 1/8 teaspoon *each* garlic powder, ground ginger and chili powder
- 1 tablespoon dried minced onion
- 1 can (11 ounces) mandarin oranges
- 1 tablespoon cornstarch
- 2 tablespoons water
- 1-1/2 cups hot cooked long grain rice

Place chicken in an 11-in. x 7-in. x 2-in. baking pan lined with heavy-duty foil. In a small bowl, whisk the salad dressing, soy sauce, bouillon, garlic powder, ginger and chili powder. Brush over chicken. Sprinkle with onion.

Drain oranges, reserving juice; set oranges aside. Pour 1/4 cup of the reserved juice around chicken. Cover and bake at 350° for 25 minutes. Uncover; bake 20-25 minutes longer or until a meat thermometer reads 180°.

In a small saucepan, combine the cornstarch and water until smooth. Stir in pan drippings and remaining reserved juice. Bring to a boil; cook and stir for 1-2 minutes or until thickened. Stir in oranges; cook 1 minute longer or until heated through. Serve over chicken and rice. **Yield:** 2 servings.

Chicken Marinara

Danielle Rogers • Greer, South Carolina

Stuffed with a creamy garlic filling, this chicken dish features plenty of cheese and angel hair pasta. It's truly a supper-time standout at my house.

2 boneless skinless chicken breast halves (6 ounces *each*)
1 package (3 ounces) cream cheese, softened
1 envelope garlic-herb soup mix, *divided*
1/3 cup water
1 tablespoon olive oil
3 ounces uncooked angel hair pasta
1-1/2 cups marinara sauce *or* spaghetti sauce, warmed
1/4 to 1/2 cup shredded part-skim mozzarella cheese

Cut a pocket in each chicken breast half, leaving meat attached on one side. In a small mixing bowl, beat cream cheese and 2 teaspoons soup mix until blended. Stuff into chicken pockets; secure with toothpicks. Place in an 8-in. square baking dish coated with nonstick cooking spray. Combine the water, oil and remaining soup mix; pour over the chicken.

Bake, uncovered, at 375° for 25-30 minutes or until juices run clear. Cook pasta according to package directions; drain. Divide pasta between two small baking dishes. Top with chicken and marinara sauce; sprinkle with cheese. Bake 5-6 minutes longer or until cheese is melted. **Yield:** 2 servings.

Spanish Chicken and Rice

Mary Nelms • Jacksonville, Florida

I've had this recipe for 50 years and have probably made it hundreds of times. This dish can be prepared quickly, the portions are just right for two and any leftovers are just as delicious the next day.

2 tablespoons all-purpose flour
1 teaspoon salt, *divided*
1/4 teaspoon pepper
2 bone-in chicken breast halves
1 tablespoon butter
1/2 cup chopped onion
1/4 cup chopped green pepper
1 garlic clove, minced
1 jar (2-1/2 ounces) sliced pimientos, drained
1/2 cup uncooked rice
1-1/4 cups chicken broth
1/2 teaspoon ground turmeric
1/8 to 1/4 teaspoon chili powder

Combine flour, 1/2 teaspoon salt and pepper in a large resealable plastic bag. Add chicken and shake until well coated. In a skillet, brown chicken in butter over medium heat. Remove chicken; set aside and keep warm.

In the pan drippings, saute onion, green pepper and garlic until tender. Add pimientos and rice. Reduce heat; cook for 2 minutes, stirring occasionally. Stir in the broth, turmeric, chili powder and remaining salt; bring to a boil.

Pour into an ungreased 2-qt. baking dish; top with chicken. Cover and bake at 350° for 45 minutes or until chicken juices run clear and rice is tender. **Yield:** 2 servings.

Turkey with Apple Slices

Mary Lou Wayman • Salt Lake City, Utah

Any day can be "Turkey Day" when you make this smaller-scale main course. The moist tenderloins and tangy apple glaze offer the goodness of turkey without a refrigerator full of leftovers.

2   turkey breast tenderloins (about 4 ounces *each*)
1   tablespoon butter
2   tablespoons maple syrup
1   tablespoon cider vinegar
1   teaspoon Dijon mustard
1/2   teaspoon chicken bouillon granules
1   medium tart apple, sliced

In a large skillet, cook turkey in butter over medium heat for 4-5 minutes on each side or until the juices run clear. Remove from the skillet; cover and keep warm.

In the same skillet, combine the syrup, vinegar, mustard and bouillon. Add the apple; cook and stir over medium heat for 2-3 minutes or until the apple is tender. Spoon over turkey. **Yield:** 2 servings.

Tortellini Primavera

Tina Green • Albany, Oregon

This pared-down pesto dish was a family favorite when my teens lived at home. I could stretch it with additional veggies for last-minute guests. It's so tasty and easy to whip up. Try it with your favorite vegetables or use whatever produce you have on hand.

1   cup frozen cheese tortellini
2   tablespoons olive oil, *divided*
3   tablespoons prepared pesto, *divided*
1/4   pound boneless skinless chicken breast, cut into 1-inch cubes
1   cup cut fresh asparagus (1-inch pieces)
1/4   cup *each* chopped sweet yellow pepper, green pepper and sweet onion
1/4   cup sliced fresh carrot
1/4   cup fresh *or* frozen snow peas
1/4   cup fresh broccoli florets
1/4   teaspoon garlic powder
1/8   teaspoon salt
1/8   teaspoon pepper
2   plum tomatoes, cut into wedges
3   tablespoons grated Parmesan cheese, *divided*
1   tablespoon water

Cook tortellini according to package directions. Meanwhile, in a small bowl, combine 4-1/2 teaspoons oil and 4-1/2 teaspoons pesto. Add chicken and toss to coat. Let stand at room temperature while cooking the vegetables.

In a large skillet, saute the asparagus, peppers, onion, carrot, peas, broccoli, garlic powder, salt and pepper in remaining oil until crisp-tender. Drain tortellini and return to the saucepan; add the vegetable mixture.

In the same skillet, cook and stir the chicken for 4-5 minutes or until juices run clear. Stir in the tomatoes, 2 tablespoons Parmesan cheese, water and remaining pesto; simmer for 2 minutes. Add tortellini mixture; toss. Sprinkle with remaining Parmesan cheese. **Yield:** 2 servings.

Tortellini Primavera

Chicken Red Pepper Saute

Taste of Home Test Kitchen • Greendale, Wisconsin

Flavored with garlic and a hint of citrus, tender strips of chicken meet sweet red pepper and green onion in this stovetop specialty.

1 tablespoon cornstarch
1/2 cup chicken broth, *divided*
1 garlic clove, minced
1/2 teaspoon lemon-pepper seasoning
1/2 pound boneless skinless chicken breasts, cut into 1/2-inch strips
1 tablespoon vegetable oil
1 medium sweet red pepper, julienned
Green onion strips *or* fresh chives

In a bowl, combine the cornstarch, 1/4 cup of broth, garlic and lemon-pepper; stir until smooth. Add the chicken strips and toss to coat.

Heat oil in a nonstick skillet over medium-high heat. Add the chicken mixture and remaining broth; cook and stir for 2 minutes. Add red pepper strips; cook and stir until the chicken is no longer pink and the peppers are crisp-tender, about 6-8 minutes. Garnish with green onions or chives. **Yield:** 2 servings.

Texas Turkey Tacos

Heidi Mahon Cook • Dallas, Texas

We really enjoy these zesty tacos. In fact, the turkey filling is so good, we've stuffed it into pita bread, mixed it with scrambled eggs and even stood over the stove and eaten it right out of the pan!

1 medium onion, chopped
2 garlic cloves, minced
1 tablespoon olive oil
1/2 pound ground turkey
1/3 cup frozen corn
3 tablespoons picante sauce
3 tablespoons chicken broth
1/2 teaspoon salt
1/4 teaspoon ground cumin
1/8 teaspoon cayenne pepper

4 flour tortillas (7 inches), warmed
Chopped tomato, shredded lettuce, shredded cheddar cheese *and/or* sour cream, optional

In a saucepan, saute onion and garlic in oil until tender. Add turkey; cook over medium until meat is no longer pink. Drain if necessary. Stir in the corn, picante sauce, broth, salt, cumin and cayenne. Cook and stir for 5 minutes or until corn is tender. Spoon over tortillas. Top with tomato, lettuce, cheese and sour cream if desired. Roll up. **Yield:** 2 servings.

GREAT GRILLING

Lily Jones of Eagle Grove, Iowa grills several pieces of chicken at once. "I do a marathon session of grilling," she says. "I refrigerate and freeze batches of the grilled chicken breasts as well as hamburgers, brats and the like. Having the cooked meat on hand, saves me from firing up the grill for one serving."

Mediterranean-Style Chicken

Mediterranean-Style Chicken

LaVonne Cunningham • Colfax, Illinois

With plenty of garlic, basil, tomatoes and olives, this flavorful skillet dinner has become a staple in my home. It's a great way to use chicken and makes a comforting meal for a pair.

2	bone-in skinless chicken thighs
1	teaspoon olive oil
2	garlic cloves, minced
1	can (14-1/2 ounces) stewed tomatoes, cut up
1	bay leaf
3/4	teaspoon sugar
3/4	teaspoon dried basil
1/4	teaspoon salt

Dash pepper

Hot cooked spaghetti

2	tablespoons sliced pimiento-stuffed olives, optional

In a skillet, brown chicken in oil over medium-high heat for about 3 minutes on each side. Add garlic; cook and stir about 45 seconds. Stir in the tomatoes, bay leaf, sugar, basil, salt and pepper. Bring to a boil. Reduce heat; cover and simmer for 20-25 minutes or until chicken juices run clear and chicken is tender.

Simmer, uncovered, until sauce reaches desired thickness. Discard bay leaf. Serve over spaghetti. Garnish with olives if desired. **Yield:** 2 servings.

PORK, SAUSAGE & LAMB

Juicy pork tenderloin, savory lamb shanks and spicy sausage dishes are all mouth-watering ways to dress up your dinner table. Sample a few of the must-try twosomes in this chapter and see just how delicious cooking with pork and lamb can be.

Pork Chops with Tomatoes and Peppers p. 154

Maple Sausage Skillet p. 164

Spinach-Pork Stuffed Shells p. 167

Pork Fried Rice p. 158

Italian Sausage Lasagna
p. 157

Broccoli Pork Stir-Fry

Broccoli Pork Stir-Fry

Wendy Nuis • Stokes Bay, Ontario

I downsized this handy, one-pot recipe years ago for my husband and me. It's delicious, versatile and so easy to double when company comes. Try substituting Italian sausage for the pork tenderloin or adding extra veggies for more color.

1	package (3 ounces) pork ramen noodles
1	cup warm water
2	teaspoons cornstarch
1/2	teaspoon garlic powder
1/4	teaspoon crushed red pepper flakes
2/3	cup cold water
1-1/2	teaspoons reduced-sodium soy sauce
1	teaspoon white vinegar
4	teaspoons canola oil
1/2	pound pork tenderloin, thinly sliced
6	large fresh mushrooms, sliced
1	cup fresh broccoli florets
1/2	cup julienned sweet red pepper
3	green onions (white portion only), sliced

Set aside 1 teaspoon of seasoning from ramen-noodle seasoning packet (discard remaining seasoning or save for another use). Break noodles into small pieces and place in a microwave-safe dish; add warm water. Microwave, uncovered, on high for 2 minutes. Drain and set aside.

In a small bowl, combine the cornstarch, garlic powder, pepper flakes and reserved seasoning. Stir in the cold water, soy sauce and vinegar until smooth; set aside.

In a large skillet or wok, heat oil; stir-fry pork and mushrooms for 5 minutes. Add broccoli and red pepper. Stir-fry for 4-5 minutes or until vegetables are crisp-tender and pork is no longer pink. Stir cornstarch mixture and stir into skillet. Add noodles and onions. Bring to a boil; cook and stir for 2 minutes or until thickened. **Yield:** 2 servings.

Editor's Note: This recipe was tested in a 1,100-watt microwave.

Chili Verde Stew

Doris McGuire • Grants Pass, Oregon

I found other recipes for green chili stew to be too bland, so I came up with this version. It makes a great dinner for two when served with corn breadsticks and a simple salad.

- 3/4   pound boneless pork roast, cut into 1-inch cubes
- 1   tablespoon canola oil
- 1/4   cup chopped green pepper
- 1/4   cup chopped onion
- 1/4   teaspoon minced garlic
- 1/4   cup dry red wine *or* beef broth
- 1   cup diced canned tomatoes, undrained
- 1/2   cup salsa
- 2   tablespoons canned chopped green chilies, *divided*
- 1/2   teaspoon ground cumin
- 1/4   teaspoon sugar

Dash ground cloves

- 2   tablespoons minced fresh parsley
- 1   small jalapeno pepper, seeded and chopped

In a large saucepan, cook the pork in oil over medium heat until no longer pink; remove and set aside. In the same pan, saute the green pepper, onion and garlic for 1-2 minutes or until tender. Stir in the pork, wine or broth, tomatoes, salsa, 1 tablespoon chilies, cumin, sugar and cloves. Cover and cook over low heat for 40 minutes, stirring occasionally.

Stir in the parsley, jalapeno and remaining chilies. Cover and cook 20-25 minutes longer or until meat is tender. **Yield:** 2 servings.

Nutrition Facts: 1-1/2 cups equals 385 calories, 17 g fat (4 g saturated fat), 102 mg cholesterol, 514 mg sodium, 16 g carbohydrate, 4 g fiber, 37 g protein.

Editor's Note: When cutting or seeding hot peppers, use rubber or plastic gloves to protect your hands. Avoid touching your face.

Ham with Currant Sauce

Sharon Shaw • Battle Creek, Michigan

This tender ham slice cooks in no time...and the glaze is so quick to make with just two ingredients. It's an easy main dish for the two of us.

- 1   bone-in fully cooked ham slice (about 1 pound)
- 1/4   cup water
- 1/3   cup currant jelly
- 1   teaspoon prepared horseradish

In a large skillet, bring ham and water to a boil. Reduce heat; cover and simmer until ham is heated through, turning once. Meanwhile, in a small microwave-safe bowl, combine jelly and horseradish. Cover and microwave on high for 2-3 minutes or until heated through, stirring occasionally. Serve over ham. **Yield:** 2 servings.

Ham with Currant Sauce

Pork Chops with Tomatoes and Peppers

Esther Lux • Lead, South Dakota

My mother created delicious dishes based on whatever she had on hand. This recipe is one she tried and kept, and it became our traditional Sunday dinner. She increased the ingredients proportionately to the number of people she invited after church each week.

2 bone-in pork loin chops (3/4 inch thick)
1 tablespoon butter
1/4 teaspoon salt
1/8 teaspoon pepper
4 thin onion slices
4 thin green pepper rings
4 thin fresh tomato slices
1/8 teaspoon dried basil
1/8 teaspoon dried thyme
Additional pepper

In a skillet, brown pork chops in butter on each side. Season with salt and pepper. Layer with onion, green pepper and tomato. Sprinkle with basil, thyme and additional pepper. Reduce heat; cover and cook for 20 minutes or until meat juices run clear. **Yield:** 2 servings.

Jaeger Schnitzel

Bob and Gail Worm • Madison, Wisconsin

Pork tenderloin gets dressed up with mushrooms, onion, white wine and gravy in this all-time classic. It's a comforting main course the two of you will turn to time and again.

1 pork tenderloin (6 to 7 ounces)
1 egg, lightly beaten
1/4 cup all-purpose flour
1/4 cup butter
1/2 cup sliced mushrooms
1/2 medium onion, thinly sliced
2 tablespoons white wine, optional
1-1/2 cups prepared brown gravy
2 tablespoons sour cream

Trim tenderloin, removing any visible fat. Cut in half lengthwise. Pound each half to 1/4-in. thickness. Dip into egg; coat with flour and shake off excess. In a skillet over medium heat, fry tenderloin in butter until no pink remains. Remove and keep warm.

Add mushrooms and onion to skillet; cook until tender. Add wine if desired. Stir in the gravy and sour cream; mix well and heat through, but do not boil. Serve with the tenderloin. **Yield:** 2 servings.

Sausage and Vegetable Skillet

Ruby Williams • Bogalusa, Louisiana

A variety of vegetables makes this an attractive, stovetop dish. The cooking time is minimal, which is wonderful when you need to set dinner on the table fast.

1/2 pound fresh Italian sausage, cut into 1/2-inch slices
1 tablespoon vegetable oil
1 cup cubed yellow summer squash (3/4-inch pieces)
1/2 cup chopped green onions
2 garlic cloves, minced
1-1/2 cups chopped fresh tomatoes
2 teaspoons Worcestershire sauce
1/8 teaspoon cayenne pepper

In a medium skillet, cook sausage in oil over medium heat until no longer pink; drain. Add squash, onions and garlic; cook for 2 minutes. Stir in the tomatoes, Worcestershire sauce and cayenne pepper; heat through. **Yield:** 2 servings.

Oven Barbecued Pork Chops

Helen Anton • West Fargo, North Dakota

This simple recipe is country cooking at its best. The down-home chops bake up tender and juicy, and the touch of lemon gives them a special flair.

- 2 bone-in pork loin chops (3/4 inch thick)
- 1/8 teaspoon salt
- 2 tablespoons brown sugar
- 2 tablespoons ketchup
- 2 thin onion slices
- 2 thin lemon slices

Oven Barbecued Pork Chops

Place pork chops in a greased 9-in. square baking dish; sprinkle with salt. In a small bowl, combine brown sugar and ketchup. Top each chop with onion, lemon and the ketchup mixture.

Cover and bake at 350° for 30 minutes. Uncover; bake 15 minutes longer or until a meat thermometer reads 160°. **Yield:** 2 servings.

Saucy Spareribs

Melanie Sanders • Kaysville, Utah

My husband likes spareribs, so when my mom gave me this stovetop recipe, I knew I had to try it. He loves the tender ribs and finger-licking barbecue sauce.

- 2 pounds bone-in pork spareribs
- 2 cans (12 ounces *each*) cola
- 1 cup ketchup
- 2 tablespoons cornstarch
- 2 tablespoons cold water

In a large nonstick skillet, brown the ribs; drain. Add the cola and ketchup; cover and simmer for 1 hour or until the meat is tender.

Remove ribs and keep warm. Transfer 2 cups of sauce to a saucepan. Bring to a boil. In a small bowl, combine the cornstarch and cold water; stir into sauce. Bring to a boil; cook for 1-2 minutes or until thickened. Serve over the ribs. **Yield:** 2 servings.

STORAGE STRATEGY

It's easy to forget what you have stashed away in the freezer. To help remember, keep a list of the frozen foods and their freeze dates on your freezer. Check the items off as you use them.

Pizza Macaroni Bake

Pizza Macaroni Bake

Barbara Kemmer • Rohnert Park, California

I found this recipe in a cookbook over 30 years ago when I was newly married. It's tasty and simple to prepare—just right for a busy couple. It's also easy to double for a family of four.

1/2 pound bulk pork sausage
1/4 cup chopped green pepper
2 tablespoons chopped onion
1/2 cup elbow macaroni, cooked and drained
1 can (8 ounces) tomato sauce
4 tablespoons grated Parmesan cheese, *divided*
2 tablespoons water
1/4 teaspoon dried oregano
Dash pepper

In a skillet, cook sausage, green pepper and onion over medium heat until meat is no longer pink; drain. Stir in the macaroni, tomato sauce, 2 tablespoons Parmesan cheese, water, oregano and pepper.

Transfer to a lightly greased 1-qt. baking dish; sprinkle with remaining cheese. Cover and bake at 350° for 25-30 minutes or until liquid is absorbed and casserole is heated through. **Yield:** 2 servings.

Italian Sausage Lasagna

Becky Harrington • Grandin, North Dakota

I received this recipe from a friend, and I have to say that it's the best lasagna that I've ever had! Best of all, it doesn't leave me with leftovers for days on end.

2 Italian sausage links, casings removed
1/4 cup chopped onion
1 garlic clove, minced
1 can (14-1/2 ounces) diced tomatoes, undrained
1/4 cup tomato paste
3/4 teaspoon sugar
1/2 teaspoon dried basil
1/4 teaspoon salt
1/8 teaspoon crushed red pepper flakes
1/8 teaspoon pepper
1 egg, beaten
3/4 cup ricotta cheese
1 tablespoon minced fresh parsley
4 lasagna noodles, cooked and drained
3/4 to 1 cup shredded part-skim mozzarella cheese
1 tablespoon grated Parmesan cheese

Crumble sausage into a small skillet. Add onion and garlic; cook over medium heat until meat is no longer pink. Drain. Add the tomatoes, tomato paste, sugar and seasonings. Bring to a boil. Reduce heat; simmer, uncovered, for 20 minutes. Combine the egg, ricotta and parsley.

Spread 1/4 cup sauce in an 8-in. x 4-in. x 2-in. loaf dish coated with nonstick cooking spray. Trim noodles to fit dish. Layer a third of the noodle pieces over sauce; top with a third of the remaining sauce, a third of the ricotta mixture and 3 tablespoons mozzarella cheese. Repeat layers twice.

Cover and bake at 375° for 30 minutes or until browned. Sprinkle with Parmesan cheese. Let stand for 15 minutes before cutting. **Yield:** 3 servings.

Pork Fried Rice

Peggy Vaught • Glasgow, West Virginia

Here's an all-time classic redone for a pair. Pretty peas and crunchy carrots add color to this savory supper staple.

☑ **Uses less fat, sugar or salt. Includes Nutrition Facts or Diabetic Exchanges.**

- 1 boneless pork loin chop (6 ounces), cut into 1/2-inch pieces
- 1/4 cup finely chopped carrot
- 1/4 cup chopped fresh broccoli
- 1/4 cup frozen peas
- 1 green onion, chopped
- 1 tablespoon butter
- 1 egg, beaten
- 1 cup cold cooked long grain rice
- 4-1/2 teaspoons reduced-sodium soy sauce
- 1/8 teaspoon garlic powder
- 1/8 teaspoon ground ginger

In a large skillet, saute the pork, carrot, broccoli, peas and onion in butter until pork is no longer pink. Remove from skillet and set aside. In same skillet, cook and stir egg over medium heat until completely set. Stir in the rice, soy sauce, garlic powder, ginger and pork mixture; heat through. **Yield:** 2 servings.

Nutrition Facts: 1 cup equals 338 calories, 13 g fat (6 g saturated fat), 163 mg cholesterol, 597 mg sodium, 29 g carbohydrate, 2 g fiber, 24 g protein. **Diabetic Exchanges:** 3 lean meat, 2 starch.

Sausage Potato Skillet

Sausage Potato Skillet

Amelia Bordas • Springfield, Virginia

During my childhood, I lived in an Italian neighborhood in New Jersey. Since both of my parents were working, I went home for lunch with my Italian girlfriend. Lunch was always the same—sausage, fried potatoes, green peppers and onions—but I could never get enough of my favorite meal.

- 2 fresh Italian sausage links, cut into 1/2-inch pieces
- 1 tablespoon vegetable oil
- 1 small onion, sliced
- 1/4 cup *each* sliced green and sweet red pepper
- 2 small potatoes, sliced
- 2 cups water

Salt and pepper to taste

In a skillet, brown sausage in oil. Add onion and peppers; saute until vegetables are tender. Add potatoes and water; bring to a boil. Reduce heat; cover and simmer for 15 minutes or until potatoes are tender. Drain; add salt and pepper. **Yield:** 2 servings.

Mushroom-Orange Chop

Joan Nichols • Sarina, Ontario

Here's a one-person entree that's big on flavor. The marmalade in the sauce gives the moist pork chop a tasty tang that I really enjoy. I hope you will, too.

- 1 butterfly pork chop (3/4 inch thick)
- 2 teaspoons vegetable oil
- 2 green onions, thinly sliced
- 2 fresh mushrooms, chopped
- 1 garlic clove, minced
- 2 tablespoons orange marmalade
- 1 teaspoon soy sauce
- 1 tablespoon sunflower kernels, optional

In a skillet over medium heat, brown pork chop in oil on both sides. Continue cooking until a meat thermometer reads 160°-170°, about 6 minutes. Remove and keep warm. In the same skillet, saute onions, mushrooms and garlic until tender. Add marmalade and soy sauce; cook and stir until heated through. Pour over chop. Sprinkle with sunflower kernels if desired. **Yield:** 1 serving.

Mushroom-Orange Chop

Sweet-and-Sour Pork

Sharon Ryzner • Girard, Ohio

On the lookout for a time-saving but tasty dinner? This tangy main course is a real find! It makes a great quick meal. We love the blend of pineapple and green pepper.

- 1 can (8 ounces) pineapple chunks
- 1/4 cup dark corn syrup
- 3 tablespoons white vinegar
- 1 tablespoon ketchup
- 1 tablespoon soy sauce
- 1/2 pound boneless pork, cut into 1-inch cubes
- 1 garlic clove, minced
- 1 tablespoon vegetable oil
- 1 small green pepper, cut into 3/4-inch chunks
- 4 to 5 teaspoons cornstarch
- 2 tablespoons cold water

Hot cooked rice

Drain pineapple, reserving juice; set pineapple aside. In a small bowl, combine the corn syrup, vinegar, ketchup, soy sauce and reserved juice; set mixture aside.

In a small skillet, stir-fry the pork and garlic in oil for 4 minutes or until pork is browned. Add green pepper; stir-fry for 2 minutes or until crisp-tender. Stir in the pineapple juice mixture; bring to a boil.

Combine the cornstarch and water until smooth; gradually stir into the skillet. Cook and stir for 1-2 minutes or until thickened. Stir in the reserved pineapple; heat through. Serve over rice. **Yield:** 2 servings.

Pear-fect Pork Supper

Pear-fect Pork Supper

Lori Jameson • Walla Walla, Washington

This hearty, meal-in-one dish nicely pairs sweet and savory flavors. It's a great change of pace, and I can make the entire meal in the time it takes to cook the rice.

1	cup water
2	tablespoons raisins
3/4	teaspoon salt, *divided*
1/2	cup uncooked long grain rice
2	bone-in pork rib chops (3/4 inch thick)
1/8	teaspoon pepper
1-1/2	teaspoons vegetable oil
1	can (8-1/2 ounces) sliced pears
1	tablespoon cornstarch
1	tablespoon soy sauce
1/4	to 1/2 teaspoon dried thyme
1	medium sweet red pepper, cut into 3/4-inch pieces
1	small onion, cut into 3/4-inch pieces
1	garlic clove, minced

In a small saucepan, bring the water, raisins and 1/4 teaspoon salt to a boil. Stir in rice. Reduce heat; cover and simmer for 18-20 minutes or until rice is tender. Meanwhile, sprinkle pork chops with pepper and remaining salt. In a skillet, brown chops on both sides in oil over medium-high heat. Remove and keep warm.

Drain pears, reserving juice; set pears aside. Add enough water to juice to measure 1 cup. Combine cornstarch, pear juice, soy sauce and thyme until blended; set aside. In the drippings in the skillet, saute red pepper, onion and garlic for 2-3 minutes or until crisp-tender. Stir in pear juice mixture. Bring to a boil; cook and stir for 1-2 minutes or until thickened.

Return chops to skillet. Cook for 4 minutes. Add pears; cook 2 minutes longer or until pork is tender and pears are heated through. Serve with rice. **Yield:** 2 servings.

Pizza Parlor Pasta

Shelley Pimlott • Nashua, Iowa

I usually serve this cheesy, sausage dish with slices of garlic bread. It reminds me of a pasta specialty at a popular pizza parlor.

1 cup uncooked medium pasta shells
1/3 pound bulk Italian sausage
1/2 small onion, finely chopped
3 tablespoons finely chopped green pepper
1-1/3 cups spaghetti sauce
1/3 cup 1% cottage cheese
1/2 cup shredded part-skim mozzarella cheese, *divided*
1/2 cup shredded Monterey Jack cheese, *divided*
2 tablespoons grated Parmesan cheese

Cook pasta according to package directions. Meanwhile, crumble the sausage into a small skillet; add onion and green pepper. Cook over medium heat until meat is no longer pink. Stir in the spaghetti sauce, cottage cheese, 1/4 cup mozzarella cheese and 1/4 cup Monterey Jack cheese.

Drain pasta; stir into sausage mixture. Transfer to a 1-qt. baking dish coated with nonstick cooking spray. Sprinkle with remaining shredded cheeses. Top with Parmesan cheese. Bake, uncovered, at 350° for 5-10 minutes or until cheese is melted. **Yield:** 3 servings.

Glazed Ham Slice

Taste of Home Test Kitchen • Greendale, Wisconsin

A pineapple-honey mixture makes a sweet glaze for ham in this no-fuss dinner. Cooked on the stovetop, it's a simple meal for two that packs a flavorful punch.

1 fully cooked ham slice (about 3/4 pound and 1/2 inch thick)
1 tablespoon butter
1 can (8 ounces) sliced pineapple
1-1/2 teaspoons cornstarch
2 tablespoons honey
1 tablespoon steak sauce
1 tablespoon Dijon mustard

Cut ham slice in half. In a skillet, cook ham in butter for 3-4 minutes on each side or until heated through. Meanwhile, drain pineapple, reserving the juice. Set aside two pineapple slices; refrigerate remaining pineapple for another use.

In a bowl, combine cornstarch, pineapple juice, honey, steak sauce and mustard until smooth. Remove ham and keep warm. Add honey mixture to skillet. Bring to a boil over medium-low heat; cook for 1-2 minutes. Return ham to skillet; top with the reserved pineapple slices. Spoon glaze over the top; heat through. **Yield:** 2 servings.

Glazed Ham Slice

Skillet Ham And Rice

Susan Zivec • Regina, Saskatchewan

Ham, rice and mushrooms make a tasty combination in this homey stovetop dish that's topped with Parmesan cheese.

Skillet Ham and Rice

1 medium onion, chopped
1 teaspoon olive oil
1 cup cubed fully cooked lean ham
1 cup sliced fresh mushrooms
1/2 cup reduced-sodium chicken broth
1/4 cup water
1/8 teaspoon pepper
3/4 cup instant rice
2 green onions, sliced
1/4 cup shredded Parmesan cheese

In a nonstick skillet, saute onion in oil until tender. Add the ham, mushrooms, broth, water and pepper; bring to a boil. Add the rice. Reduce heat; cover and simmer for 5 minutes or until rice is tender. Gently fluff rice. Serve with green onions and Parmesan cheese. **Yield:** 2 servings.

Stuffed Pork Tenderloin

Taste of Home Test Kitchen • Greendale, Wisconsin

Cooking for two doesn't mean preparing boring foods! Here's a beautiful entree sized right for a couple. Single-serving tenderloins are marinated for a few hours before being filled with apples, pecans and more.

1/3 cup apple jelly
2 tablespoons lemon juice
2 tablespoons soy sauce
2 tablespoons vegetable oil
1/2 teaspoon ground ginger
2 pork tenderloins (about 1/2 pound *each*)
1/2 cup chopped tart apple
1/2 cup soft bread crumbs
2 tablespoons finely chopped celery
2 tablespoons chopped pecans
1/2 cup apple juice

In a small saucepan, combine the first five ingredients. Cook and stir until the jelly is melted; cover and refrigerate 4-1/2 teaspoons.

Slice each tenderloin lengthwise to within 1/2 in. of the bottom. Place in a large resealable plastic bag. Add remaining jelly mixture. Seal and refrigerate for 4 hours or overnight.

Place meat in a 9-in. square baking dish; discard marinade. In a bowl, combine apple, bread crumbs, celery, pecans and reserved jelly mixture. Spoon apple mixture down the center of tenderloins; secure with toothpicks. Drizzle with apple juice.

Cover and bake at 375° for 30 minutes or until a meat thermometer reads 160°. Discard toothpicks. Let stand for 10 minutes before slicing. **Yield:** 2 servings.

Grilled Veggie Pork Bundles

Linda Turner Ludwig • Columbiana, Ohio

Stacked with veggies and wrapped in bacon, these pork chops make for great summer dining on our deck. We enjoy the colorful bundles with rice and iced tea. For variety, try the recipe with provolone cheese or red sweet peppers...or substitute chicken breasts for the pork.

4	bacon strips
2	boneless pork loin chops (4 ounces *each*)
1/8	teaspoon salt
1/8	teaspoon pepper
2	slices onion (1/4 inch thick)
2	slices tomato (1/2 inch thick)
1/2	medium green pepper, cut in half
2	slices Swiss cheese

Cross two bacon strips to form an X; repeat. Sprinkle pork chops with salt and pepper; place over bacon strips. Layer with onion, tomato and green pepper. Wrap bacon strips over vegetables and secure with a wooden toothpick.

Coat the grill rack with nonstick cooking spray before starting the grill for indirect heat, using a drip pan. Place pork bundles over the drip pan. Grill, covered, over indirect medium heat for 20-25 minutes or until a meat thermometer reads 160°.

Place cheese slices over bundles; cover and grill 1 minute longer or until cheese is melted. Discard toothpicks before serving. **Yield:** 2 servings.

Pork Meatballs

Joan Newberry • Indiana, Pennsylvania

This recipe is a favorite. Mom made the moist, flavorful meatballs often, and they were part of our traditional dinner the night before Lent, served with homemade gnocchi.

1	egg, lightly beaten
1	slice bread, crumbled
1	garlic clove, minced
1/4	cup grated Romano *or* Parmesan cheese
1/2	teaspoon salt
1/2	teaspoon dried parsley flakes
1/4	teaspoon pepper
3/4	pound ground pork
1	can (14-1/2 ounces) beef broth

In a bowl, combine the first seven ingredients. Crumble meat over mixture and mix well. Shape into ten 2-in. balls.

In a saucepan, bring broth to a boil. Place meatballs in the broth. Reduce heat; cover and simmer for 15 minutes. Turn the meatballs; cook 15 minutes long or until meat is no longer pink. Remove with a slotted spoon. **Yield:** 2 servings.

Pork Meatballs

Maple Sausage Skillet

Dottie Tarlton • Malvern, Arkansas

Maple syrup adds a welcomed bit of sweetness to this yummy stir-fry. I sometimes work in a little broccoli, too, for a change of pace. Add a green salad and a crusty loaf of bread for a complete meal in minutes.

✓ **Uses less fat, sugar or salt. Includes Nutrition Facts or Diabetic Exchanges.**

1/2	pound fully cooked kielbasa *or* **Polish sausage, sliced**
1	teaspoon canola oil
1	medium green pepper, thinly sliced
1	small onion, halved and sliced
1-1/2	cups sliced fresh mushrooms
1	celery rib, sliced
2	tablespoons maple syrup
1/4	teaspoon pepper

Hot cooked rice

In a large skillet, cook sausage in oil for 3-4 minutes or until lightly browned. Add vegetables; stir-fry 3-4 minutes longer or until crisp-tender. Stir in the syrup and pepper; heat through. Serve with rice. **Yield:** 2 servings.

Nutrition Facts: 1-1/2 cups sausage mixture (calculated without rice) equals 472 calories, 34 g fat (11 g saturated fat), 76 mg cholesterol, 1,244 mg sodium, 26 g carbohydrate, 3 g fiber, 17 g protein.

Rack of Lamb

Rack of Lamb

Margery Bryan • Moses Lake, Washington

We've raised sheep for years, so lamb has been a staple entree in our house as well as a favorite to serve when company comes. We do our own butchering and can cut the meat any way, but we've found the rack yields a perfect amount of meat for just the two of us.

1	tablespoon olive oil
2	garlic cloves, minced
1	tablespoon minced fresh parsley
1	teaspoon minced fresh rosemary *or* 1/4 to 1/2 teaspoon dried rosemary, crushed
1	teaspoon minced fresh thyme *or* 1/4 to 1/2 teaspoon dried thyme
1	French-style rack of lamb (8 chops), about 1 pound

In a bowl, combine the oil, garlic, parsley, rosemary and thyme. Rub oil mixture over lamb.

Place meat side up on a rack in a greased 11-in. x 7-in. x 2-in. baking pan. Bake, uncovered, at 400° for 20-30 minutes or until meat reaches desired doneness (for medium-rare, a meat thermometer should read 145°; medium, 160°; well-done, 170°). **Yield:** 2 servings.

Sausage-Spinach Pasta Supper

Sausage-Spinach Pasta Supper

Daphine Smith • Baytown, Texas

You won't miss the marinara sauce once you taste this pasta dish flavored with chicken broth and Italian sausage. The sauce simmers away on its own, without much work on your part. My husband likes it so much that I make it once a week.

2	Italian sausage links, cut into 1/2-inch slices
1	small onion, chopped
1	garlic clove, minced
1	teaspoon olive oil
1	can (14-1/2 ounces) chicken broth
4	ounces uncooked angel hair pasta, broken in half
1	package (10 ounces) fresh spinach, trimmed and coarsely chopped
1	tablespoon all-purpose flour
1/8	teaspoon pepper
3	tablespoons heavy whipping cream

In a large saucepan, cook the sausage, onion and garlic in oil over medium heat until sausage is browned; drain.

Add broth; bring to a boil. Add pasta; cook for 3 minutes, stirring frequently. Gradually add spinach. Cook and stir for 2-3 minutes or until pasta is tender and spinach is wilted. In a small bowl, combine flour, pepper and cream until smooth; stir into pasta mixture. Bring to a boil; cook and stir for 1-2 minutes or until thickened. **Yield:** 2 servings.

Hearty Lima Bean Bake

Cathy Elands • Hightstown, New Jersey

*Sausage and chili powder spice up yummy baked beans in this casserole.
I often increase the recipe to take to picnics. Everyone loves it.*

✓ **Uses less fat, sugar or salt. Includes Nutrition Facts or Diabetic Exchanges.**

- 1/2 medium green pepper, diced
- 1/3 cup chopped onion
- 1/4 cup chopped celery
- 1 tablespoon olive oil
- 1/4 pound turkey Italian sausage links, cut into 1/4-inch slices
- 1 cup frozen lima beans, thawed
- 3/4 cup canned diced tomatoes
- 3 tablespoons water
- 2 teaspoons brown sugar
- 1 teaspoon chili powder
- 1 teaspoon minced fresh oregano
- 1/2 teaspoon ground mustard

Dash salt and pepper

In a large nonstick skillet, saute the green pepper, onion and celery in oil until tender. Add sausage; cook and stir over medium heat for 3 minutes or until no longer pink. Stir in the remaining ingredients. Cover and simmer for 5 minutes.

Transfer to an ungreased 1-qt. baking dish. Bake, uncovered, at 325° for 45-50 minutes or until heated through, stirring once. **Yield:** 2 servings.

Nutrition Facts: 1-1/4 cups equals 316 calories, 13 g fat (3 g saturated fat), 30 mg cholesterol, 610 mg sodium, 34 g carbohydrate, 9 g fiber, 17 g protein.
Diabetic Exchanges: 2 starch, 1-1/2 lean meat, 1 vegetable, 1 fat.

Spiced Ham Steak

Spiced Ham Steak

Karla Foisy • Minneapolis, Minnesota

My husband loves ham, but I get bored cooking it the same old way. I came up with this zippy sauce that really perks up plain ham steak.

- 1 fully cooked ham steak (about 8 ounces and 1/2 inch thick)
- 4-1/2 teaspoons lime juice
- 1 tablespoon grated Parmesan cheese
- 1 tablespoon sour cream
- 1-1/2 teaspoons all-purpose flour
- 1 teaspoon vegetable oil
- 1/4 teaspoon garlic salt
- 1/4 teaspoon Cajun seasoning
- 1/4 teaspoon curry powder
- 1/4 teaspoon dried savory

Place ham steak on a lightly greased broiler pan; broil 4 in. from the heat for 5 minutes. In a small bowl, combine the remaining ingredients; mix well. Turn ham steak; spread with sauce. Broil 5 minutes longer or until lightly browned and bubbly. Cut in half to serve. **Yield:** 2 servings.

Sausage Casserole For Two

Kathryn Curtis • Lakeport, California

I don't know if my mother made up this recipe or if it was handed down to her, but it's scrumptious. Best of all, the small-portion hot dish is just enough to satisfy two.

Sausage Casserole for Two

2	smoked cooked Polish sausages (about 6 ounces)
1/4	cup sliced fresh mushrooms
1/4	cup finely chopped onion
1	tablespoon butter
2	tablespoons heavy whipping cream
1-1/2	teaspoons Dijon mustard
1/8	teaspoon garlic powder
1/2	cup shredded cheddar cheese
4	tomato slices

Cut sausages in half lengthwise; place in a greased 1-1/2-qt. baking dish. In a medium saucepan, saute mushrooms and onion in butter until lightly browned. Stir in cream, mustard and garlic powder; bring to a boil. Cook and stir until slightly thickened. Pour over sausages; top with cheese. Bake, uncovered, at 450° for 15-20 minutes or until cheese is melted. Garnish with tomato slices. **Yield:** 2 servings.

Spinach-Pork Stuffed Shells

Becky Burch • Marceline, Missouri

Everyone loves Italian-style shells, and this recipe is popular because its pared down to serve just two folks.

6	uncooked jumbo pasta shells
1/4	pound ground pork
4	cups water
3	cups torn fresh spinach
1	egg, lightly beaten
3	tablespoons shredded Parmesan cheese, *divided*
2	tablespoons heavy whipping cream
1	garlic clove, minced
1/4	teaspoon salt
1/8	teaspoon ground nutmeg
1/8	teaspoon pepper
1	cup meatless spaghetti sauce

Cook pasta shells according to package directions. Meanwhile, in a small skillet, cook pork over medium heat until no longer pink; drain and set aside. In a saucepan, bring water to a boil. Add spinach; boil for 1-2 minutes or until wilted. Drain and squeeze dry; chop the spinach.

In a bowl, combine the pork, spinach, egg, 1 tablespoon Parmesan cheese, cream, garlic, salt, nutmeg and pepper. Drain shells; stuff with the pork mixture. Spread 1/4 cup spaghetti sauce in an ungreased 1-qt. baking dish.

Place stuffed shells in dish; drizzle with remaining spaghetti sauce. Sprinkle with remaining Parmesan cheese. Cover and bake at 400° for 15 minutes. Uncover; bake 10-15 minutes longer or until heated through. **Yield:** 2 servings.

Pork and Veggie Saute

Ethel Martin • Warwick, Rhode Island

I'm always trying to cut calories, and this is one of my favorite ways to do it.
This dish is so tasty, particularly when it's served over noodles. Enjoy!

☑ **Uses less fat, sugar or salt. Includes Nutrition Facts or Diabetic Exchanges.**

- 1 cup reduced-sodium chicken broth
- 1/4 cup reduced-sodium soy sauce
- 3 garlic cloves, minced
- 1/2 teaspoon ground allspice
- 1 to 2 teaspoons grated fresh gingerroot
- 1/2 pound pork tenderloin, cut into 1/4-inch slices
- 2 bay leaves
- 2 teaspoons canola oil
- 1/2 cup sliced fresh mushrooms
- 1/2 cup julienned sweet red pepper
- 1/3 cup thinly sliced celery
- 2 teaspoons cornstarch
- 2 teaspoons honey
- Hot cooked rice, optional

In a bowl, combine the first five ingredients. Pour 1/2 cup marinade into a large resealable plastic bag; add pork and one bay leaf. Seal bag and turn to coat; refrigerate for at least 4 hours. Add remaining bay leaf to the remaining marinade; cover and refrigerate.

Drain and discard marinade from pork; discard bay leaf. In a nonstick skillet, saute pork in oil for 4-5 minutes or until no longer pink. Remove and keep warm.

In the same skillet, saute the mushrooms, red pepper and celery until crisp-tender. Discard bay leaf from reserved marinade. Combine cornstarch, honey and marinade until smooth. Stir into skillet. Bring to a boil; cook and stir for 1-2 minutes or until thickened. Return pork to the pan; heat through. Serve over rice if desired. **Yield:** 2 servings.

Nutrition Facts: 1 cup pork mixture (calculated without rice) equals 249 calories, 9 g fat (2 g saturated fat), 74 mg cholesterol, 846 mg sodium, 15 g carbohydrate, 2 g fiber, 27 g protein. **Diabetic Exchanges:** 3 lean meat, 1 starch.

Braised Pork with Red Chili Sauce

Kara de la Vega • Somerset, California

Spiced-up pork and rice make a great duo in this meal-in-one. I got the recipe from
my mom. It is also really good scooped into flour tortillas.

- 3/4 pound pork chop suey meat
- 1 teaspoon canola oil
- 1 medium onion, chopped
- 1 garlic clove, minced
- 1-1/2 to 2 teaspoons chili powder
- 1/2 teaspoon dried oregano
- 1/2 teaspoon ground cumin
- 2/3 cup water
- 1 tablespoon tomato paste
- 1/2 teaspoon sugar
- 1/4 teaspoon salt
- 1/4 cup heavy whipping cream

In a large skillet, brown pork in oil. Remove and keep warm. In the same skillet, saute the onion, garlic, chili powder, oregano and cumin for 2-3 minutes or until onion is tender. Stir in the pork, water, tomato paste, sugar and salt. Cover and simmer for 18-20 minutes or until pork is tender; skim fat. Stir in the cream; bring to a boil, stirring constantly. **Yield:** 2 servings.

Pork and Veggie Saute

Pork Tenderloin with Raspberry Sauce

Pork Tenderloin with Raspberry Sauce

Kathleen Boulanger • Williston, Vermont

*I altered the original version of this recipe by substituting spreadable fruit for some of the butter.
I've found this is a good way to lighten up any pork dish...and it improves the taste, too!*

✓ Uses less fat, sugar or salt. Includes Nutrition Facts or Diabetic Exchanges.

- 1   pork tenderloin (3/4 pound)
- 1/2 teaspoon lemon-pepper seasoning
- 1/8 teaspoon cayenne pepper
- 1   tablespoon reduced-fat butter

SAUCE:
- 3   tablespoons 100% raspberry spreadable fruit
- 1   tablespoon red wine vinegar
- 2   teaspoons ketchup
- 1   garlic clove, minced
- 1/4 teaspoon prepared horseradish
- 1/4 teaspoon reduced-sodium soy sauce

Cut tenderloin into eight slices, about 1-1/4 in. thick. Sprinkle with lemon-pepper and cayenne. In a large nonstick skillet, cook pork in butter over medium-high heat for 3-4 minutes on each side or until juices run clear. Remove and keep warm.

Combine sauce ingredients; add to the skillet. Cook and stir for 2-3 minutes or until bubbly and slightly thickened, scraping to loosen browned bits. Serve over pork. **Yield:** 2 servings.

Nutrition Facts: 5 ounces cooked pork with 2 tablespoons sauce equals 276 calories, 9 g fat (4 g saturated fat), 121 mg cholesterol, 327 mg sodium, 11 g carbohydrate, 1 g fiber, 36 g protein. **Diabetic Exchanges:** 4 lean meat, 1 fruit.

Ham with Potatoes and Onions

Mrs. Maynard Robinson • Cleveland, Minnesota

A browned potato and onion mixture is a nice complement to ham in this country-style dinner. This recipe has made the rounds in my family for a number of years.

1   **large baking potato**
1   **medium red onion**
2   **tablespoons vegetable oil**
1   **tablespoon red wine vinegar**
1/2 **teaspoon salt**
1/8 **to 1/4 teaspoon pepper**
1/8 **teaspoon dried thyme**
1   **ham steak (about 1/2 pound)**

Peel potato; slice lengthwise into quarters, then crosswise into 1/4-in. slices. Repeat with onion. In a skillet over medium heat, saute potato and onion in oil for 2 minutes. Reduce heat; cover and cook for 10 minutes or until potato is crisp-tender.

Uncover; increase heat to high. Cook and stir for 6-8 minutes or until potato is browned. Sprinkle with vinegar, salt, pepper and thyme. Meanwhile, in another skillet, saute ham steak over medium heat until browned and heated through. To serve, place ham on a platter and spoon potato and onion over the top. **Yield:** 2 servings.

Sausage-Stuffed Potatoes

Margaret Allen • Abingdon, Virginia

I came up with this recipe because I wanted to add flavor to plain baked potatoes. I combined several ideas, experimented and ended up with this version. It's so satisfying that the potatoes can be a meal all by themselves.

2   **large baking potatoes**
1/4 **pound smoked Polish sausage, cut into 1/4-inch slices**
1   **tart green apple, chopped**
3   **garlic cloves, minced**
1   **can (8 ounces) sauerkraut, rinsed and drained**
1/2 **teaspoon caraway seed**
1/2 **cup sour cream**

Bake the potatoes at 400° for 1 hour or until tender. In a medium skillet, brown sausage for 2-3 minutes. Add apple and garlic; cook over low heat for 3-4 minutes or until apple is tender. Add sauerkraut and caraway; cook 4-5 minutes longer or until heated through. Stir in sour cream.

To serve, cut an X in the top of each potato. Fluff pulp with a fork; spoon sausage mixture over potatoes. **Yield:** 2 servings.

Sausage-Stuffed Potatoes

FISH & SEAFOOD

You're sure to net a bucket of compliments with any of the deep-sea specialties found in this chapter. From breaded and baked fish favorites to seafood stir-fries and pasta dishes, the following recipes are loaded with flavor and sized right for two.

Fish in Foil
p. 181

Pesto Salmon
p. 186

Dilly Red Snapper
p. 180

Herbed Tomato Fish Bake
p. 188

Pecan-Crusted Salmon
p. 185

Honey-Dijon Salmon and Asparagus

Honey-Dijon Salmon and Asparagus

Betty Stewart • Leola, Pennsylvania

Here is our all-time favorite salmon recipe. It's a fast, nutritious and delicious meal-in-one. Plus, cleanup is always a snap!

✓ Uses less fat, sugar or salt. Includes Nutrition Facts or Diabetic Exchanges.

1-1/2   teaspoons cornstarch
2-1/4   teaspoons butter, melted
      1   teaspoon Worcestershire sauce
      2   tablespoons honey
      1   tablespoon Dijon mustard
Dash white pepper
      2   salmon fillets (4 ounces *each*)
   1/4   cup chopped walnuts
   1/2   pound fresh asparagus, trimmed

In a small bowl, combine cornstarch, butter and Worcestershire sauce until smooth. Stir in the honey, mustard and pepper.

Place each salmon fillet on a double thickness of heavy-duty foil (about 18 in. x 12 in.). Drizzle with honey mixture and sprinkle with walnuts. Place asparagus around salmon. Fold foil around salmon and seal tightly. Grill, covered, over medium heat for 15-20 minutes or until fish flakes easily with a fork. **Yield:** 2 servings.

Nutrition Facts: 1 serving equals 437 calories, 26 g fat (6 g saturated fat), 78 mg cholesterol, 335 mg sodium, 25 g carbohydrate, 2 g fiber, 28 g protein.

Stir-Fried Scallops

Stephany Gocobachi • San Rafuel, California

Sea scallops are a hit in this mild, tomato-based stovetop supper. Try serving the saucy mixture over rice or angel hair pasta...and garnish with fresh cilantro if you like.

✓ **Uses less fat, sugar or salt. Includes Nutrition Facts or Diabetic Exchanges.**

- 1 small onion, chopped
- 3 garlic cloves, minced
- 1 tablespoon olive oil
- 3/4 pound sea scallops, halved
- 2 medium plum tomatoes, chopped
- 2 tablespoons lemon juice
- 1/4 teaspoon salt
- 1/8 teaspoon pepper

Hot cooked pasta *or* rice, optional

In a nonstick skillet or wok, stir-fry onion and garlic in hot oil until tender. Add scallops; stir-fry until scallops turn opaque. Add tomatoes; cook and stir 1-2 minutes longer or until heated through.

Stir in lemon juice, salt and pepper. Serve over pasta or rice if desired. **Yield:** 2 servings.

Nutrition Facts: 1 cup stir-fry mixture (calculated without pasta or rice) equals 246 calories, 8 g fat (1 g saturated fat), 56 mg cholesterol, 575 mg sodium, 13 g carbohydrate, 1 g fiber, 30 g protein. **Diabetic Exchanges:** 4 very lean meat, 2 vegetable, 1-1/2 fat.

Shrimp Dijonnaise

Wanda Penton • Franklinton, Louisiana

This is a very easy dish to prepare for two. After the shrimp have marinated, dinner can be on the table in minutes! It's a refreshing departure from meat, and the mixture of flavors is delicious.

- 1/2 cup lemon juice
- 1/4 cup butter, melted
- 2 tablespoons vegetable oil
- 2 tablespoons Dijon mustard
- 1 tablespoon Worcestershire sauce
- 3 garlic cloves, minced
- 3/4 pound uncooked large shrimp, peeled and deveined

In a large resealable bag, combine the lemon juice, butter, oil, mustard, Worcestershire sauce and garlic. Add shrimp; seal bag and turn to coat. Refrigerate for 4 hours, turning occasionally.

Drain and discard marinade. Broil shrimp 4 in. from the heat for 4 minutes or until pink. **Yield:** 2 servings.

Shrimp Dijonnaise

Confetti Salmon Steaks

Mary Kay Dixson • Decatur, Alabama

I turn to my microwave to help cook up salmon in a jiffy. With its sprinkling of bright peppers, the mildly seasoned dish makes a pretty entree for the two of us.

✓ **Uses less fat, sugar or salt. Includes Nutrition Facts or Diabetic Exchanges.**

2   salmon steaks (6 ounces *each*)
1/2   teaspoon Worcestershire sauce
1/2   teaspoon lemon juice
1/2   teaspoon Cajun *or* Creole seasoning
1/4   teaspoon salt, optional
1/2   cup diced green pepper
1/2   cup diced sweet red pepper

Place the salmon in an ungreased 8-in. square microwave-safe dish. Rub with Worcestershire sauce and lemon juice; sprinkle with Cajun seasoning and salt if desired. Sprinkle peppers on top. Cover and microwave on high for 5-1/2 to 6 minutes, turning once, or until fish flakes easily with a fork. Let stand, covered, for 2 minutes. **Yield:** 2 servings.

Nutrition Facts: One serving (prepared without salt) equals 192 calories, 9 g fat (0 saturated fat), 68 mg cholesterol, 185 mg sodium, 5 g carbohydrate, 0 fiber, 22 g protein. **Diabetic Exchanges:** 3 lean meat, 1 vegetable.

Editor's Note: This recipe was tested in an 850-watt microwave.

Crab Alfredo

Crab Alfredo

Esther Pittello • Chicopee, Massachusetts

I improvised this pasta recipe when I was looking for quick Lenten meals, but it has become a favorite for my husband and me all year long.

1/4   cup chopped onion
1   tablespoon butter
1   cup sliced fresh mushrooms
1   cup prepared Alfredo sauce
2   tablespoons chicken broth
1   package (8 ounces) imitation crabmeat, flaked
2   cups hot cooked fettuccine *or* pasta of your choice

In a skillet, saute onion in butter until tender. Add mushrooms; cook and stir for 3 minutes or until tender. Stir in the sauce and broth until blended. Add the crab. Reduce heat; cook for 10 minutes or until heated through, stirring occasionally. Serve over pasta. **Yield:** 2 servings.

Baked Fish

Lynn Mathieu • Great Mills, Maryland

After enjoying a seafood dish with Parmesan cheese sprinkled on top at a restaurant, I created a similar recipe. The cheese added extra zip and gave me the idea to try it at home. With only three ingredients, it's a fast fix for two.

☑ **Uses less fat, sugar or salt. Includes Nutrition Facts or Diabetic Exchanges.**

Baked Fish

1/2	pound panfish fillets (perch, trout *or* whitefish)
4	teaspoons grated Parmesan cheese
1/2	teaspoon dill weed

Place fish in a 10-in. pie plate that has been coated with nonstick cooking spray. Sprinkle with Parmesan cheese and dill. Bake, uncovered, at 350° for 8-10 minutes or until fish flakes easily with a fork. **Yield:** 2 servings.

Nutrition Facts: One serving (prepared with perch) equals 119 calories, 2 g fat (0 saturated fat), 104 mg cholesterol, 131 mg sodium, 0 carbohydrate, 0 fiber, 23 g protein. **Diabetic Exchange:** 3 very lean meat.

Cream Cheese-Stuffed Catfish

Anneliese Deising • Plymouth, Michigan

I like to wrap strips of bacon and fish fillets around a rich cream cheese filling for this entree that tastes like we're pampering ourselves.

4	bacon strips
1/2	cup soft bread crumbs
4-1/2	teaspoons cream cheese, softened
2	teaspoons lemon juice, *divided*
1-1/2	teaspoons finely chopped onion
1-1/2	teaspoons finely chopped celery
1-1/2	teaspoons dried parsley flakes
1/2	teaspoon dried thyme
1/4	teaspoon pepper, *divided*
1/8	teaspoon salt
2	catfish fillets (6 ounces *each*)

In a skillet, cook bacon over medium heat until cooked but not crisp. Remove to paper towels; keep warm. In a bowl, combine the bread crumbs, cream cheese, 1-1/2 teaspoons lemon juice, onion, celery, parsley, thyme, 1/8 teaspoon pepper and salt. Sprinkle catfish fillets with remaining lemon juice and pepper. Spread crumb mixture over each fillet; roll from one end. Wrap two strips of bacon around each fillet and secure with toothpicks.

Place in a greased 8-in. square baking dish. Bake at 350° for 25-30 minutes or until fish flakes easily with a fork. Remove toothpicks before serving. **Yield:** 2 servings.

Weeknight Catfish Wraps

Weeknight Catfish Wraps

Monica A. Perry • Boise, Idaho

Tuck catfish "nuggets" and a convenient coleslaw mix into tortillas for these handheld greats. The fish gets a slight kick from the Creole seasoning.

1-1/2 cups coleslaw mix
2 tablespoons finely chopped onion
1/8 teaspoon pepper
1 teaspoon Creole *or* Cajun seasoning, *divided*
1/4 cup coleslaw salad dressing
2 tablespoons pancake mix
1/2 pound catfish fillets, cut into 2-inch pieces
1 teaspoon canola oil
4 flour tortillas (6 inches), warmed

In a small bowl, combine the coleslaw mix, onion, pepper and 1/4 teaspoon seasoning. Stir in dressing. Cover and refrigerate for at least 30 minutes.

In a resealable plastic bag, combine the pancake mix and remaining seasoning. Add fish and toss to coat. In a small skillet, cook fish in oil over medium heat for 6 minutes or until lightly browned on each side and fish flakes easily with a fork. Spoon coleslaw mixture onto tortillas; top with fish and roll up. **Yield:** 2 servings.

Shrimp-Topped Red Snapper

Marsha Sullins • Longview, Texas

We first experimented with this recipe using fresh crappie. We liked it so much, the next night I used it with bass. When my friend tried it on red snapper, I realized that it's just awesome with any fish!

2 red snapper fillets (about 7 ounces *each*)
1 tablespoon lemon juice
Dash pepper
1/2 cup sliced fresh mushrooms
3 to 4 garlic cloves, minced
1/4 cup butter
1/4 pound uncooked medium shrimp, peeled and deveined
2 tablespoons sliced green onion

Place the fillets in a shallow 2-qt. baking dish coated with nonstick cooking spray. Sprinkle with lemon juice and pepper. Bake, uncovered, at 350° for 20-25 minutes or until fish flakes easily with a fork.

Meanwhile, in a small skillet, saute the mushrooms and garlic in butter until tender. Add shrimp; cook for 2-4 minutes or until shrimp turn pink. Spoon over fish. Sprinkle with onion. **Yield:** 2 servings.

SEAFOOD SENSATION

Tuna steaks are a tasty change-of-pace entree for one or two. Laurie Todd of Columbus, Mississippi suggests easily seasoning them with bottled Italian salad dressing, salsa or a specialty mustard.

Crispy Salmon Steaks

Maxine Pheasant • Mt. Airy, Maryland

My husband and I had always enjoyed fish, but I could never make it quite right until I found this recipe. The first time I made it, I knew I had a winner.

Crispy Salmon Steaks

1/4	cup butter, melted
1/2	teaspoon salt

Pinch paprika

1/2	cup crushed saltines
1/2	cup crushed potato chips
2	salmon steaks (1 inch thick)

In a shallow bowl, combine the butter, salt and paprika. In another bowl, combine saltines and chips. Dip both sides of salmon steaks in butter mixture, then coat with crumbs. Broil 4-6 in. from the heat for 5-6 minutes on each side or until fish flakes easily with a fork. **Yield:** 2 servings.

Dilly Red Snapper

Sharon Semph • Salem, Oregon

A light and creamy dill sauce lends lovely flavor to these tender fillets. I like to serve the easy entree with a green salad and asparagus or a rice side dish.

✓ Uses less fat, sugar or salt. Includes Nutrition Facts or Diabetic Exchanges.

1	medium lemon, thinly sliced
2	green onions, sliced
2	dill sprigs
2	red snapper fillets (6 ounces *each*)
1/8	teaspoon salt

Dash pepper

DILL SAUCE:

1/3	cup mayonnaise
1	garlic clove, minced
1/2	teaspoon snipped fresh dill *or* 1/8 teaspoon dill weed
1/2	teaspoon lemon juice
1/2	teaspoon minced green onion

Place the lemon slices, onions and dill sprigs in a foil-lined baking pan. Top with fish fillets; sprinkle with salt and pepper. Fold foil around fish and seal tightly.

Bake at 400° for 20-25 minutes or until fish flakes easily with a fork. In a small bowl, combine the sauce ingredients. Serve with fish. **Yield:** 2 servings.

Nutrition Facts: One fillet with 2-1/2 tablespoons sauce (prepared with fat-free mayonnaise) equals 216 calories, 3 g fat (1 g saturated fat), 67 mg cholesterol, 580 mg sodium, 10 g carbohydrate, 2 g fiber, 35 g protein. **Diabetic Exchanges:** 5 very lean meat, 1/2 starch.

Fish in Foil

Bill Davis • Casper, Wyoming

This recipe proves that cooking a satisfying supper for one can be fuss-free. Cooked this way, fish stays moist and flavorful. Plus, there are no dishes to wash!

✓ Uses less fat, sugar or salt. Includes Nutrition Facts or Diabetic Exchanges.

- 1   halibut steak (6 ounces)
- 4   medium mushrooms
- 2   cherry tomatoes, halved
- 2   lemon slices
- 1/2   medium green pepper, sliced
- 1/4   cup diet Mountain Dew

Crushed pepper

Place fish in the center of a 20-in. x 14-in. piece of heavy-duty foil. Place mushrooms, tomatoes, lemon and green pepper around fish. Slightly fold up the edges of the foil; pour soda over fish. Fold the foil to seal tightly.

Bake at 375° for 20-25 minutes or until fish flakes easily with a fork. Open foil carefully to allow steam to escape. Sprinkle with pepper. **Yield:** 1 serving.

Nutrition Facts: 1 serving equals 205 calories, 4 g fat (0 saturated fat), 49 mg cholesterol, 95 mg sodium, 8 g carbohydrate, 0 fiber, 34 g protein. **Diabetic Exchanges:** 4 very lean meat, 1-1/2 vegetable.

Lemon Shrimp Ravioli Toss

Emma Magielda • Amsterdam, New York

Treat yourself to this attractive, single-serving main course that relies on shrimp and cheese ravioli. Being an avid crafter and quilter, I'm usually running short on time, so I make it quite often.

- 1-1/2   cups refrigerated cheese ravioli
- 2   tablespoons butter, melted
- 1   tablespoon lemon juice
- 3/4   teaspoon snipped fresh basil
- 1/2   teaspoon grated lemon peel
- 1-1/3   cups cooked medium shrimp, peeled and deveined

Cook ravioli according to package directions; drain. In a microwave-safe 1-qt. dish, combine the butter, lemon juice, basil and lemon peel. Add shrimp and ravioli; toss to coat. Cover and microwave on high for 2-4 minutes or until heated through. **Yield:** 1 serving.

Editor's Note: This recipe was tested in an 850-watt microwave.

Lemon Shrimp Ravioli Toss

Veggie Shrimp Fettuccine

Angie Medearis • Lemoore, California

This dish is easy, fast and good. The colorful combination of pretty zucchini rounds, fresh tomato and flavorful shrimp is sure to make an everyday meal seem like a special occasion.

4   ounces uncooked fettuccine
1   medium onion, chopped
1   medium zucchini, cut into 1/4-inch slices
1   medium tomato, seeded and chopped
1   garlic clove, minced
2   tablespoons butter
1/2   pound uncooked medium shrimp, peeled and deveined
2   tablespoons white wine *or* chicken broth
1/4   teaspoon salt
1/8   teaspoon pepper

Cook fettuccine according to package directions. Meanwhile, in a skillet, saute the onion, zucchini, tomato and garlic in butter for 8-10 minutes or until crisp-tender. Add the shrimp, wine or broth, salt and pepper. Cook 3-4 minutes longer or until shrimp turn pink. Drain fettuccine; top with shrimp mixture. **Yield:** 2 servings.

Scallop & Potato Saute

Scallop & Potato Saute

Mildred Sherrer • Fort Worth, Texas

This complete dinner comes together on the stovetop and is just perfect for one. Slices of red potatoes make a great addition to bay scallops that are seasoned with garlic and lemon juice.

2   small red potatoes, sliced 1/4 inch thick
2   tablespoons olive oil, *divided*
1/4   pound bay scallops
1   garlic clove, minced
1   tablespoon lemon juice
1   tablespoon chopped fresh parsley
1/8   teaspoon salt

Dash pepper

Lemon slice *or* wedge, optional

In a small skillet over medium heat, cook potatoes in 1 tablespoon oil until golden brown and tender, about 12 minutes. Remove and keep warm. In the same skillet, heat remaining oil. Cook and stir scallops for 2 minutes. Add garlic and lemon juice; cook and stir 1-2 minutes longer or until scallops are firm and opaque.

Add parsley, salt and pepper. Return potatoes to pan; heat through. Serve with lemon if desired. **Yield:** 1 serving.

Tuna Potato Supper

Tuna Potato Supper

Rosella Peters • Gull Lake, Saskatchewan

Tuna lovers will find this a real treat. My husband and I enjoy it as a nice change from ordinary baked potatoes. Along with a salad, it makes a simple lunch or dinner.

2   large baking potatoes
1   can (6 ounces) light water-packed tuna, drained and flaked
1   celery rib with leaves, finely chopped
1   green onion, chopped
1/3 cup creamy cucumber salad dressing
1/8 teaspoon *each* salt and pepper
1/4 cup shredded Colby-Monterey Jack cheese

Scrub and pierce potatoes; place on a microwave-safe plate. Microwave, uncovered, on high for 7-9 minutes or until tender, turning once. Cool slightly. Cut a thin slice off the top of each potato and discard. Scoop out the pulp, leaving a thin shell.

In a bowl, mash the pulp. Stir in the tuna, celery, onion, salad dressing, salt and pepper. Spoon into potato shells. Sprinkle with cheese. Place on a baking sheet. Broil 4-6 in. from the heat for 5-6 minutes or until cheese is melted. **Yield:** 2 servings.

Editor's Note: This recipe was tested in a 1,100-watt microwave.

Shrimp Creole

Edna Boothe • Richmond, Virginia

Years ago, when we visited relatives on the eastern coast of North Carolina, they served this Creole specialty. I asked for the recipe, and it became one of our most-loved meals.

Shrimp Creole

1/2	cup chopped green pepper
1/4	cup chopped onion
1	celery rib, chopped
1	garlic clove, minced
1-1/2	teaspoons vegetable oil
1	can (15 ounces) tomato sauce
1	teaspoon dried oregano
1	bay leaf
1/2	pound cooked medium shrimp, peeled and deveined

Hot cooked rice

In a skillet, saute the green pepper, onion, celery and garlic in oil until tender. Add the tomato sauce, oregano and bay leaf. Reduce heat; simmer, uncovered, for 20 minutes.

Stir in the shrimp; cook 3 minutes longer. Discard bay leaf. Serve over rice. **Yield:** 2 servings.

Baked Orange Roughy with Veggies

Shannon Messmer • Oklahoma City, Oklahoma

This is a nice supper for two, but the recipe is easily doubled to serve four when you're having a few friends over for a small dinner party.

3/4	teaspoon lemon-pepper seasoning
1/8	teaspoon salt
2	orange roughy, red snapper, cod *or* haddock fillets (6 ounces *each*)
1/2	cup sliced fresh mushrooms
1/4	cup thinly sliced green onions
1/4	cup chopped seeded tomato
1/4	cup finely chopped green pepper
2	tablespoons butter, melted
1-1/2	teaspoons orange juice
1	cup hot cooked rice
4-1/2	teaspoons grated Parmesan cheese, optional

Combine lemon-pepper and salt; sprinkle over both sides of fillets. Place in a greased 11-in. x 7-in. x 2-in. baking dish. Combine the mushrooms, onions, tomato and green pepper; spoon over fillets. Combine butter and orange juice; pour over fish and vegetables.

Cover and bake at 350° for 20-25 minutes or until fish flakes easily with a fork. Serve over rice. Sprinkle with Parmesan cheese if desired. **Yield:** 2 servings.

Pecan-Crusted Salmon

Cheryl Bykowski • Punta Gorda, Florida

Let this nutty coating and refreshing sauce turn salmon into something extra special. My husband was thrilled the first time I served it.

- 2 salmon fillets (6 ounces *each*)
- 2 tablespoons mayonnaise
- 1/2 cup finely chopped pecans
- 1/3 cup seasoned bread crumbs
- 2 tablespoons grated Parmesan cheese
- 1 tablespoon minced fresh parsley
- 1 tablespoon butter, melted

CUCUMBER SAUCE:
- 1/2 cup chopped seeded peeled cucumber
- 1/2 cup vanilla yogurt
- 1/2 teaspoon snipped fresh dill *or* 1/4 teaspoon dill weed
- 1/8 teaspoon garlic powder

Place salmon skin side down in a greased 11-in. x 7-in. x 2-in. baking dish. Spread 1 tablespoon mayonnaise over each fillet. Combine the pecans, bread crumbs, Parmesan cheese, parsley and butter; spoon over salmon. Bake at 425° for 10-15 minutes or until fish flakes easily with a fork.

Meanwhile, in a small bowl, combine the cucumber sauce ingredients. Serve with the salmon. **Yield:** 2 servings.

Stuffed Haddock

Jeannette Wojtowicz • Buffalo, New York

I entertain at least once a month. After I served this at a party for eight, I decided to reduce the recipe to serve two. It turned out just as delicious.

- 1 tablespoon chopped onion
- 1 tablespoon butter
- 5 butter-flavored crackers, crushed
- 1 haddock, sole *or* cod fillet (about 1 pound)
- 1/3 cup condensed cream of celery soup, undiluted
- 1 tablespoon sour cream

Paprika

In a skillet, saute onion in butter until tender. Stir in crackers and just enough water to hold mixture together. Cut a pocket into side of fillet; stuff with cracker mixture.

Place in a greased baking dish. Combine soup and sour cream; spread over fish. Sprinkle with paprika. Bake, uncovered, at 350° for 25-30 minutes or until fish flakes easily with a fork. **Yield:** 2 servings.

Stuffed Haddock

Shrimp Pasta Primavera

Shari Neff • Silver Spring, Maryland

They say the way to a man's heart is through his stomach, so when I invite that special guy to dinner, I like to prepare something equally special. This well-seasoned pasta dish has lots of flavor, and it won't hurt your budget!

4	ounces uncooked angel hair pasta
8	jumbo shrimp, peeled and deveined
6	fresh asparagus spears, trimmed and cut into 2-inch pieces
12	garlic cloves, minced
1/4	cup olive oil
1/2	cup sliced fresh mushrooms
1/2	cup chicken broth
1	small plum tomato, peeled, seeded and diced
1/4	teaspoon salt
1/8	teaspoon crushed red pepper flakes
1	tablespoon *each* minced fresh basil, oregano, thyme and parsley
1/4	cup grated Parmesan cheese

Cook pasta according to package directions. Meanwhile, in a large skillet, saute the shrimp, asparagus and garlic in oil for 3-4 minutes or until shrimp turn pink.

Add the mushrooms, broth, tomato, salt and pepper flakes; simmer, uncovered, for 2 minutes.

Drain pasta. Add the pasta and seasoning to skillet; toss to coat. Sprinkle with Parmesan cheese. **Yield:** 2 servings.

Pesto Salmon

Lee Bremson • Kansas City, Missouri

A flavorful, homemade pesto helps keep this fish entree moist, and toasted bread crumbs give it the perfect finishing touch. I like to use fresh basil from the garden when I can.

✓ Uses less fat, sugar or salt. Includes Nutrition Facts or Diabetic Exchanges.

1	slice bread
1/4	cup lightly packed fresh basil
2	tablespoons packed fresh parsley
2-1/2	teaspoons olive oil
1/2	teaspoon pine nuts
1/4	teaspoon minced garlic
Dash salt	
Dash coarsely ground pepper	
2	salmon fillets (6 ounces *each*)

For pesto, tear bread into pieces; place in a miniature food processor. Pulse until fine crumbs form. Set aside 1 tablespoon. To the remaining bread crumbs, add the basil, parsley, oil, pine nuts, garlic, salt and pepper; cover and process until finely chopped.

Place salmon on a baking sheet coated with nonstick cooking spray. Spread with pesto. Sprinkle with reserved bread crumbs. Bake at 400° for 20-22 minutes or until fish flakes easily with a fork and crumbs are lightly browned. **Yield:** 2 servings.

Nutrition Facts: 1 serving equals 406 calories, 25 g fat (5 g saturated fat), 101 mg cholesterol, 252 mg sodium, 8 g carbohydrate, 1 g fiber, 35 g protein.

Shrimp Pasta Primavera

Herbed Tomato Fish Bake

Linda Buiter • Lansing, Illinois

We appreciate Italian cuisine that has a healthy flair, so this recipe is a keeper. The fish gets a little tartness from the lemon. I like to serve it alongside risotto and steamed broccoli.

✓ **Uses less fat, sugar or salt. Includes Nutrition Facts or Diabetic Exchanges.**

3/4	pound cod, haddock *or* orange roughy fillets
1/3	cup canned Italian diced tomatoes, drained
3	tablespoons chopped green pepper
1	tablespoon finely chopped onion
1-1/2	teaspoons lemon juice
1/2	teaspoon honey
1/8	teaspoon salt
1/8	teaspoon dried marjoram
1/8	teaspoon hot pepper sauce, optional
3	teaspoons minced fresh basil, *divided*

Place the fillets in a 1-qt. baking dish coated with nonstick cooking spray. Combine the next eight ingredients. Pour over fillets. Sprinkle with 2 teaspoons basil.

Bake, uncovered, at 400° for 15-20 minutes or until fish flakes easily with a fork. Sprinkle with remaining basil. **Yield:** 2 servings.

Nutrition Facts: 1 serving equals 160 calories, 1 g fat (trace saturated fat), 73 mg cholesterol, 301 mg sodium, 5 g carbohydrate, 1 g fiber, 31 g protein.
Diabetic Exchanges: 4 very lean meat, 1 vegetable.

Tarragon Flounder

Tarragon Flounder

Donna Smith • Fairport, New York

Tarragon and a hint of ground mustard makes this a super dinner for one. The flounder bakes in the buttery sauce with savory results.

✓ **Uses less fat, sugar or salt. Includes Nutrition Facts or Diabetic Exchanges.**

1/4	pound flounder fillets
1/4	cup chicken broth
1	tablespoon butter, melted
1-1/2	teaspoons minced fresh tarragon *or* 1/2 teaspoon dried tarragon
1/2	teaspoon ground mustard

Place fillets in a greased 11-in. x 7-in. x 2-in. baking dish. Combine remaining ingredients; pour over fish. Bake, uncovered, at 350° for 20-25 minutes or until fish flakes easily with a fork. Remove to a serving plate with a slotted spatula. Serve immediately. **Yield:** 1 serving.

Nutrition Facts: One serving (prepared with low-sodium broth and reduced-fat margarine) equals 192 calories, 10 g fat (0 saturated fat), 61 mg cholesterol, 250 mg sodium, 1 g carbohydrate, 0 fiber, 25 g protein.
Diabetic Exchange: 3-1/2 lean meat.

Salmon with Chive Mayonnaise

Taste of Home Test Kitchen • Greendale, Wisconsin

It's easy to stir together a thick sauce to dress up broiled salmon steaks. The fish seems special but is really no fuss to prepare. Serve it with crisp deli coleslaw and store-bought lemon cake for dessert...or try it with a Caesar salad and slices of frozen key lime pie.

1/2	cup mayonnaise
3	tablespoons white wine *or* chicken broth
1/4	cup minced chives
1	tablespoon minced fresh thyme
1	tablespoon snipped fresh dill *or* 1 teaspoon dill weed
1/8	teaspoon pepper
2	salmon steaks (3/4 inch thick)

In a bowl, combine the first six ingredients; set aside 1/3 cup for serving. Place salmon steaks on a broiler rack. Broil 4 in. from the heat for 9 minutes. Brush with remaining mayonnaise mixture. Turn salmon over; broil 9 minutes longer or until fish flakes easily with a fork. Serve with the reserved mayonnaise mixture. **Yield:** 2 servings.

Salmon with Chive Mayonnaise

Tuna Macaroni Toss

Peggy Burdick • Burlington, Michigan

The no-fuss, from-scratch sauce almost steals the show from my tuna classic. I like it served over hot cooked noodles, but feel free to try it with rice or shell pasta.

1/3	cup chopped onion
2	tablespoons butter
1	tablespoon all-purpose flour
3/4	cup milk
1	chicken bouillon cube
1/4	teaspoon salt, optional
1/8	teaspoon pepper
1	can (3-1/4-ounces) tuna, drained and flaked
1/2	cup frozen peas
2	teaspoons diced pimientos

Cooked noodles
Chopped fresh parsley

In a saucepan, saute onion in butter until tender. Stir in the flour, forming a smooth paste; cook and stir for 1 minute. Gradually stir in milk. Add bouillon, salt if desired and pepper; cook until thickened. Stir in tuna, peas and pimientos; heat through. Serve over noodles and garnish with parsley. **Yield:** 1 serving.

SCALED-DOWN SIDE DISHES

Nothing beats the memory-making flavor of a homemade specialty...so why open a can or boxed mix when it comes to preparing a side dish? Whether you're serving beef or chicken, ham or fish, you'll find that the recipes offered here make perfect dinner accompaniments.

Fettuccine Primavera
p. 210

Green Bean Fritters
p. 202

Mushroom Rice Pilaf
p. 207

Quick Cheese Puffs
p. 197

Tomato 'n' Cheese Pasta
p. 193

Grilled Vegetable Skewers

Grilled Vegetable Skewers

Susan Bourque • Danielson, Connecticut

My mother and I love to eat fresh vegetables the most flavorful way...grilled! Seasoned with several herbs, these kabobs showcase the best of summer's gorgeous bounty.

✓ Uses less fat, sugar or salt. Includes Nutrition Facts or Diabetic Exchanges.

- 1 medium ear fresh *or* frozen sweet corn, thawed and quartered
- 1 small zucchini, quartered
- 1/4 small red onion, halved
- 4 cherry tomatoes
- 1/4 teaspoon dried basil
- 1/4 teaspoon dried rosemary, crushed
- 1/4 teaspoon dried thyme
- 1/8 teaspoon garlic powder
- 1/8 teaspoon salt
- 1/8 teaspoon pepper

Place the corn on a microwave-safe plate. Cover with waxed paper. Microwave on high for 2 minutes.

Coat grill rack with nonstick cooking spray before starting the grill. On two metal or soaked wooden skewers, alternately thread the corn, zucchini, onion and tomatoes. Lightly coat vegetables with nonstick cooking spray. In a small bowl, combine the seasonings; sprinkle over vegetables.

Grill, covered, over medium heat for 3 minutes on each side or until vegetables are tender, turning three times. **Yield:** 2 servings.

Nutrition Facts: 1 kabob equals 69 calories, 1 g fat (trace saturated fat), 0 cholesterol, 131 mg sodium, 16 g carbohydrate, 3 g fiber, 3 g protein. **Diabetic Exchanges:** 1 vegetable, 1/2 starch.

Tomato 'n' Cheese Pasta

Dawn Dhooghe • Concord, North Carolina

Garlic, basil and oregano add pizzazz to this savory casserole. The pasta is tender and moist, and there's plenty of cheese flavor. I like to serve it with steaks.

1 cup uncooked small tube pasta
1 small onion, chopped
2 garlic cloves, minced
1 tablespoon olive oil
1 can (14-1/2 ounces) Italian diced tomatoes
1/2 teaspoon dried basil
1/2 teaspoon dried oregano
1/4 teaspoon sugar
1/4 teaspoon pepper
1/4 cup shredded part-skim mozzarella cheese
1/4 cup grated Parmesan cheese

Cook pasta according to package directions. In a small saucepan, saute onion and garlic in oil until tender. Stir in the tomatoes, basil, oregano, sugar and pepper. Bring to a boil.

Reduce heat; simmer, uncovered, for 15 minutes. Drain pasta; stir into saucepan.

Transfer to a greased 1-qt. baking dish. Top with cheeses. Bake, uncovered, at 375° for 10-15 minutes or until cheese is melted. **Yield:** 2 servings.

Dutch Potatoes

Perlene Hoekema • Lynden, Washington

I whip up mashed potatoes with carrots and sour cream for this stick-to-your-ribs side dish. Cook it up for the meat-and-potato lover in your home.

☑ **Uses less fat, sugar or salt. Includes Nutrition Facts or Diabetic Exchanges.**

1/4 cup chopped onion
2 teaspoons butter
2 cups cubed peeled potatoes
1 cup sliced fresh carrots
1/4 cup sour cream
1/4 teaspoon salt
Minced chives

In a small skillet, saute onion in butter for 8-10 minutes or until golden brown. Meanwhile, place potatoes and carrots in a large saucepan and cover with water. Bring to a boil. Reduce heat; cover and cook for 10-15 minutes or until tender. Drain.

In a small mixing bowl, mash potatoes and carrots. Beat in onion, sour cream and salt. Sprinkle with chives. **Yield:** 2 servings.

Dutch Potatoes

Nutrition Facts: 1 cup (prepared with reduced-fat butter and reduced-fat sour cream) equals 225 calories, 5 g fat (3 g saturated fat), 17 mg cholesterol, 368 mg sodium, 41 g carbohydrate, 5 g fiber, 6 g protein.

Seasoned Fan Potatoes

Tressa Surdick • Bethel Park, Pennsylvania

For a festive presentation, I slice baking potatoes and fan them. Featuring butter and herbs, the potatoes get raves from anyone who tries them.

✓ Uses less fat, sugar or salt. Includes Nutrition Facts or Diabetic Exchanges.

2	medium baking potatoes
1	teaspoon Italian seasoning
1/2	teaspoon salt
1	tablespoon butter, melted
2	tablespoons finely shredded cheddar cheese
1	tablespoon grated Parmesan cheese
1	tablespoon minced fresh parsley

With a sharp knife, slice potatoes thinly but not all the way through, leaving slices attached at the bottom. Fan potatoes slightly.

Place in an ungreased 8-in. square baking dish. Sprinkle with Italian seasoning and salt. Drizzle with butter. Bake, uncovered, at 425° for 50 minutes. Sprinkle with cheeses and parsley; bake 10-15 minutes longer or until lightly browned. **Yield:** 2 servings.

Nutrition Facts: One potato (prepared with reduced-fat butter and reduced-fat cheese) equals 227 calories, 5 g fat (4 g saturated fat), 17 mg cholesterol, 731 mg sodium, 39 g carbohydrate, 4 g fiber, 8 g protein.

Green Beans with Red Peppers

Green Beans with Red Peppers

Chris Kallies • Oldsmar, Florida

Balsamic vinegar adds zing to these pretty, sauteed veggies that cook in a flash. Trim the beans and julienne the red pepper ahead to cook this dish at the last minute.

✓ Uses less fat, sugar or salt. Includes Nutrition Facts or Diabetic Exchanges.

1/4	pound fresh green beans, trimmed
1/2	cup julienned sweet red pepper
1/2	teaspoon olive oil
1	teaspoon balsamic vinegar
1/8	to 1/4 teaspoon dried basil
1/8	teaspoon pepper

In a nonstick skillet coated with nonstick cooking spray, saute beans and red pepper in oil for 4 minutes or until crisp-tender. Stir in the vinegar, basil and pepper. **Yield:** 2 servings.

Nutrition Facts: 2/3 cup equals 79 calories, 3 g fat (1 g saturated fat), 0 cholesterol, 10 mg sodium, 14 g carbohydrate, 3 g fiber, 3 g protein. **Diabetic Exchanges:** 2 vegetable, 1/2 fat.

Orange-Kissed Beets

Bonnie Baumgardner • Sylva, North Carolina

This is an original recipe that I developed myself a few years ago. It's one of my husband's favorites.

1/3   cup orange juice
2   tablespoons light brown sugar
1   tablespoon butter
1/2   teaspoon cornstarch
1/8   teaspoon ground ginger
1/8   teaspoon salt
1/8   teaspoon pepper
1   can (8-1/4 ounces) sliced beets, drained
2   tablespoons golden raisins

Strips of orange peel

In a saucepan over medium heat, cook and stir orange juice, brown sugar, butter, cornstarch, ginger, salt and pepper until thick. Add the beets and raisins; heat through. Garnish with orange peel. **Yield:** 2 servings.

Orange-Kissed Beets

Sweet Onion Blossom

Judy Stratton • Duluth, Minnesota

Using fresh asparagus from my garden, I created this side dish for lunch one day...and was delighted by the change-of-pace combination of vegetables, colors and flavors.

✓ Uses less fat, sugar or salt. Includes Nutrition Facts or Diabetic Exchanges.

1   small Vidalia *or* sweet onion
2   teaspoons butter, *divided*
1/4   cup shredded part-skim mozzarella cheese
3/4   cup sliced fresh mushrooms
4   fresh asparagus spears, trimmed and cut into 1-inch pieces

Cut onion into 1/4-in. slices to within 1 in. of bottom. Repeat cuts in opposite direction. Place in an ungreased 2-cup baking dish. Top with 1 teaspoon butter.

Bake, uncovered, at 350° for 60-70 minutes or until tender (cover with foil if top browns too quickly). Sprinkle with cheese. Bake 3-4 minutes longer or until cheese is melted.

Meanwhile, in a small skillet, saute mushrooms in remaining butter until tender; keep warm. Place asparagus in a steamer basket; place in a saucepan over 1 in. of water. Bring to a boil; cover and steam for 3-4 minutes or until crisp-tender. Place onion on a serving plate; spoon mushrooms and asparagus around onion. **Yield:** 1 serving.

Nutrition Facts: 1 serving equals 223 calories, 13 g fat (8 g saturated fat), 37 mg cholesterol, 222 mg sodium, 18 g carbohydrate, 4 g fiber, 12 g protein.
Diabetic Exchanges: 2 vegetable, 2 fat, 1 lean meat, 1/2 starch.

Corn Medley

Corn Medley

Donna Brockett • Kingfisher, Oklahoma

I clipped this recipe many years ago, and it remains one of my most requested. My husband and I love all the items in it, plus it doesn't require much prep time. With a simple green salad, it can even make a light yet complete meal.

2 bacon strips
1 cup whole kernel corn
2 tablespoons finely chopped onion
1/2 cup chopped fresh tomato
1/4 teaspoon dried basil
Salt and pepper to taste

In a medium skillet, cook bacon until crisp. Remove to paper towel to drain; reserve 1 tablespoon of drippings. Add corn and onion to skillet; cook and stir over medium-low heat until onion is tender.

Add tomato and basil. Reduce heat to low; cover and cook for 5-7 minutes or until vegetables are tender, stirring occasionally. Crumble bacon; add to the vegetables. Season with salt and pepper. **Yield:** 2 servings.

Quick Cheese Puffs

Janet Scherffius • Mountain Home, Arkansas

These golden puffs are a favorite when it comes to lunches and meatless meals. For extra flavor, I'll sometimes use homemade bread or a specialty loaf such as Italian, French or sourdough.

2 tablespoons butter, softened
3 slices white bread
2 eggs
1 cup milk
1/2 cup shredded cheddar cheese
1/4 teaspoon onion salt
8 to 10 drops hot pepper sauce

Spread butter on one side of each slice of bread. Cut bread into strips; place strips, buttered side down, on the bottom and around the sides of two greased 10-oz. baking dishes. In a bowl, beat eggs and milk. Add cheese, onion salt and hot pepper sauce.

Pour over bread. Place the dishes on a baking sheet. Bake, uncovered, at 350° for 30-35 minutes or until puffed and golden brown. Serve immediately. **Yield:** 2 servings.

Colorful Fried Rice

Linda Rae Lee • San Francisco, California

This recipe was given to me by a dear friend many years ago. The variety of ingredients makes a pretty presentation, and the preparation is simple using cooked rice. I make it all the time.

1-1/2 cups cold cooked rice
2 green onions, chopped
1 small carrot, diced
1/4 cup fresh *or* frozen peas, thawed
4 teaspoons soy sauce
1 tablespoon minced fresh parsley
1 tablespoon vegetable oil

1 egg, beaten
Salt and pepper to taste

In a skillet, cook and stir the rice, onions, carrot, peas, soy sauce and parsley in oil until onions are tender and rice is heated through. Add egg; cook and stir until egg is completely set. Season with salt and pepper. **Yield:** 2 servings.

Apricot-Ginger Asparagus

Taste of Home Test Kitchen • Greendale, Wisconsin

Here's a succulent side dish that goes great with any entree. It's so easy to dress up asparagus with apricot preserves and a few simple seasonings.

Apricot-Ginger Asparagus

1/2	pound fresh asparagus, trimmed
1/4	cup apricot preserves
1	tablespoon red wine vinegar
1/8	teaspoon ground cinnamon
1/8	teaspoon minced fresh gingerroot

In a large skillet, bring 1 in. of water to a boil; place asparagus in a steamer basket over water. Cover and steam for 5 minutes or until crisp-tender; drain and keep warm.

In a small skillet over medium heat, bring the preserves, vinegar, cinnamon and ginger to a boil. Reduce heat; simmer, uncovered, for 2-4 minutes or until glaze begins to thicken. Pour over asparagus. **Yield:** 2 servings.

Italian-Style Rice

Kathry Manwiller • Wyomissing, Pennsylvania

Turmeric and Parmesan cheese boost the flavor of long grain rice in this kitchen staple. It's a mouth-watering dish for two that's perfect on busy weeknights.

1	tablespoon chopped onion
1	tablespoon butter
1/3	cup uncooked long grain rice
1-1/4	cups chicken broth
Dash ground turmeric	
1/4	cup shredded Parmesan cheese

In a saucepan, saute onion in butter until tender. Add rice; cook over medium heat for 2 minutes, stirring constantly. Stir in broth and turmeric; bring to a boil. Reduce heat; cover and simmer for 20-25 minutes or until liquid is absorbed. Stir in cheese. **Yield:** 2 servings.

SWIFT SPUDS

Mashed potatoes usually freeze well. If you just can't pare down your favorite recipe, freeze the leftovers in 1/2-cup servings on a baking sheet. The frozen mounds can be stored in a resealable bag, allowing you to microwave individual servings whenever you'd like.

Summer Squash Bundles

Juanita Daugherty • Cadet, Missouri

We love zucchini and my husband enjoys cooking summer meals on the grill, so I came up with this idea to add to our outdoor dining menu. We increased the recipe and served the pretty bundles at a family reunion cookout...and they were a big hit!

✓ Uses less fat, sugar or salt. Includes Nutrition Facts or Diabetic Exchanges.

- 1   green onion
- 1   medium yellow squash (6 to 8 inches long)
- 1   medium zucchini (6 to 8 inches long)
- 1/4   cup chopped leek (white portion only)
- 2   tablespoons grated Parmesan cheese
- 2   teaspoons Italian seasoning
- 2   teaspoons butter, melted
- 1/4   teaspoon salt

Remove white portion of green onion (discard or save for another use). Trim the onion tops to 8- or 9-in. lengths. In a saucepan, bring water to a boil. Add onion tops; boil for 1 minute or until softened. Drain and immediately place in ice water. Drain and pat dry; set aside.

Cut squash and zucchini in half lengthwise. Scoop out pulp from zucchini halves, leaving a 3/8-in. shell. Discard pulp. In a bowl, combine the remaining ingredients; fill zucchini shells. Place yellow squash halves, cut side down, over filled zucchini halves. Tie each bundle with a blanched onion top.

Wrap each bundle in a double thickness of heavy-duty foil (12 in. square). Fold foil around squash and seal tightly. Grill, covered, over medium heat for 15-20 minutes or until tender. **Yield:** 2 servings.

Nutrition Facts: 1 squash bundle equals 114 calories, 6 g fat (3 g saturated fat), 14 mg cholesterol, 439 mg sodium, 12 g carbohydrate, 5 g fiber, 6 g protein. **Diabetic Exchanges:** 2 vegetable, 1 fat.

Spicy Roasted Potatoes

Linda Tepper • Clifton Park, New York

I came up with this recipe when I had some leftover taco seasoning mix and wanted to spice up homemade oven fries. They were an immediate success!

- 3   medium red potatoes, cut into 1-inch pieces
- 1   tablespoon taco seasoning
- 1   tablespoon canola oil

In a large resealable plastic bag, combine all ingredients; shake to coat. Place potatoes in a 9-in. square baking pan coated with nonstick cooking spray. Bake, uncovered, at 450° for 25-30 minutes or until tender, stirring once. **Yield:** 2 servings.

Spicy Roasted Potatoes

Pasta with Broccoli

Jan Vallely • Fullerton, California

This dish is not only delicious and attractive, but it saves time because you can prepare the pasta and broccoli in one saucepan.

2 garlic cloves, minced
1 tablespoon olive oil
3/4 cup water
2 ounces uncooked spaghetti *or* linguine, broken into 2-inch pieces
Dash crushed red pepper flakes
1-1/2 cups small fresh broccoli florets
1/4 teaspoon salt
Pepper to taste
2 tablespoons grated Parmesan cheese

In a saucepan, saute garlic in oil until tender. Add the water, pasta and pepper flakes. Bring to a boil, stirring occasionally. Reduce heat; cover and simmer for 6 minutes, stirring occasionally.

Add the broccoli; cook 4-5 minutes longer or until pasta and broccoli are tender. Drain and transfer to a serving bowl. Season with salt and pepper; sprinkle with Parmesan cheese. **Yield:** 2 servings.

Nutrition Facts: 1 cup equals 214 calories, 10 g fat (3 g saturated fat), 3 mg cholesterol, 312 mg sodium, 25 g carbohydrate, 2 g fiber, 8 g protein. **Diabetic Exchanges:** 2 vegetable, 2 fat, 1 starch.

Cheesy Baked Onions

Cheesy Baked Onions

Louise Elliott • Gallipolis, Ohio

I found this recipe in the newspaper many years ago. It has been a family favorite ever since. Because it goes well with any meat, it's a good "dish to pass" when doubled and brought to potluck suppers. Someone will always ask, "Who brought the onions?"

1 medium onion
1 tablespoon butter
1 tablespoon all-purpose flour
1/4 teaspoon salt
1/2 cup milk
1/3 cup shredded cheddar cheese

Slice onion and separate into rings; place in a greased 1-qt. baking dish and set aside. In a small saucepan over low heat, melt the butter. Stir in the flour and salt until smooth. Gradually add milk; bring to a boil over medium heat. Cook and stir for 2 minutes. Remove from the heat; stir in cheese until melted.

Pour over onions. Bake, uncovered, at 350° for 45-50 minutes or until onions are tender and cheese is browned. **Yield:** 2 servings.

Twice-Baked Sweet Potatoes

Twice-Baked Sweet Potatoes

Lorraine Menard • Omaha, Nebraska

*I like this irresistible dish so much that I sometimes make it with deli ham
when I don't have leftover baked ham. The sweet potatoes are a nice change of pace.*

✓ Uses less fat, sugar or salt. Includes Nutrition Facts
or Diabetic Exchanges.

- 2   large sweet potatoes (3/4 pound *each*)
- 1   pineapple tidbits snack cup (4 ounces)
- 2   tablespoons reduced-fat butter
- 2   tablespoons brown sugar
- 2/3 cup cubed fully cooked lean ham

Prick sweet potatoes with a fork; place on a microwave-safe plate. Microwave on high for 4-5 minutes or until tender. Cool slightly. Drain pineapple, reserving 2 tablespoons juice; set aside.

Cut a thin slice off the top of each potato and discard. Scoop out the pulp, leaving a thin shell. In a bowl, mash the pulp with butter. Stir in brown sugar and reserved pineapple juice. Fold in ham and half of the pineapple. Spoon into potato shells. Top with remaining pineapple.

Place on a baking sheet. Broil 4-6 in. from the heat for 3-5 minutes or until browned and heated through. **Yield:** 2 servings.

Nutrition Facts: One stuffed potato equals 551 calories, 9 g fat (5 g saturated fat), 34 mg cholesterol, 650 mg sodium, 103 g carbohydrate, 11 g fiber, 17 g protein.

Editor's Note: This recipe was tested in a 1,100-watt microwave.

Raspberry-Pecan Dressing

Beverly Coyde • Gasport, New York

Stuffing isn't just for company! Here's a downsized recipe that proves it. With a sweet raspberry flavor and pecan-packed crunch, it is ideal for pairing up with pork or poultry.

4   slices day-old bread, cubed
1/2 cup chopped pecans, toasted
1/2 cup chopped green onions
1   egg, beaten
2   tablespoons butter, melted
1   teaspoon raspberry *or* cider vinegar
Salt and pepper to taste
1   cup fresh raspberries

Place the bread cubes, pecans and onions in a large bowl. Combine the egg, butter, vinegar, salt and pepper. Pour over bread mixture; toss to combine. Gently fold in raspberries.

Transfer to a greased 1-qt. baking dish. Cover and bake at 350° for 20-25 minutes or until a knife inserted near the center comes out clean. **Yield:** 2 servings.

Green Bean Fritters

Sharon Dyck • Roxton Falls, Quebec

You've just got to try this fun take on green beans. Wrapped in strips of green onions, bundles of beans are coated in a simple batter and fried to perfection. I serve them with a finger-licking, homemade salsa.

2   green onions
3/4 pound fresh green beans, trimmed
1   teaspoon salt, *divided*
6   eggs, *separated*
2/3 cup all-purpose flour
1/4 teaspoon pepper
Oil for deep-fat frying
SALSA:
2   medium tomatoes, seeded and chopped
3   tablespoons finely chopped onion
1   jalapeno pepper, seeded and chopped
2   tablespoons minced fresh parsley
1   garlic clove, minced
1   tablespoon olive oil
1   tablespoon cider vinegar
Salt and pepper to taste

Cut green tops from onions (save white portion for another use). Cut tops into narrow strips; soften in boiling water for 30 seconds. Drain and rinse in cold water. Wrap each strip round a bundle of eight green beans; gently tie a knot.

Place 1/2 in. of water in a large skillet; add bean bundles and 1/2 teaspoon salt. Bring to a boil. Reduce heat; cover and simmer for 8-10 minutes or until beans are crisp-tender. Drain on paper towels.

In a mixing bowl, beat egg yolks until lemon-colored. Stir in the flour, pepper and remaining salt. In another mixing bowl, beat egg whites until stiff peaks form. Fold into flour mixture.

In an electric skillet or deep-fat fryer, heat oil to 375°. Dip bean bundles in batter; fry a few at a time for 7 minutes or until golden brown. Drain on paper towels.

In a bowl, combine salsa ingredients. Serve with fritters. **Yield:** 2 servings.

Editor's Note: When cutting or seeding hot peppers, use rubber or plastic gloves to protect your hands. Avoid touching your face.

Raspberry-Pecan Dressing

Macaroni 'n' Cheese For Two

Mrs. Lick • Boyne Falls, Michigan

This is the simplest of dishes. It's so well received on cold, frosty evenings. The combination of sour cream and cheese gives this macaroni classic a distinctive taste of its own.

- 1/3 cup sour cream
- 1/3 cup milk
- 1 cup (4 ounces) shredded sharp cheddar cheese
- 3/4 cup elbow macaroni, cooked and drained
- 2 tablespoons chopped onion, optional

Paprika

In a bowl, combine sour cream and milk. Stir in the cheese, macaroni and onion if desired. Transfer to a greased 2-1/2-cup baking dish; sprinkle with the paprika. Cover and bake at 325° for 25 minutes or until heated through. **Yield:** 2 servings.

Macaroni 'n' Cheese for Two

Ginger Veggie Stir-Fry

Jennifer Maslowski • New York, New York

I created this combination from the last remaining items in our refrigerator before a long vacation. The green beans blend nicely with broccoli, carrot, red onion and sweet potato for a well-seasoned dish.

- 1 teaspoon cornstarch
- 1/4 cup orange juice
- 2 tablespoons soy sauce
- 1 medium carrot, julienned
- 1 cup fresh broccoli florets
- 1 cup cut fresh green beans (2-inch pieces)
- 2 tablespoons olive oil
- 1 cup julienned peeled sweet potato
- 1 cup thinly sliced red onion
- 1 garlic clove, minced
- 1/2 teaspoon dried rosemary, crushed
- 1/4 teaspoon ground ginger
- 1/8 teaspoon crushed red pepper flakes, optional

In a small bowl, combine cornstarch, orange juice and soy sauce until smooth; set aside. In a large skillet or wok, stir-fry carrot, broccoli and beans in oil for 8 minutes. Add sweet potato and onion; stir-fry until vegetables are crisp-tender.

Stir the soy sauce mixture; add to the skillet with garlic, rosemary, ginger, and pepper flakes if desired. Bring to a boil; cook and stir for 1 minute or until thickened. **Yield:** 2 servings.

Potato Wedges with Dip

Deborah Lacher • Deerfield, Ohio

I make these potato wedges all the time because my husband won't eat anything fried. I couldn't find the bacon dip in the grocery store that I wanted, so I made my own.

 1 **large baking potato**
Olive oil-flavored nonstick cooking spray
 1/4 **teaspoon salt**
Dash garlic salt
Dash cayenne pepper
BACON HORSERADISH DIP:
 1/3 **cup sour cream**
 1/2 **teaspoon prepared horseradish**
 1 **bacon strip, cooked and crumbled**

Pierce potato and place on a microwave-safe plate. Microwave on high for 3 minutes or until still firm but almost tender. Cut into eight wedges; place on a baking sheet coated with nonstick cooking spray. Spritz wedges with olive oil-flavored spray; sprinkle with salt, garlic salt and cayenne. Bake at 425° for 20-25 minutes or until golden brown.

In a small bowl, combine the dip ingredients. Serve with potato wedges. **Yield:** 1 serving.

Editor's Note: This recipe was tested in a 1,100-watt microwave.

Sweet-Sour Red Cabbage

Karen Gorman • Gunnison, Colorado

The first time I bought a red cabbage, I didn't quite know what to do with it, but after some experimenting, I came up with this recipe. It has now become my fall comfort food. This side dish is compatible with a variety of meats, but I especially like it with a pork roast.

 2 **tablespoons cider vinegar**
 1 **tablespoon brown sugar**
 1/4 **teaspoon caraway seed**
 1/4 **teaspoon celery seed**
 2 **cups shredded red cabbage**
 1/2 **cup thinly sliced onion**
Salt and pepper to taste

In a small bowl, combine the vinegar, brown sugar, caraway seed and celery seed; set aside. Place cabbage and onion in a saucepan; add a small amount of water. Cover and steam until tender, about 15 minutes.

Add the vinegar mixture and toss to coat. Season with the salt and pepper. Serve warm. **Yield:** 2 servings.

Sweet-Sour Red Cabbage

Colorful Zucchini Spears

Colorful Zucchini Spears

Jan Caldwell • Shingle Springs, California

A bit of bacon lends country flavor to this garden-fresh side dish, while reduced-fat cheese helps keep the calories and fat in check.

☑ **Uses less fat, sugar or salt. Includes Nutrition Facts or Diabetic Exchanges.**

1	bacon strip, cut into 1-inch pieces
1	medium zucchini
1/8	teaspoon salt
1/8	teaspoon dried oregano
1/8	teaspoon garlic powder
1/8	teaspoon pepper
1	plum tomato, halved and sliced
1/4	cup sliced onion
1/4	cup shredded reduced-fat sharp cheddar cheese

In a small nonstick skillet, cook bacon over medium heat until cooked but not crisp. Using a slotted spoon, remove bacon to paper towels to drain. Cut zucchini in half widthwise; cut halves lengthwise into quarters. Place in an ungreased shallow 1-qt. baking dish.

Combine the salt, oregano, garlic powder and pepper; sprinkle half over the zucchini. Top with tomato, onion, remaining seasonings and bacon. Bake, uncovered, at 350° for 15 minutes. Sprinkle with cheese; bake 5-10 minutes longer or until zucchini is tender. **Yield:** 2 servings.

Nutrition Facts: 1 serving equals 85 calories, 5 g fat (3 g saturated fat), 13 mg cholesterol, 202 mg sodium, 6 g carbohydrate, 2 g fiber, 6 g protein. **Diabetic Exchanges:** 1 vegetable, 1 fat.

Mushroom Rice Pilaf

Anita Miller • Sartell, Minnesota

I used to prepare this no-fuss recipe when we were first married, and now that the kids are grown and we're retired, I'm using it again. Canned mushrooms do a super job of dressing up the long grain rice.

✓ **Uses less fat, sugar or salt. Includes Nutrition Facts or Diabetic Exchanges.**

1/4	cup chopped green pepper
2	tablespoons chopped onion
2	teaspoons butter
1	can (7 ounces) mushroom stems and pieces, drained
2/3	cup water
1/3	cup uncooked long grain rice
1	teaspoon chicken bouillon granules
1	teaspoon dried parsley flakes
1/8	teaspoon salt

Dash pepper

In a saucepan, saute green pepper and onion in butter until tender. Add mushrooms; heat through. Stir in the water, rice, bouillon, parsley, salt and pepper. Bring to a boil. Reduce heat; cover and simmer for 14-16 minutes or until liquid is absorbed and rice is tender. **Yield:** 2 servings.

Nutrition Facts: 3/4 cup equals 183 calories, 4 g fat (2 g saturated fat), 11 mg cholesterol, 973 mg sodium, 31 g carbohydrate, 3 g fiber, 5 g protein. **Diabetic Exchanges:** 2 starch, 1/2 fat.

Spinach Cheddar Bake

Julie Dixon • Hazelwood, Missouri

Spinach is one of my favorite foods, so I make this easy recipe often, using the frozen or canned spinach that I keep on hand.

1	package (10 ounces) frozen chopped spinach, thawed and undrained
1/3	cup crushed saltines (about 6 crackers)
1	egg, beaten
1/2	teaspoon onion powder

Salt to taste

1	cup (4 ounces) shredded cheddar cheese, *divided*

In a bowl, combine the spinach, saltines, egg, onion powder and salt. Stir in 1/2 cup cheese.

Transfer to a greased 2-cup baking dish; sprinkle with remaining cheese. Bake, uncovered, at 350° for 30 minutes or until cheese is melted and bubbly. **Yield:** 2 servings.

Spinach Cheddar Bake

Sweet Potato Souffles

Mary Kay Dixson • Decatur, Alabama

Looking for something special to serve with dinner? Try these delightful souffles made hearty with sweet potato, nutmeg and butter.

4   teaspoons sugar, *divided*
1   large sweet potato (about 12 ounces), peeled and cubed
1   teaspoon lemon juice
1/2 to 3/4 teaspoon salt
1/8 teaspoon ground nutmeg
1   tablespoon butter
4   teaspoons all-purpose flour
1/2 cup milk
2   eggs, *separated*
1/4 cup miniature marshmallows

Grease two 2-cup souffle dishes or custard cups; sprinkle each with 1/2 teaspoon of sugar. Set aside. Place sweet potato in a saucepan; cover with water. Cover and cook until tender, about 10-15 minutes; drain well.

Add lemon juice, salt and nutmeg. Mash potato mixture; set aside to cool. In another saucepan, melt butter; stir in flour and remaining sugar until smooth. Gradually add milk; cook and stir until thickened and bubbly. Remove from the heat.

Beat egg yolks in a small bowl; stir in mashed potato. Combine potato and milk mixture; set aside. In a mixing bowl, beat egg whites until stiff peaks form; gently fold into potato mixture.

Spoon into prepared dishes. Top with marshmallows. Bake, uncovered, at 350° for 35-38 minutes or until a knife inserted in the center comes out clean. Serve immediately. **Yield:** 2 servings.

Lemon Basil Carrots

Lemon Basil Carrots

Donna Smith • Fairport, New York

This recipe is a winner! The subtle hint of lemon really enhances the flavor of the carrots. Seasoned with basil, the sweet, tender carrot coins add color to any main course.

1-1/2 cups sliced carrots
1   tablespoon butter
1   tablespoon lemon juice
1/2 teaspoon garlic salt, optional
1/2 teaspoon dried basil
Dash pepper

In a saucepan, cook carrots in a small amount of water until tender. Drain and set aside. In the same pan, melt butter; stir in lemon juice, garlic salt if desired, basil and pepper. Return carrots to the pan and heat through. **Yield:** 2 servings.

Baked Beans For Two

Eldora Yoder • Versailles, Missouri

Want to enjoy some baked beans without having to deal with a big pot of leftovers? Try this tangy idea. Perfect with grilled foods, it's one side dish recipe that you'll reach for over and over again. Best of all, the recipe simply dresses up a can of pork and beans, keeping your time in the kitchen to an absolute minimum!

Baked Beans for Two

1	can (16 ounces) pork and beans
3	tablespoons ketchup
2	tablespoons chopped onion
2	to 3 teaspoons brown sugar
2	to 3 teaspoons honey
1	teaspoon prepared mustard
1/2	teaspoon Worcestershire sauce
1/8	teaspoon prepared horseradish

Combine all ingredients in an ungreased 1-qt. baking dish. Bake, uncovered, at 350° for 30-40 minutes. **Yield:** 2 servings.

Parmesan Asparagus

Sarah Porter • Pagosa Springs, Colorado

This delicious side dish will turn anyone into an asparagus lover. My husband used to turn up his nose at asparagus. Now he asks me to make this regularly. It's perfect with chicken or turkey.

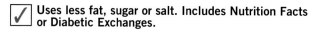 Uses less fat, sugar or salt. Includes Nutrition Facts or Diabetic Exchanges.

10	medium fresh asparagus spears, trimmed
4	teaspoons olive oil
1	tablespoon grated Parmesan cheese
1/8	teaspoon garlic salt

Brush asparagus spears with oil; place on a baking sheet coated with nonstick cooking spray. Bake, uncovered, at 400° for 6 minutes; turn asparagus. Bake 6 minutes longer or until asparagus is tender.

Combine Parmesan cheese and garlic salt; sprinkle over asparagus. **Yield:** 2 servings.

Nutrition Facts: 5 spears equals 116 calories, 10 g fat (2 g saturated fat), 2 mg cholesterol, 171 mg sodium, 5 g carbohydrate, 2 g fiber, 4 g protein. **Diabetic Exchanges:** 2 fat, 1 vegetable.

Cheesy Carrot Casserole

Diane Hixon • Niceville, Florida

Since all of our children are grown, I like to make simple foods for my husband and me. I usually have cheese, carrots and rice on hand, so this is a side dish I can whip up any time. The cashews add a fun crunch and a great flavor.

- 1 cup cooked rice
- 1/2 cup shredded carrots
- 1/2 cup shredded process American cheese
- 1 egg
- 2 tablespoons finely chopped salted cashews
- 1 teaspoon dried parsley flakes

In a bowl, combine rice, carrots, cheese and egg; mix well. Spoon into a greased 2-cup baking dish. Combine the cashews and parsley; sprinkle on top. Bake, uncovered, at 350° for 20-25 minutes or until lightly browned. **Yield:** 2 servings.

Editor's Note: Two 8-oz. baking dishes may be used for this recipe; bake for 15-20 minutes.

Cheesy Carrot Casserole

Fettuccine Primavera

Cassandra Corridon • Frederick, Maryland

This popular dish is chock-full of crisp-tender vegetables that are seasoned with garlic, cheese and chicken broth. You can serve it either as a delicious dinner accompaniment or a simple main course.

- 4 ounces uncooked fettuccine
- 1/2 cup cauliflowerets
- 1/2 cup fresh snow peas
- 1/2 cup broccoli florets
- 1/4 cup julienned carrot
- 1 tablespoon vegetable oil
- 1/2 cup julienned zucchini
- 1/4 cup julienned sweet red pepper
- 2 to 3 garlic cloves, minced
- 1/3 cup chicken broth
- 1/4 cup grated Romano cheese

Cook fettuccine according to package directions. Meanwhile, in a skillet or wok, stir-fry the cauliflower, peas, broccoli and carrot in oil for 2 minutes. Add the zucchini, red pepper and garlic; stir-fry until vegetables are crisp-tender. Stir in broth. Reduce heat; cover and simmer for 2 minutes. Drain the fettuccine; toss with vegetables. Sprinkle with cheese. **Yield:** 2 servings.

Veggie-Stuffed Potatoes

Jennifer Andrzejewski • Grizzly Flats, California

Marinated artichoke hearts are a unique but tasty addition to these stuffed potatoes. Bacon, sour cream and broccoli help round out the flavor.

2 medium baking potatoes
1/2 cup sour cream
1 cup (4 ounces) shredded cheddar cheese
1/2 cup frozen chopped broccoli, thawed
1/2 cup chopped marinated artichoke hearts
2 tablespoons crumbled cooked bacon
1/2 teaspoon garlic salt
1/4 teaspoon lemon-pepper seasoning

Place potatoes on a microwave-safe plate; pierce several times with a fork. Microwave on high for 6-8 minutes or until tender. When cool enough to handle, cut a thin slice off the top of each potato and discard. Scoop out pulp, leaving a thin shell.

In a bowl, mash the pulp with sour cream. Stir in the cheese, broccoli, artichoke hearts, bacon, garlic salt and lemon-pepper seasoning. Spoon into potato shells. Microwave, uncovered, on high for 1-2 minutes or until heated through. **Yield:** 2 servings.

Editor's Note: This recipe was tested in a 1,100-watt microwave.

Potato Nests With Peas

Margery Bryan • Royal City, Washington

I serve potatoes with just about every meal. Besides using this recipe as a side dish, I discovered I could serve it as a main course for a light supper. It satisfies the appetite well, especially for us older folks.

1 cup hot mashed potatoes (with added milk and butter)
1 egg yolk, beaten
1/4 cup shredded cheddar cheese
Dash dill weed
2 teaspoons butter
1 can (8-1/2 ounces) peas, drained

In a bowl, combine potatoes and egg yolk; mix well. Stir in the cheese.

Spoon two mounds onto a greased baking sheet. With the back of a spoon, shape each mound into a 4-in. nest. Sprinkle with dill; dot with butter. Bake at 350° for 30-35 minutes or until potatoes are golden brown. Fill nest with peas. Bake 10 minutes longer or until heated through. **Yield:** 2 servings.

Potato Nests with Peas

Stewed Tomatoes with Dumplings

Stewed Tomatoes with Dumplings

Viola Stutz • Greenwood, Delaware

When I was young and did not feel well, my mother would always make this dish because it was one of my favorites. Just smelling it cook made me feel better, along with her tender loving care.

1   **can (14-1/2 ounces) diced tomatoes, undrained**
1   **tablespoon sugar**
1/4   **teaspoon salt**
1/4   **teaspoon pepper**
2   **tablespoons butter**
1/2   **cup biscuit/baking mix**
3   **tablespoons milk**

In a saucepan, combine the tomatoes, sugar, salt, pepper and butter. Bring to a boil over medium heat, stirring occasionally. In a bowl, combine the biscuit mix and milk. Drop batter in four mounds onto the tomatoes. Reduce heat; cover and simmer for 10 minutes or until a toothpick inserted in a dumpling comes out clean. (Only lift cover for toothpick test.) **Yield:** 2 servings.

Pea Pods with Onion

Heather Sauter • Silver Spring, Maryland

This simple side is a welcomed alternative to green beans, and the pea pods look so pretty tossed with chopped onion. It tastes like a million bucks!

1/2   **pound fresh pea pods**
2   **tablespoons water**
1/4   **cup chopped onion**
3   **tablespoons butter,** *divided*
Salt and pepper to taste

Place the pea pods and water in a microwave-safe bowl; cover and cook on high for 3-5 minutes or until crisp-tender. Meanwhile, in a small skillet, cook onion in 2 tablespoons butter over medium heat until crisp-tender.

Drain peas; add to onion mixture. Add salt, pepper and remaining butter; toss to coat. Cook and stir until heated through. **Yield:** 2 servings.

Editor's Note: This recipe was tested in a 1,100-watt microwave.

Garlic Brussels Sprouts

Chris Tucker • Portland, Oregon

Parmesan cheese tops these buttery sprouts for one. They come together quickly on the stove so I can fit them into nearly any meal I'm preparing.

5   **brussels sprouts, halved**
1   **garlic clove, minced**
1   **teaspoon butter, melted**
1   **tablespoon shredded Parmesan cheese, optional**

Place brussels sprouts and garlic in a small saucepan; add 1 in. of water. Bring to a boil; reduce heat. Cover and simmer for 6-8 minutes or until sprouts are crisp-tender; drain. Drizzle with butter. Sprinkle with Parmesan cheese if desired. **Yield:** 1 serving.

Cracker Dressing

Jan Woodruff • Chandler, Arizona

Nicely seasoned, Cracker Dressing is a great alternative to other side dish recipes that call for dry bread crumbs or croutons. Try it tonight and see for yourself!

1/2	cup chopped celery
1/2	cup chopped onion
2	tablespoons butter
1	egg
2/3	cup milk
1	tablespoon minced fresh parsley
1/2	teaspoon rubbed sage
1/4	teaspoon dried thyme
1/4	teaspoon salt

Dash pepper

2 cups coarsely crushed saltines (about 27 crackers)

In a skillet over medium heat, saute celery and onion in butter until tender.

In a bowl, combine the egg, milk, parsley, sage, thyme, salt and pepper. Add the crackers and celery mixture; toss lightly.

Place in a greased 1-qt. baking dish. Bake, uncovered, at 350° for 25-30 minutes or until browned. **Yield:** 2 servings.

Pasta with Tomatoes

Pasta with Tomatoes

Earlene Ertelt • Woodburn, Oregon

I found the recipe for this side dish in the newspaper a few years ago and have used it frequently ever since. My husband and I are busy on our farm, so quick and easy foods like this are very important to me.

2	large tomatoes, chopped
2	tablespoons snipped fresh basil *or* 2 teaspoons dried basil
1	garlic clove, minced
1/2	teaspoon salt
1/4	teaspoon pepper
4	ounces bow tie pasta *or* spaghetti

Fresh basil and grated Parmesan cheese, optional

Combine the tomatoes, basil, garlic, salt and pepper. Set aside at room temperature.

Prepare pasta according to directions. Drain. Serve tomato mixture over hot pasta. If desired, garnish with basil and sprinkle with Parmesan cheese. **Yield:** 2 servings.

Brown Rice Veggie Stir-Fry

Maxine Driver • Littleton, Colorado

My husband and I first tasted this colorful combination while visiting my sister. We enjoyed it so much that I often double the recipe and make it for family and friends.

- 2 tablespoons water
- 2 tablespoons reduced-sodium soy sauce
- 1 tablespoon olive oil
- 1 cup sliced zucchini
- 1 cup shredded cabbage
- 1/2 cup sliced fresh mushrooms
- 1/2 cup chopped onion
- 1 cup cooked brown rice
- 1/4 cup diced fresh tomato
- 1/4 cup grated carrot
- 2 tablespoons slivered almonds

Brown Rice Veggie Stir-Fry

In a large skillet or wok, combine the water, soy sauce and oil. Add the zucchini, cabbage, mushrooms and onion; stir-fry for 4-5 minutes or until crisp-tender. Add the rice, tomato and carrot; stir-fry for 2-3 minutes or until heated through. Sprinkle with almonds. **Yield:** 4 servings.

Orange Sweet Potato Bake

Dorothy Pritchett • Wills Point, Texas

Orange slices liven up a sweet potato in this comforting item. Topped with a buttery, brown-sugar glaze and chopped pecans, it'll quickly become a favorite in your home.

☑ **Uses less fat, sugar or salt. Includes Nutrition Facts or Diabetic Exchanges.**

- 1 medium sweet potato, peeled and cut into 3/4-inch slices
- 1/2 medium navel orange, peeled and thinly sliced
- 2 tablespoons brown sugar
- 1-1/2 teaspoons reduced-fat butter
- 1 teaspoon water

Dash nutmeg

Dash salt

- 1/8 teaspoon grated orange peel
- 1 to 2 teaspoons chopped pecans, optional

Place sweet potato in a saucepan and cover with water. Bring to a boil. Reduce heat; cover and simmer for 10 minutes or until almost tender. Drain. Arrange potato and orange slices in a 2-cup baking dish.

In a microwave-safe bowl, combine the brown sugar, butter, water, nutmeg and salt. Cover and microwave on high for 30 seconds or until mixture is melted and smooth, stirring once. Stir in orange peel. Pour over potato and orange.

Bake, uncovered, at 350° for 15-20 minutes or until potato is tender, spooning glaze over potato and orange occasionally. Sprinkle with pecans if desired. **Yield:** 2 servings.

Nutrition Facts: 1 serving equals 167 calories, 2 g fat (1 g saturated fat), 5 mg cholesterol, 105 mg sodium, 39 g carbohydrate, 4 g fiber, 2 g protein.

THE BREAD BASKET

The comforting aroma of freshly baked breads, biscuits and muffins doesn't have to be lost on those cooking for a pair. The following baked goods yield just the right amount for cozy, two-person homes.

Banana Apple Muffins
p. 227

Traditional Hot Cross
Buns p. 230

Cranberry Pumpkin
Bread p. 221

Apricot Scones
p. 220

Cheesy Onion Biscuits
p. 218

Cheesy Onion Biscuits

Taste of Home Test Kitchen • Greendale, Wisconsin

These four, scone-shaped biscuits have a savory onion-and-cheddar flavor and a golden look. Serve them with a pat of butter alongside your favorite soup or bubbling casserole.

☑ **Uses less fat, sugar or salt. Includes Nutrition Facts or Diabetic Exchanges.**

1/4	cup chopped onion
3/4	cup all-purpose flour
1/8	teaspoon baking powder
1/8	teaspoon baking soda
1/8	teaspoon salt
1	tablespoon shortening
1/4	cup shredded cheddar cheese
1/3	cup buttermilk

Place onion in a small microwave-safe bowl; cover and microwave on high for 1-2 minutes or until tender. In a small bowl, combine the flour, baking powder, baking soda and salt. Cut in shortening until mixture resembles coarse crumbs. Stir in cheese and onion. Stir in buttermilk just until moistened.

Turn onto a lightly floured surface; knead 8-10 times. Pat or roll out into a 4-in. circle; cut into four wedges. Place 2 in. apart on a baking sheet coated with nonstick cooking spray. Bake at 450° for 8-12 minutes or until golden brown. Serve warm. **Yield:** 4 biscuits.

Nutrition Facts: 1 biscuit equals 150 calories, 5 g fat (2 g saturated fat), 8 mg cholesterol, 190 mg sodium, 20 g carbohydrate, 1 g fiber, 5 g protein.
Diabetic Exchanges: 1 starch, 1 fat.

Editor's Note: This recipe was tested in a 1,100-watt microwave.

Popovers

Popovers

Emma Magielda • Amsterdam, New York

A local restaurant was noted for the giant popovers they served with their meals. I decided to do the same for special birthdays and other occasions. These popovers soon became family favorites, and because the recipe only makes two, they've truly become one of my specialties.

1/2	cup milk, room temperature
1	egg, room temperature
1/2	cup all-purpose flour
1/4	teaspoon salt

In a bowl, beat all ingredients just until smooth. Pour into four greased muffin cups. Fill the remaining muffin cups two-thirds full with water.

Bake at 450° for 15 minutes. Reduce heat to 350° (do not open door). Bake 20 minutes longer or until deep golden brown (do not underbake). **Yield:** 2 servings.

Sugar-Dusted Blueberry Muffins

Sugar-Dusted Blueberry Muffins

Janis Plagerman • Lynden, Washington

*I top these fruity, golden-brown muffins with cinnamon and sugar for a tasty treat any time of day.
If you don't like blueberries, feel free to substitute them with the berry of your choice.*

1/4   **cup old-fashioned oats**
1/4   **cup orange juice**
1   **egg**
1/4   **cup canola oil**
3/4   **cup all-purpose flour**
1/4   **cup plus 1 tablespoon sugar,** *divided*
1/2   **teaspoon baking powder**
1/4   **teaspoon salt**
1/8   **teaspoon baking soda**
1/2   **cup fresh** *or* **frozen unsweetened blueberries**
1/8   **teaspoon ground cinnamon**

In a small bowl, combine the oats and orange juice; let stand for 5 minutes. Stir in egg and oil until blended. Combine the flour, 1/4 cup sugar, baking powder, salt and baking soda; stir into oat mixture just until moistened. Fold in blueberries.

Coat muffin cups with nonstick cooking spray or use paper liners; fill two-thirds full with batter. Combine cinnamon and remaining sugar; sprinkle over batter. Bake at 400° for 18-22 minutes or until a toothpick comes out clean. Cool for 5 minutes before removing from pan to a wire rack. **Yield:** 6 muffins.

Editor's Note: If using frozen blueberries, do not thaw before adding to batter.

Moist Bran Muffins

Mildred Ross • Badin, North Carolina

Here's a wonderfully wholesome recipe that bakes up just four hearty muffins. You'll be surprised how very easily the ingredients come together.

1/2	cup All-Bran
1/2	cup milk
2	tablespoons vegetable oil
1/2	cup all-purpose flour
2	tablespoons sugar
1	teaspoon baking powder
1/4	teaspoon salt

In a bowl, combine the bran and milk; let stand for 5 minutes. Stir in the oil. Combine the remaining ingredients; stir into bran mixture just until moistened.

Fill greased or paper-lined muffin cups half full. Bake at 400° for 18-22 minutes or until a toothpick comes out clean. Cool for 5 minutes before removing from pan to a wire rack. **Yield:** 4 muffins.

Moist Bran Muffins

Apricot Scones

Linda Swanson • Riverside, Washington

Besides farming and raising cattle, our family has a home bakery that serves area restaurants and health food stores. With a sweet oat filling, these golden scones are popular.

1-1/2	cups all-purpose flour
1/2	cup quick-cooking oats
1/4	cup sugar
2-1/2	teaspoons baking powder
1/4	teaspoon salt
1/3	cup cold butter, cubed
2	eggs
1/4	cup sour cream
1	tablespoon milk
3/4	cup finely chopped dried apricots

FILLING:

3	tablespoons brown sugar
1	tablespoon quick-cooking oats
1	tablespoon butter, softened

Additional sugar

In a bowl, combine the first five ingredients; cut in butter until mixture resembles fine crumbs. In a small bowl, beat eggs; set aside 1 tablespoon for glaze. In another bowl, combine the sour cream, milk and remaining beaten eggs; add apricots. Stir into the crumb mixture until the dough clings together.

Turn onto a lightly floured surface; knead 12-15 times. Divide dough in half. Pat one portion into a 7-in. circle on a greased baking sheet. Combine the brown sugar, oats and butter; sprinkle over dough. Roll out remaining dough into a 7-in. circle; place over filling.

Brush with reserved egg; sprinkle with additional sugar. Cut into wedges but do not separate. Bake at 400° for 15-20 minutes or until scones are golden brown. Cool slightly; cut again if necessary. Serve warm. **Yield:** 6 servings.

Cranberry Pumpkin Bread

Taste of Home Test Kitchen • Greendale, Wisconsin

These miniature pumpkin loaves offer a taste of cranberry and spice and everything nice. The tiny breads freeze well, too, making them ideal for gift giving or keeping on hand for last-minute needs.

1/2   cup plus 2 tablespoons all-purpose flour
1/2   cup sugar
1/2   teaspoon baking soda
1/4   teaspoon salt
1/4   teaspoon ground cinnamon
1/4   teaspoon ground nutmeg
1/2   cup canned pumpkin
1/4   cup canola oil
  1   egg, lightly beaten
  3   tablespoons buttermilk
1/4   teaspoon butter flavoring
1/4   teaspoon vanilla extract
1/4   cup dried cranberries

In a large bowl, combine the flour, sugar, baking soda, salt, cinnamon and nutmeg. Combine the pumpkin, oil, egg, buttermilk, butter flavoring and vanilla; stir into dry ingredients just until moistened. Fold in cranberries.

Transfer to three 4-1/2-in. x 2-1/2-in. x 1-1/2-in. loaf pans coated with nonstick cooking spray. Bake at 350° for 25-30 minutes or until a toothpick inserted near the center comes out clean. Cool for 10 minutes before removing from pans to wire racks to cool completely. **Yield:** 3 loaves.

Sour Cream Biscuits

Nell Jones • Smyrna, Georgia

It's hard to imagine that only four ingredients lead to these delightful biscuits. I hope you enjoy them as much as we do.

  1   cup self-rising flour
1/4   teaspoon baking soda
3/4   cup sour cream
  2   teaspoons vegetable oil

In a bowl, combine flour and baking soda. Add sour cream and oil; stir just until moistened. Turn the dough onto a floured surface; knead 4-6 times. Roll out to 3/4-in. thickness; cut with a 2-1/2-in. biscuit cutter.

Place on a greased baking sheet. Lightly spray tops with nonstick cooking spray. Bake at 425° for 10-12 minutes or until golden brown. **Yield:** 4 biscuits.

Editor's Note: As a substitute for 1 cup of self-rising flour, place 1-1/2 teaspoons baking powder and 1/2 teaspoon salt in a measuring cup. Add all-purpose flour to measure 1 cup.

Sour Cream Biscuits

Garlic Crescent Rolls

Garlic Crescent Rolls

Pat Habiger • Spearville, Kansas

Delicious baked goods can really embellish a dinner, and it only takes a minute to prepare the treats with convenient refrigerator rolls. I experimented and created several flavor combinations to complement menus. This version is a favorite.

1 package (4 ounces) refrigerated crescent rolls
2 teaspoons grated Parmesan cheese
1/4 to 1/2 teaspoon garlic powder
1 egg, beaten
1/2 teaspoon sesame *and/or* poppy seeds

Separate crescent dough into four triangles. Sprinkle with Parmesan cheese and garlic powder. Beginning at the wide end, roll up dough. Place with point down on a greased baking sheet.

Brush with egg; sprinkle with sesame and/or poppy seeds. Bake at 375° for 11-13 minutes or until golden brown. Serve warm. **Yield:** 2 servings.

Basil Garlic Bread

Stephanie Moon • Green Bay, Wisconsin

Grilling a small loaf of French bread makes the crust extra crispy, but it's the delicious herbed butter that makes the slices so irresistible.

1/4 cup butter
2 tablespoons minced fresh parsley
1-1/2 teaspoons minced fresh basil *or* 1/2 teaspoon dried basil
1 garlic clove, minced
1/4 cup grated Parmesan cheese
1 loaf (8 ounces) French bread

In a microwave-safe bowl, combine butter, parsley, basil and garlic. Cover and microwave until butter is melted. Stir in Parmesan cheese.

Cut the bread in half lengthwise; place cut side down on an uncovered grill over medium heat for 2 minutes or until lightly toasted. Brush cut side with the butter mixture. Grill 1-2 minutes longer. **Yield:** 4 servings.

Cinnamon-Raisin Buttermilk Biscuits

Myrna Itterman • Aberdeen, South Dakota

I modeled this recipe after a favorite restaurant treat. The sweet biscuits are excellent at brunch with a steaming cup of tea or coffee.

1 cup all-purpose flour
1 tablespoon sugar
2 teaspoons baking powder
1/2 teaspoon ground cinnamon
1/3 cup butter-flavored shortening
1/3 cup buttermilk
1/4 cup golden raisins
GLAZE:
1/2 cup confectioners' sugar
1 tablespoon milk
1/4 teaspoon vanilla extract

In a bowl, combine the flour, sugar, baking powder and cinnamon; cut in shortening until crumbly. Stir in buttermilk just until moistened. Turn onto a lightly floured surface. Sprinkle raisins over dough; knead 2 or 3 times. Pat to 3/4-in. thickness. Cut with a floured 2-1/2-in. biscuit cutter.

Place on an ungreased baking sheet. Bake at 400° for 12-15 minutes or until golden brown. Combine glaze ingredients; drizzle over biscuits. Serve warm. **Yield:** 4 biscuits.

Cinnamon-Sugar Fan Biscuits

Doris Heath • Franklin, North Carolina

The recipe for these layered, homemade biscuits came from a friend in Florida years ago. They're so easy when you need a breakfast treat but don't want to bake a large batch of anything.

- 2 cups all-purpose flour
- 3 tablespoons sugar
- 4 teaspoons baking powder
- 1/2 teaspoon salt
- 1/2 teaspoon cream of tartar
- 1/2 cup shortening
- 2/3 cup milk

FILLING:
- 3 tablespoons butter, softened
- 3 tablespoons sugar
- 1 teaspoon ground cinnamon

In a bowl, combine the flour, sugar, baking powder, salt and cream of tartar. Cut in shortening until mixture resembles coarse crumbs. Stir in milk just until moistened.

Turn onto a lightly floured surface; knead 8-10 times. Roll or pat into a 12-in. x 10-in. rectangle. Spread with butter. Combine sugar and cinnamon; sprinkle over butter.

Cut into five 2-in. strips; stack strips on top of each other. Cut into six 2-in. pieces; place cut side down in six greased muffin cups. Bake at 425° for 11-14 minutes or until golden brown. Remove from pan to wire racks. Serve warm. **Yield:** 6 biscuits.

Whipped Cream Biscuits

Whipped Cream Biscuits

Linda Murrow • Aurora, Colorado

Since there is no shortening to cut in, these light, airy biscuits are quick to make. I try to time the baking so that they're out of the oven when we sit down to eat.

- 1 cup all-purpose flour
- 1-1/2 teaspoons baking powder
- 1/4 teaspoon salt
- 1/2 cup heavy whipping cream, whipped

In a bowl, combine the flour, baking powder and salt. Stir in cream. Turn dough onto a floured surface; knead 10 times. Roll to 3/4-in. thickness; cut with a 2-1/4-in. round biscuit cutter.

Place on an ungreased baking sheet. Bake at 425° for 10 minutes or until lightly browned. Serve warm. **Yield:** 5 biscuits.

Poppy Seed Doughnuts

Taste of Home Test Kitchen • Greendale, Wisconsin

This from-scratch doughnut recipe provides a few extra servings but the results freeze well; though, you may find it difficult not to eat them all at once!

✓ Uses less fat, sugar or salt. Includes Nutrition Facts or Diabetic Exchanges.

1	cup all-purpose flour
1/2	cup sugar
1	tablespoon poppy seeds
3/4	teaspoon baking powder
3/4	teaspoon baking soda
1/4	teaspoon salt
1	egg
1/3	cup buttermilk
1/3	cup reduced-fat plain yogurt
1	tablespoon canola oil
2	teaspoons lemon juice
1	teaspoon grated lemon peel
1/2	teaspoon vanilla extract
2	teaspoons confectioners' sugar, *divided*

Poppy Seed Doughnuts

In a small bowl, combine the first six ingredients. Combine the egg, buttermilk, yogurt, oil, lemon juice, peel and vanilla; stir into dry ingredients just until moistened.

Coat six 4-in. tube pans with nonstick cooking spray and dust with 1 teaspoon confectioners' sugar. Divide batter among pans.

Bake at 400° for 10-12 minutes or until a toothpick inserted near the center comes out clean. Cool for 5 minutes before removing from pans to wire racks. Dust with remaining confectioners' sugar. **Yield:** 6 servings.

Nutrition Facts: 1 doughnut equals 199 calories, 4 g fat (1 g saturated fat), 37 mg cholesterol, 341 mg sodium, 36 g carbohydrate, 1 g fiber, 5 g protein.
Diabetic Exchanges: 2 starch, 1/2 fruit.

STORAGE SECRETS

If you have a small household but like to bake bread, remember that all-purpose, self-rising and bread flour can be stored in an airtight container in a cool, dry place for an entire year. Whole wheat and rye flours keep best in a moisture-proof container in the refrigerator for up to 6 months. It's not a good idea to store most types of flour in the freezer.

Savory Crescent Bundles

Savory Crescent Bundles

Margaret Pache • Mesa, Arizona

Each time I prepare these full-flavored bundles, I'm reminded fondly of my mother, who made the bites often. It was one of her favorites—and now it's ours, too.

1	package (3 ounces) cream cheese, softened
3	tablespoons butter, melted, *divided*
2	cups cooked cubed chicken *or* turkey
2	tablespoons milk
1	tablespoon chopped chives
1	tablespoon chopped pimientos
1/4	teaspoon salt
1/8	teaspoon pepper
1	tube (8 ounces) refrigerated crescent rolls
1/2	cup seasoned bread crumbs

Additional chives

In a mixing bowl, beat cream cheese and 2 tablespoons butter until smooth. Stir in chicken, milk, chives, pimientos, salt and pepper.

Separate crescent dough into four rectangles; firmly press perforations to seal. Spoon 1/2 cup chicken mixture into center of each rectangle. Bring four corners of dough together and twist; pinch edges to seal.

Brush tops of bundles with remaining butter. Sprinkle with bread crumbs. Place on an ungreased baking sheet. Bake at 350° for 20-25 minutes or until golden brown. Tie a chive around each. **Yield:** 4 servings.

Banana Apple Muffins

Alice Muradliyan • Covina, California

Here's a light, tasty muffin that stays moist. It's flavorful whether served plain, with butter and jam or dipped in cinnamon-sugar fresh out of the oven.

3/4 cup old-fashioned oats
1/2 cup all-purpose flour
3 tablespoons sugar
1 teaspoon baking powder
1/4 teaspoon salt
1/4 teaspoon ground allspice
1/4 teaspoon ground cinnamon
1 egg
1/3 cup milk
1 tablespoon vegetable oil
1/2 cup grated peeled tart apple
1/4 cup mashed ripe banana

In a bowl, combine the first seven ingredients. In another bowl, beat the egg, milk and oil. Stir into dry ingredients just until moistened. Fold in apple and banana.

Fill greased muffin cups about three-fourths full. Bake at 375° for 25-30 minutes or until a toothpick comes out clean. Cool for 5 minutes before removing from pan to a wire rack. **Yield:** 6 muffins.

Rye Drop Biscuits

Nancy Zimmerman • Cape May Court House, New Jersey

These rich but rugged biscuits are so easy to make since you don't have to knead them or use a biscuit cutter. They go with any meal.

1/3 cup all-purpose flour
1/4 cup rye flour
1 tablespoon brown sugar
1 teaspoon baking powder
1/4 teaspoon dried parsley flakes
1/8 teaspoon salt
1/4 cup cold butter
1 egg
1 tablespoon milk

In a bowl, combine the flours, sugar, baking powder, parsley and salt. Cut in butter until mixture resembles coarse crumbs. Stir in the egg and milk just until combined.

Drop by 1/4 cupfuls 2 in. apart onto a greased baking sheet. Bake at 400° for 7-10 minutes or until golden brown. Remove from pan to a wire rack. Serve warm. **Yield:** 4 biscuits.

Rye Drop Biscuits

Zucchini Muffins

Peg Gausz • Watchung, New Jersey

These yummy currant and walnut muffins are an excellent way to use up your garden overload of zucchini.

Zucchini Muffins

3/4   cup all-purpose flour
1/2   cup sugar
1/4   teaspoon baking powder
1/4   teaspoon baking soda
1/4   teaspoon salt
1/4   teaspoon ground cinnamon
  1   egg
1/4   cup canola oil
  1   cup finely shredded unpeeled zucchini
1/2   cup chopped walnuts
1/4   cup dried currants *or* chopped raisins

In a bowl, combine the first six ingredients. Combine the egg and oil; stir into dry ingredients just until moistened. Fold in the zucchini, walnuts and currants.

Coat muffin cups with nonstick cooking spray or use paper liners; fill three-fourths full with batter. Bake at 350° for 22-25 minutes or until a toothpick comes out clean. Cool for 5 minutes before removing from pan to a wire rack. **Yield:** 6 muffins.

Apple Streusel Muffins

Elizabeth Calabrese • Yucaipa, California

I was looking for something warm to make for my daughter before school on a rainy morning. I jazzed up a boxed muffin mix with a chopped apple, nuts, brown sugar and a fast-to-fix vanilla glaze. The tasty results really hit the spot.

    1   package (6-1/2 ounces) apple cinnamon muffin mix
    1   large tart apple, peeled and diced
  1/3   cup chopped walnuts
    3   tablespoons brown sugar
4-1/2   teaspoons all-purpose flour
    1   tablespoon butter, melted
GLAZE:
  3/4   cup confectioners' sugar
  1/2   teaspoon vanilla extract
    1   to 2 tablespoons milk

Prepare muffin mix according to package directions; fold in apple. Fill greased muffin cups three-fourths full. In a small bowl, combine the walnuts, brown sugar, flour and butter; sprinkle over batter.

Bake at 400° for 15-20 minutes or until a toothpick comes out clean. Cool for 5 minutes before removing from pan to a wire rack. Combine the glaze ingredients; drizzle over warm muffins. **Yield:** 6 muffins.

Editor's Note: This recipe was tested with Betty Crocker apple cinnamon muffin mix.

Cinnamon-Orange Swirl Bread

Nancy Means • Moline, Illinois

*Offering ribbons of cinnamon and orange peel and a sweet topping,
this delightful mini loaf is as pretty as it is scrumptious.*

1/4	cup butter-flavored shortening
1/2	cup plus 2 tablespoons sugar, *divided*
1	egg
1/3	cup sour cream
1/2	teaspoon vanilla extract
1	cup all-purpose flour
3/4	teaspoon baking powder
1/2	teaspoon baking soda
1/4	teaspoon salt
1	teaspoon ground cinnamon
1	teaspoon grated orange peel

In a small mixing bowl, cream shortening and 1/2 cup sugar. Add the egg, sour cream and vanilla; mix well. Combine the flour, baking powder, baking soda and salt; stir into creamed mixture just until moistened.

Pour half of the batter into a 5-3/4-in. x 3-in. x 2-in. loaf pan coated with nonstick cooking spray. Combine the cinnamon, orange peel and remaining sugar; set aside 1-1/2 teaspoons for topping. Sprinkle remaining cinnamon mixture over batter. Carefully top with remaining batter; cut through batter with a knife to swirl. Sprinkle with reserved cinnamon mixture.

Bake at 350° for 30-35 minutes or until a toothpick inserted near the center comes out clean. Cool for 10 minutes before removing from pan to a wire rack. **Yield:** 1 mini loaf (6 slices).

Editor's Note: Batter may be divided between two 5-1/4-in. x 2-1/2-in. x 1-3/4-in. loaf pans; bake for 20-25 minutes.

Cheesy Texas Toast

LaDonna Reed • Ponca City, Oklahoma

My husband and I love garlic bread, but it's such a waste for just the two of us. That's why I came up with this cheesy version. You can prepare it in a few minutes, and it's tasty, too!

2	tablespoons butter, softened
4	slices French bread (1 inch thick)
1/4	to 1/2 teaspoon garlic powder
1	cup (4 ounces) shredded part-skim mozzarella cheese

Chopped green onions *or* parsley, optional

Spread butter over bread. Sprinkle with garlic powder and cheese. Place on an ungreased baking sheet. Bake at 400° for 5-7 minutes or until cheese is melted. Sprinkle with onions or parsley if desired. Serve warm. **Yield:** 2 servings.

Cheesy Texas Toast

Orange Pan Rolls

Jackie Riley • Holland, Michigan

A hint of citrus flavor in the dough makes these rolls refreshingly different. Similar in texture to a biscuit, they bake to a beautiful golden brown. I make them any time I want something warm from the oven to accompany a meal.

1	tablespoon sugar
1/8	teaspoon ground nutmeg
1/2	cup all-purpose flour
3/4	teaspoon baking powder
1/8	teaspoon cream of tartar
1/8	teaspoon salt
1/2	teaspoon grated orange peel
2	tablespoons shortening
3	tablespoons milk
1	tablespoon butter, melted

In a small bowl, combine sugar and nutmeg; set aside. In a medium bowl, combine flour, baking powder, cream of tartar and salt. Add orange peel; cut in shortening until the mixture resembles coarse crumbs. Stir in milk just until moistened.

Divide dough into fourths. With floured hands, roll each piece of dough into a ball; dip in butter, then in sugar mixture. Evenly space in a greased 9-in. round baking pan. Bake at 450° for 10-12 minutes or until golden brown. **Yield:** 4 rolls.

Traditional Hot Cross Buns

Barbara Jean Lull • Fullerton, California

We looked forward to eating my mother's hot cross buns on Easter morning for many years. This scaled-down version makes just six buns that have all of the flavor of Mom's specialty.

✓ **Uses less fat, sugar or salt. Includes Nutrition Facts or Diabetic Exchanges.**

2	teaspoons active dry yeast
1/2	cup warm 2% milk (110° to 115°)
1	tablespoon butter, softened
1	egg
4	teaspoons sugar
1/4	teaspoon salt
1-1/2	to 1-3/4 cups all-purpose flour
2	tablespoons raisins
2	tablespoons dried currants
1/4	teaspoon ground cinnamon

Dash ground allspice

1	egg yolk
1	tablespoon water

ICING:

1/4	cup confectioners' sugar
1/8	teaspoon vanilla extract
3/4	to 1 teaspoon 2% milk

In a small mixing bowl, dissolve yeast in milk. Stir in butter, egg, sugar and salt. Combine 3/4 cup flour, raisins, currants, cinnamon and allspice; add to the yeast mixture and mix well. Stir in enough remaining flour to form a soft dough.

Turn onto a floured surface; knead until smooth and elastic, about 4-6 minutes. Place in a greased bowl, turning once to grease top. Cover and let rise in a warm place until doubled, about 1 hour.

Punch dough down; shape into six 2-in. balls. Place 2 in. apart on a baking sheet coated with nonstick cooking spray. Using a sharp knife, cut a cross on top of each bun. Cover and let rise until doubled, about 30 minutes.

Beat egg yolk and water; brush over buns. Bake at 375° for 13-15 minutes or until golden brown. Cool on wire racks. Combine icing ingredients; pipe over buns. **Yield:** 6 buns.

Nutrition Facts: One bun equals 215 calories, 4 g fat (2 g saturated fat), 78 mg cholesterol, 142 mg sodium, 38 g carbohydrate, 2 g fiber, 6 g protein.

Orange Pan Rolls

Honey-Nut Breakfast Twists

Holly Baird • Zurich, Montana

These homemade delights are always well received. A nutty filling and sweet glaze make them a regular in my kitchen.

1   **package (1/4 ounce) active dry yeast**
1/4   **cup warm water (110° to 115°)**
2   **tablespoons sugar**
1   **teaspoon salt**
2   **tablespoons butter, melted**
1   **cup (8 ounces) sour cream**
1   **egg**
2-1/2 **to 3 cups all-purpose flour**
GLAZE:
1/3   **cup packed brown sugar**
3   **tablespoons butter, melted**
3   **tablespoons honey, warmed**
3   **tablespoons heavy whipping cream**
FILLING:
1/3   **cup butter, softened**
1/4   **cup finely chopped nuts**
1/4   **cup honey**

In a mixing bowl, combine yeast and water; let stand 5 minutes. Stir in sugar, salt and butter. Add sour cream and egg; beat until smooth. Add 1-1/2 cups flour; blend at low speed until moistened. Beat 3 minutes at medium speed, scraping bowl twice. By hand, stir in enough remaining flour to make a soft dough.

Turn out onto a floured surface; knead until smooth and elastic, about 5 minutes. Place in a greased bowl, turning once to grease top. Cover and let rise in a warm place until doubled, about 1 hour. Combine glaze ingredients; spread evenly in a 13-in. x 9-in. x 2-in. baking dish; set aside.

Punch dough down. Roll into a 24-in. x 9-in. rectangle. Combine filling ingredients; spread over dough. Fold dough lengthwise over filling, forming 12-in. x 9-in. x 2-in. pieces. Twist each piece loosely and place over glaze in baking dish. Cover and let rise until doubled, about 1 hour.

Bake at 350° for 25-30 minutes or until golden brown. Invert pan onto a large platter; let set 1 minute before removing. Serve warm or refrigerate overnight. **Yield:** 6 twists.

Biscuit Bites

Biscuit Bites

Joy Beck • Cincinnati, Ohio

These savory mini biscuits are wonderful with soup, a main dish or even as a snack to munch on while watching television. They come together easily with three ingredients, including convenient refrigerated biscuits.

1   **tube (12 ounces) refrigerated buttermilk biscuits**
2   **tablespoons grated Parmesan cheese**
1   **teaspoon onion powder**

Cut each biscuit into thirds; place on a greased baking sheet. Combine Parmesan cheese and onion powder; sprinkle over biscuits. Bake at 400° for 7-8 minutes or until golden brown. **Yield:** 5 servings.

Buttermilk Scones

Ruth LeBlanc • Nashua, New Hampshire

I was glad to find this recipe. The small quantity is just what I was looking for in my quest for recipes for two. Happily, there are often a few left over for a snack later.

Buttermilk Scones

- 1   cup all-purpose flour
- 2   tablespoons plus 1/2 teaspoon sugar, *divided*
- 1   teaspoon baking soda
- 1/4   cup butter
- 1/3   cup buttermilk
- 3   tablespoons raisins *or* dried currants
- 1/4   teaspoon grated lemon *or* orange peel
- 1/8   teaspoon ground cinnamon

In a bowl, combine the flour, 2 tablespoons sugar, baking powder and baking soda. Cut in butter until mixture resembles coarse crumbs. Stir in the buttermilk, raisins and lemon peel until a soft dough forms.

Turn onto a lightly floured surface; knead gently 5-6 times or until no longer sticky. On a lightly greased baking sheet, pat dough into a 5-in. circle about 3/4 in. thick.

Score the top, making six wedges. Combine cinnamon and remaining sugar; sprinkle over the top. Bake at 375° for 23-25 minutes or until golden brown. Break into wedges. Serve warm. **Yield:** 6 scones.

Dried-Cherry Muffins

Sandra Wagner • Chicago, Illinois

For a casual breakfast, formal lunch or even an afternoon tea, consider these muffins. They star sweet-tart dried cherries that offer a little color.

☑ Uses less fat, sugar or salt. Includes Nutrition Facts or Diabetic Exchanges.

- 4-1/2   teaspoons shortening
- 1/3   cup sugar
- 1   egg
- 3/4   cup all-purpose flour
- 1/2   teaspoon baking soda
- 1/4   teaspoon salt
- 1/4   cup buttermilk
- 1/4   cup dried cherries *or* cranberries, halved

In a small mixing bowl, beat shortening and sugar. Beat in egg. Combine the flour, baking soda and salt; add to egg mixture alternately with buttermilk. Fold in cherries.

Coat muffin cups with nonstick cooking spray or line with paper liners; fill three-fourths full. Bake at 350° for 20-25 minutes or until a toothpick comes out clean. Cool for 5 minutes before removing to a wire rack. **Yield:** 6 muffins.

Nutrition Facts: One muffin equals 184 calories, 4 g fat (1 g saturated fat), 36 mg cholesterol, 226 mg sodium, 32 g carbohydrate, 1 g fiber, 4 g protein.
Diabetic Exchanges: 2 starch, 1/2 fat.

TABLE FOR TWO

The next time you need a complete menu for two, turn to this colorful chapter! You'll find 15 three-course meals, from casual to elegant, that feature all of the down-home flavors you crave the most.

Pork Chop Dinner
p. 242

Hearty Steak Supper
p. 240

Salad and Sandwich
Specialty p. 260

Comforting Potpie Meal
p. 236

Cornish Hen
Delight for Two
p. 246

Chicken Vegetable Potpie

Marva Vandivier • Battle Ground, Washington

I actually created this recipe when I was a little girl. Since then, I've found it's a good way to use up the second pastry when I make a one-crust pie. When I tell my husband, "It's chicken potpie tonight," he lights up and thinks I've worked in the kitchen all day!

2   medium carrots, sliced
1   medium potato, peeled and cubed
1   small onion, chopped
1   celery rib, chopped
1   cup water
1/2 cup frozen peas, thawed
1   cup cubed cooked chicken
1   can (10-3/4 ounces) condensed cream of chicken soup, undiluted

Pastry for single-crust pie (9 inches)

In a saucepan, cook the carrots, potato, onion and celery in water for 10 minutes or until tender; drain. Stir in the peas, chicken and soup.

Pour into a greased 1-1/2-qt. deep baking dish. Roll out pastry to fit top of dish; place over filling. Trim, seal and flute edges. Cut slits in pastry. Bake at 350° for 50 minutes or until crust is golden and filling is bubbly. **Yield:** 2 servings.

Crunchy Macaroni Salad

Ruth Griggs • South Hill, Virginia

This salad is ideal for one or two people, but I've often increased the recipe to take to potlucks. For variety, I'll sometimes add chopped pickles or shredded cheese. In summer, fresh tomatoes lend color.

1   cup cooked elbow macaroni
1   hard-cooked egg, chopped
2   tablespoons chopped celery
2   tablespoons chopped onion
3   tablespoons mayonnaise
1   teaspoon sugar
1   teaspoon cider vinegar
1/2 teaspoon prepared mustard

1/4 teaspoon salt
Pinch pepper

In a bowl, combine the macaroni, egg, celery and onion. In another bowl, combine the remaining ingredients. Pour over macaroni mixture and toss gently. Cover and chill for 2 hours before serving. **Yield:** 2 servings.

Whole Wheat Biscuits

Edna Hoffman • Hebron, Indiana

I love cooking and baking and am always creating something new by experimenting with recipes. I thought the use of whole wheat flour gave these biscuits a slightly different taste.

1/3 cup all-purpose flour
1/3 cup whole wheat flour
1   tablespoon sugar
3/4 teaspoon baking powder
1/4 teaspoon baking soda
1/4 teaspoon salt
2   tablespoons cold butter
1/4 cup buttermilk

In a bowl, combine the first six ingredients. Cut in butter until crumbly. Stir in buttermilk just until moistened.

Turn onto a floured surface; knead 6-8 times. Pat to 1-in. thickness; cut with a 2-1/2-in. biscuit cutter. Place on a greased baking sheet. Bake at 375° for 18-20 minutes or until lightly browned. **Yield:** 4 biscuits.

Pancakes with Orange Syrup

Kimberly Rayfield • Cleveland, Tennessee

When I ran out of milk for pancake batter, I substituted orange juice with terrific results. I think they were the best I'd ever made!

✓ **Uses less fat, sugar or salt. Includes Nutrition Facts or Diabetic Exchanges.**

- 1 cup self-rising flour
- 2 tablespoons sugar
- 1 egg
- 1/2 cup 2% milk
- 2 tablespoons orange juice
- 1 tablespoon canola oil
- 1/2 teaspoon vanilla extract

ORANGE SYRUP:
- 1 tablespoon sugar
- 1-1/2 teaspoons cornstarch
- 1/2 cup orange juice

In a bowl, combine the flour and sugar. Whisk the egg, milk, orange juice, oil and vanilla until blended; stir into dry ingredients just until moistened.

Pour batter by 1/3 cupfuls onto a hot griddle coated with nonstick cooking spray. Turn when bubbles form on top; cook until second side is golden brown.

Meanwhile, for syrup, combine the sugar, cornstarch and orange juice in a saucepan until smooth. Bring to a boil over medium heat; cook and stir for 1-2 minutes or until thickened. Serve warm with pancakes. **Yield:** 2 servings.

Nutrition Facts: 2 pancakes with 1/4 cup syrup equals 469 calories, 11 g fat (2 g saturated fat), 111 mg cholesterol, 857 mg sodium, 78 g carbohydrate, 2 g fiber, 12 g protein.

Editor's Note: As a substitute for 1 cup of self-rising flour, place 1-1/2 teaspoons baking powder and 1/2 teaspoon salt in a measuring cup. Add all-purpose flour to measure 1 cup.

Raspberry Cream Cheese Strata

Vickie Fletcher • Lewisburg, Pennsylvania

Here's a fruity strata recipe pared down for you and a friend. The strata is best when topped with a little of the raspberry syrup. It's a yummy dish that easily impresses.

- 4 slices bread, cut into 1-inch cubes, *divided*
- 1 package (3 ounces) cream cheese, cut into 1/2-inch cubes
- 1/2 cup fresh *or* frozen unsweetened raspberries
- 3 eggs
- 1 tablespoon maple syrup
- 1/2 cup milk

RASPBERRY SYRUP:
- 1/4 cup sugar
- 1-1/2 teaspoons cornstarch
- 1/4 cup water
- 1/4 cup fresh *or* frozen unsweetened raspberries
- 1 teaspoon butter

Place half of the bread cubes in a shallow 1-qt. baking dish coated with nonstick cooking spray. Top with cream cheese and raspberries. In a small mixing bowl, combine the eggs, syrup, milk and remaining bread cubes; spoon over raspberries. Cover and refrigerate overnight.

Remove from the refrigerator 30 minutes before baking. Bake at 350° for 30 minutes. Uncover; bake 15-20 minutes longer or until set.

Meanwhile, for syrup, combine the sugar, cornstarch and water in a saucepan until smooth. Bring to a boil over medium heat. Reduce heat; simmer, uncovered, for 2-3 minutes or until syrup reaches desired consistency. Add berries; mash slightly. Remove from the heat; stir in butter. Pour over strata. Serve immediately. **Yield:** 2 servings.

Bacon Cheddar Frittata

Carrie Bonikowske • Stevens Point, Wisconsin

Most frittatas feed a bunch, but not this version! The recipe helped me get a good grade in home-ec class years ago. Not only is it delicious, but it's easy to put together and bakes in a jiffy.

☑ **Uses less fat, sugar or salt. Includes Nutrition Facts or Diabetic Exchanges.**

- 3 eggs
- 1/2 cup milk
- 1 green onion, chopped
- 1 tablespoon butter, melted
- 1/4 teaspoon salt
- Dash pepper
- 1/2 cup shredded cheddar cheese
- 1 bacon strip, cooked and crumbled

In a bowl, whisk the eggs, milk, onion, butter, salt and pepper. Pour into a shallow 3-cup baking dish coated with nonstick cooking spray. Sprinkle with cheese and bacon. Bake, uncovered, at 400° for 12-15 minutes or until eggs are set. **Yield:** 2 servings.

Nutrition Facts: 1 serving (prepared with egg substitute, fat-free milk, reduced-fat butter and reduced-fat cheese) equals 227 calories, 14 g fat (7 g saturated fat), 35 mg cholesterol, 757 mg sodium, 5 g carbohydrate, trace fiber, 22 g protein.

Mushroom Strip Steaks

Kay Riedel • Topeka, Kansas

When you want to dress up steak in a hurry, try this idea. My husband and I enjoy the succulent combination of beef, mushrooms, cheese and onion soup regularly.

2 boneless New York strip steaks (about 1/2 pound)
1 to 2 tablespoons vegetable oil
1 can (10-1/2 ounces) condensed French onion soup, undiluted
1 jar (6 ounces) sliced mushrooms, drained
1/2 cup shredded part-skim mozzarella cheese

In a large skillet over medium-high heat, cook steaks in oil for 4-6 minutes on each side or until meat reaches desired doneness (for medium-rare, a meat thermometer should read 145°; medium, 160°; well-done, 170°). Drain.

Top each steak with the soup, mushrooms and mozzarella cheese. Cover and cook for 2-4 minutes or until the cheese is melted. **Yield:** 2 servings.

Editor's Note: Steak may be known as Kansas City steak, Ambassador Steak or Club Steak.

Sesame Brussels Sprouts

Melanie DuLac • Worcester, Massachusetts

I love brussels sprouts, and preparing them this way offers a bit of crunch from sesame seeds in addition to the savory seasoning.

✓ Uses less fat, sugar or salt. Includes Nutrition Facts or Diabetic Exchanges.

1/2 pound fresh brussels sprouts, halved
1-1/4 cups water, *divided*
1 teaspoon chicken bouillon granules
1 teaspoon sugar
1 teaspoon cornstarch
4 teaspoons soy sauce
2 garlic cloves, minced
1 teaspoon sesame seeds, toasted

In a large saucepan, cook the brussels sprouts in 1 cup water and bouillon for 6-8 minutes or until tender; drain and keep warm. In the same pan, combine the sugar, cornstarch, soy sauce, garlic and remaining water until blended. Bring to a boil over medium heat; cook and stir for 1 minute or until thickened. Add sprouts and toss to coat. Sprinkle with sesame seeds. **Yield:** 2 servings.

Nutrition Facts: 1/2-cup serving (prepared with reduced-sodium soy sauce) equals 88 calories, 1 g fat (trace saturated fat), trace cholesterol, 1,008 mg sodium, 16 g carbohydrate, 4 g fiber, 5 g protein.
Diabetic Exchange: 3 vegetable.

Peanut Butter Cream Parfaits

Debbie Roberts • Lake City, Minnesota

We think these cool, creamy treats taste similar to peanut butter pie, but they're so much easier to make, and they're sized right for two.

1 carton (8 ounces) frozen whipped topping, thawed
1/2 cup peanut butter
18 milk chocolate kisses

In a bowl, stir half of the whipped topping into peanut butter. Stir in the remaining topping until blended. Set aside two chocolate kisses; coarsely chop the remaining chocolates.

Divide a third of the topping mixture between two parfait glasses; top each with a fourth of the chopped chocolate. Repeat layers. Top with remaining topping mixture and reserved kisses. Chill until serving. **Yield:** 2 servings.

Stuffed Pork Chops

Shirley Inz • Fredericksburg, Texas

It's usually just my husband and I who enjoy these moist chops, but I've been known to triple the recipe when our grown children and their families come by for dinner.

2 tablespoons chopped celery
2 tablespoons chopped onion
2 tablespoons butter, *divided*
1/2 cup seasoned stuffing croutons
3 tablespoons milk
1 teaspoon minced fresh parsley
1/4 teaspoon paprika
1/8 teaspoon salt
1/8 teaspoon pepper
2 boneless pork loin chops (1 inch thick)
3/4 cup beef broth
1 to 2 tablespoons cornstarch
2 tablespoons cold water

In a skillet, saute celery and onion in 1 tablespoon butter until tender. Transfer to a bowl. Add croutons, milk, parsley, paprika, salt and pepper. Cut a pocket in each pork chop; fill with stuffing.

In a skillet, brown chops in remaining butter. Transfer to a greased 9-in. square baking dish. Pour broth into dish. Cover and bake at 350° for 30-35 minutes or until a meat thermometer reads 160°. Remove chops and keep warm.

Pour the pan drippings into a saucepan; bring to a boil. Combine cornstarch and water until smooth; gradually stir into drippings. Cook and stir for 2 minutes or until thickened. Serve with the pork chops. **Yield:** 2 servings.

Li'l Pecan Pies

Christine Boitos • Livonia, Michigan

These tempting little tarts have all the traditional taste of a full-size pecan pie.

1/2 cup all-purpose flour
1/8 teaspoon salt
3 tablespoons shortening
4 teaspoons cold water
FILLING:
1/3 cup pecan halves
1 egg
1/3 cup corn syrup
1/3 cup packed brown sugar
1/2 teaspoon vanilla extract
Whipped cream, optional

In a bowl, combine flour and salt; cut in shortening until crumbly. Gradually add water, tossing with fork until dough forms a ball. Cover and refrigerate for at least 30 minutes.

Divide dough in half. Roll each half into a 6-in. circle. Transfer to two 4-1/2-in. tart pans; fit pastry into pans, trimming if necessary. Arrange pecans in shells.

In a bowl, combine egg, corn syrup, brown sugar and vanilla; mix well. Pour over pecans. Place shells on a baking sheet. Bake at 375° for 35-40 minutes or until a knife inserted near the center comes out clean. Cool on a wire rack. Top with whipped cream if desired. **Yield:** 2 servings.

SWEET SECRETS

Before assembling the Li'l Pecan Pies, make sure that your brown sugar hasn't turned hard. If you need to soften it, place a slice of soft bread in a container with the sugar for a few days.

Maple Carrots

Beatrice Fulton • Bellevue, Washington

Nutritious carrots are extra sweet and appealing in this three-item side dish. Tarragon and maple syrup might seem like an odd combination, but the flavors combine well with the carrots.

1-1/2   cups sliced carrots
1   tablespoon maple syrup
1/8   to 1/4 teaspoon dried tarragon

Place 1 in. of water in a saucepan; add carrots. Bring to a boil. Reduce heat; cover and simmer for 3-4 minutes or until tender. Drain. Stir in syrup and tarragon. **Yield:** 2 servings.

Hearty Ham Omelet

Charlotte Baillargeon • Hinsdale, Massachusetts

We operate a bed-and-breakfast, and omelet recipes are truly lifesavers. Omelets are sort of the "stew" of breakfast time. You can add almost any leftover vegetable or meat into the filling. This is one of our favorite combinations.

3	tablespoons butter, *divided*
1	cup diced fully cooked ham
1	cup diced cooked potato
1/4	cup shredded cheddar cheese
1	tablespoon milk
1/2	teaspoon prepared horseradish
1	bacon strip, cooked and crumbled
4	eggs
2	tablespoons water
1/4	teaspoon salt

Dash pepper

In a 10-in. nonstick skillet, melt 2 tablespoons butter over medium heat. Add ham and potato; cook and stir until potato is lightly browned. Stir in the cheese, milk, horseradish and bacon; cook until cheese is melted. Remove and keep warm.

In the same skillet, melt remaining butter. In a bowl, beat the eggs, water, salt and pepper. Pour into skillet; cook over medium heat. As eggs set, lift the edges, letting uncooked portion flow underneath. When eggs are nearly set, spoon potato mixture over half of the omelet. Fold omelet over filling. Cover and cook for 1-2 minutes or until heated through. **Yield:** 2 servings.

Applesauce Oat Muffins

Cassandra Corridon • Frederick, Maryland

It's true! You can enjoy delicious muffins without having to make a dozen or more at a time. Just try these old-fashioned favorites to see what I mean.

✓ Uses less fat, sugar or salt. Includes Nutrition Facts or Diabetic Exchanges.

1/2	cup all-purpose flour
1/4	cup quick-cooking oats
3	tablespoons brown sugar
1	teaspoon baking powder
1/4	teaspoon ground cinnamon
1/8	teaspoon salt
1	egg
1/4	cup milk
2	tablespoons unsweetened applesauce
1	tablespoon canola oil

In a bowl, combine the first six ingredients. In another bowl, combine the egg, milk, applesauce and oil. Stir into dry ingredients just until moistened.

Fill four greased muffin cups two-thirds full. Bake at 400° for 12-15 minutes or until a toothpick comes out clean. Cool for 5 minutes before removing from pan to a wire rack. Serve warm. **Yield:** 4 muffins.

Nutrition Facts: One muffin (prepared with fat-free milk) equals 173 calories, 5 g fat (1 g saturated fat), 53 mg cholesterol, 160 mg sodium, 27 g carbohydrate, 1 g fiber, 5 g protein. **Diabetic Exchanges:** 1-1/2 starch, 1 fat.

Four-Fruit Compote

Genise Krause • Sturgeon Bay, Wisconsin

This refreshing combination of fruit is a welcomed side dish that we enjoy with breakfast or lunch. The light dressing lets the goodness of the fruit come through.

☑ **Uses less fat, sugar or salt. Includes Nutrition Facts or Diabetic Exchanges.**

- 1 **can (8 ounces) unsweetened pineapple chunks**
- 1 **medium pink grapefruit, peeled and sectioned**
- 1 **medium red apple, cubed**
- 1 **tablespoon sugar**
- 1 **teaspoon cornstarch**
- 1/8 **teaspoon salt**
- 1 **tablespoon lime juice**

Drain pineapple, reserving 1/4 cup juice. In a bowl, combine the pineapple, grapefruit and apple. In a saucepan, combine the sugar, cornstarch and salt. Gradually stir in lime juice and reserved pineapple juice until smooth. Bring to a boil; cook and stir for 1-2 minutes or until thickened. Pour over fruit and toss to coat. Serve immediately. **Yield:** 2 servings.

Nutrition Facts: 1 cup equals 145 calories, trace fat (trace saturated fat), 0 cholesterol, 148 mg sodium, 37 g carbohydrate, 4 g fiber, 1 g protein. **Diabetic Exchange:** 2-1/2 fruit.

Stuffed Cornish Hens

Wanda Jean Sain • Hickory, North Carolina

Seasoned with tarragon and filled with a comforting combination of long grain rice, butter and herbs, these pretty Cornish hens turn any meal into something special.

2 tablespoons finely chopped onion
1/3 cup uncooked long grain rice
4 tablespoons butter, *divided*
1/2 cup condensed cream of celery soup
3/4 cup water
1 tablespoon lemon juice
1 teaspoon dried chives
1 teaspoon dried parsley flakes
1 chicken bouillon cube
2 Cornish game hens (1 to 1-1/4 pounds *each*)
Salt and pepper to taste
1/2 teaspoon dried tarragon

In a skillet, cook and stir onion and rice in 2 tablespoons butter until rice is browned. Add the soup, water, lemon juice, chives, parsley and bouillon; bring to a boil. Reduce heat; cover and simmer for 25 minutes or until rice is tender and liquid is absorbed. Remove from heat and cool slightly.

Sprinkle hen cavities with salt and pepper; stuff with rice mixture. Place with breast side up on a rack in an ungreased 13-in. x 9-in. x 2-in. baking pan. Melt remaining butter and add tarragon; brush some over the hens. Cover loosely and bake at 375° for 30 minutes. Uncover and bake 30 minutes more or until tender, basting frequently with the tarragon butter. **Yield:** 2 servings.

Scalloped Sweet Potatoes

Marjorie Wilkerson • Dighton, Kansas

Now that our three boys are grown, I cook for just my husband and me. This satisfying casserole features sweet potatoes, apples and pecans but has a small yield, so you won't end up with a pan of leftovers.

1 large sweet potato, peeled and sliced
1 large apple, peeled and sliced
1/3 cup dry bread crumbs
1/3 cup light corn syrup
1/8 teaspoon salt
1 tablespoon butter
1 tablespoon chopped pecans

In a greased 1-qt. baking dish, layer half the sweet potato slices, apple slices and crumbs. Repeat layers. Pour corn syrup over top; sprinkle with salt. Dot with butter; sprinkle with nuts. Cover and bake at 400° for 35 minutes. **Yield:** 2 servings.

Simple Green Salad

Wanda Jean Sain • Hickory, North Carolina

You'd be surprised at how easy it is to stir up this homemade salad dressing for two. I mix red wine vinegar with garlic powder, Italian seasoning and a few other ingredients for this no-fuss recipe.

2 to 3 cups torn lettuce
2 tablespoons olive oil
2 tablespoons red wine vinegar
1/2 teaspoon Italian seasoning
1/2 teaspoon sugar
1/4 teaspoon salt
1/8 teaspoon garlic powder
1/8 teaspoon pepper

Divide lettuce among two plates. Combine remaining ingredients in a small bowl; drizzle over lettuce and serve immediately. **Yield:** 2 servings.

**Autumn Chicken
Horseradish Dill Potatoes**

Autumn Chicken

Kelly Kirby • Westville, Nova Scotia

*Whole-berry cranberry sauce makes this chicken dish a great choice for crisp fall nights,
but feel free to enjoy it all year. It's a satisfying dish you'll quickly come to rely on.*

✓ **Uses less fat, sugar or salt. Includes Nutrition Facts
or Diabetic Exchanges.**

  **2 boneless skinless chicken breast halves
     (4 ounces *each*)**
1/2 cup whole-berry cranberry sauce
  1 tablespoon brown sugar
  1 tablespoon reduced-sodium soy sauce
1-1/2 teaspoons lemon juice
1/4 teaspoon ground mustard
1/4 teaspoon ground ginger
1/4 teaspoon minced garlic

In a nonstick skillet coated with nonstick cooking spray, brown chicken on both sides. Place in a 1-qt. baking dish coated with nonstick cooking spray. Combine the remaining ingredients; pour over chicken. Cover and bake at 350° for 25-30 minutes or until a meat thermometer reads 170°. **Yield:** 2 servings.

Nutrition Facts: 1 chicken breast half with 1/3 cup sauce equals 257 calories, 3 g fat (1 g saturated fat), 63 mg cholesterol, 375 mg sodium, 34 g carbohydrate, 1 g fiber, 24 g protein. **Diabetic Exchanges:** 3 lean meat, 2 fruit.

Apple Crisp Cheesecake

Kelly Kirby • Westville, Nova Scotia

Thanks to the 6-inch springform pans on the market today, it's easy to bake up a delectable cheesecake, perfectly sized for two, three or four friends. All you need is a great recipe like this one that offers lots of apple flavor with a fun topping.

Apple Crisp Cheesecake

1/2 cup graham cracker crumbs
1/4 cup quick-cooking oats
4 teaspoons brown sugar
3 tablespoons butter, melted

FILLING:
2 packages (3 ounces *each*) cream cheese, softened
1/4 cup packed brown sugar
1 egg, lightly beaten
3 tablespoons sour cream
1/2 teaspoon ground cinnamon
1/8 teaspoon ground ginger
2/3 cup sliced peeled apple

TOPPING:
1 tablespoon all-purpose flour
1 tablespoon quick-cooking oats
1 tablespoon brown sugar
1/4 teaspoon ground cinnamon
2 teaspoons cold butter

In a small bowl, combine the cracker crumbs, oats and brown sugar; stir in butter. Press onto the bottom of a 6-in. springform pan coated with nonstick cooking spray; set aside.

For filling, in a small mixing bowl, beat cream cheese and brown sugar until smooth. Add egg; beat on low speed just until combined. Stir in the sour cream, cinnamon and ginger. Pour over crust. Arrange apple slices over filling. For topping, combine the flour, oats, brown sugar and cinnamon in a bowl. Cut in butter until crumbly. Sprinkle over apple. Place pan on a baking sheet.

Bake at 350° for 40-45 minutes or until center is almost set. Cool on a wire rack for 10 minutes. Carefully run a knife around edge of pan to loosen; cool 1 hour longer. Refrigerate overnight. Just before serving, remove sides of pan. Refrigerate leftovers. **Yield:** 4 servings.

Horseradish Dill Potatoes

Kelly Kirby • Westville, Nova Scotia

A little horseradish does a great job of livening up red potatoes in this satisfying side dish. A hint of lemon, dill weed and pepper round out the flavors.

✓ **Uses less fat, sugar or salt. Includes Nutrition Facts or Diabetic Exchanges.**

4 small red potatoes (about 1/2 pound)
2 tablespoons butter, melted
1-1/2 teaspoons lemon juice
1/2 teaspoon prepared horseradish
1/4 teaspoon salt
1/4 teaspoon dill weed
1/8 teaspoon pepper

Remove a thin strip of peel around the center of each potato. Place in a small saucepan and cover with water. Bring to a boil. Reduce heat; cover and cook for 15-20 minutes or until tender. Combine the remaining ingredients. Drain potatoes; add butter mixture and stir to coat. **Yield:** 2 servings.

Nutrition Facts: 1 serving equals 184 calories, 12 g fat (7 g saturated fat), 31 mg cholesterol, 422 mg sodium, 19 g carbohydrate, 2 g fiber, 2 g protein.
Diabetic Exchanges: 2 fat, 1 starch.

Special Strip Steaks

Janice Mitchell • Aurora, Colorado

I use my wonderful cast-iron skillet, inherited from my mother, when preparing this delicious steak.

- 2 beef strip steaks (8 ounces *each*)
- 1 garlic clove, halved
- 1/4 teaspoon salt
- 1/4 teaspoon pepper
- 1 tablespoon butter
- 1/4 cup sherry *or* beef broth
- 1/4 teaspoon Worcestershire sauce
- 2 tablespoons chopped green onion

Rub steaks with garlic and sprinkle with salt and pepper; set aside. Melt butter in a large skillet.

Add the sherry or broth, Worcestershire sauce and onion. Bring to a boil. Reduce heat; simmer, uncovered, for 5 minutes.

Add the steaks and cook over medium heat for 3-7 minutes on each side or until the meat reaches desired doneness (for medium-rare, a meat thermometer should read 145°, medium, 160°, well-done, 170°). **Yield:** 2 servings.

Editor's Note: Steak may be known as strip steak, Kansas City steak, New York Strip steak, Ambassador Steak or boneless Club Steak in your region.

Herbed Zucchini 'n' Carrots

Tamra Duncan • Centerton, Arkansas

Here's a blend of garden veggies and herbs that works well with just about any main course.

✓ **Uses less fat, sugar or salt. Includes Nutrition Facts or Diabetic Exchanges.**

- 1 small zucchini, halved lengthwise and cut into 1/2-inch slices
- 1/8 teaspoon *each* dried marjoram, thyme and chervil
- 1/8 teaspoon salt
- 1/8 teaspoon pepper
- 2 teaspoons reduced-fat butter
- 1 cup baby carrots
- 1/4 cup water

In a nonstick skillet, cook the zucchini and seasonings in butter over medium heat for 8 minutes or until zucchini is tender.

Meanwhile, place the carrots and water in a 1-qt. microwave-safe dish. Cover and microwave on high for 1-2 minutes or until carrots are tender, stirring once; drain. Stir carrots into zucchini mixture. **Yield:** 2 servings.

Nutrition Facts: 3/4 cup equals 52 calories, 2 g fat (1 g saturated fat), 7 mg cholesterol, 203 mg sodium, 8 g carbohydrate, 2 g fiber, 2 g protein. **Diabetic Exchanges:** 1 vegetable, 1/2 fat.

Parmesan Basil Spaghetti

Sarah Briggs • Greenfield, Wisconsin

Try this lemony pasta dish with everything from poached fish to grilled steak.

- 3 ounces uncooked thin spaghetti
- 1 tablespoon olive oil
- 1 tablespoon lemon juice
- 2 tablespoons minced fresh basil *or* 1 teaspoon dried basil
- 1/8 teaspoon salt
- Dash pepper
- 1/3 cup shredded Parmesan cheese

Cook spaghetti according to package directions. In a small custard cup, combine the oil and lemon juice. Microwave on high 20 seconds. Stir in the basil, salt and pepper. Drain spaghetti and place in a serving bowl. Add basil mixture; toss to coat. Sprinkle with Parmesan cheese. **Yield:** 2 servings.

Chicken with Cranberry Sauce

Taste of Home Test Kitchen • Greendale, Wisconsin

You don't have to eat the same foods night after night just because you're cooking for two. For this elegant entree, golden chicken is coated in a pretty cranberry sauce with delicious results.

✓ **Uses less fat, sugar or salt. Includes Nutrition Facts or Diabetic Exchanges.**

2	boneless skinless chicken breast halves (5 ounces *each*)
1	tablespoon all-purpose flour
1/4	teaspoon salt, *divided*
1/8	teaspoon pepper
1	tablespoon olive oil
3/4	cup reduced-sodium chicken broth
1	cup fresh *or* frozen cranberries, thawed
2	tablespoons brown sugar
1	tablespoon red wine vinegar
1-3/4	teaspoons cornstarch
1	tablespoon cold water

Flatten chicken to 1/2-in. thickness. In a shallow bowl, combine flour, 1/8 teaspoon salt and pepper. Coat chicken with flour mixture. In a nonstick skillet, cook chicken in oil for 4-5 minutes on each side or until juices run clear. Remove chicken and keep warm.

In the same skillet, bring broth to a boil; scrape up any browned bits. Stir in the cranberries, brown sugar, vinegar and remaining salt.

Combine cornstarch and water until smooth; stir into cranberry mixture. Bring to a boil; cook and stir for 1 minute or until thickened. Return chicken to the pan and heat through. **Yield:** 2 servings.

Nutrition Facts: 1 chicken breast half with 1/2 cup sauce equals 318 calories, 10 g fat (2 g saturated fat), 78 mg cholesterol, 602 mg sodium, 25 g carbohydrate, 2 g fiber, 30 g protein. **Diabetic Exchanges:** 4 very lean meat, 2 fat, 1 fruit, 1/2 starch.

Pilgrim Pudding

Cynthia Kempski • Milwaukee, Wisconsin

With a pleasant pumpkin flavor, caramel and almonds, this rich and creamy treat tastes decadent, but it's surprisingly light.

✓ **Uses less fat, sugar or salt. Includes Nutrition Facts or Diabetic Exchanges.**

3/4	cup cold fat-free milk
1/3	cup canned pumpkin
2	tablespoons sugar-free instant vanilla pudding mix
1/2	cup plus 1 tablespoon fat-free whipped topping, *divided*
1-1/2	teaspoons fat-free caramel ice cream topping
1	teaspoon sliced almonds, toasted

In a large mixing bowl, combine milk and pumpkin. Add pudding mix; whisk for 2 minutes or until slightly thickened. Let stand for 2 minutes or until soft-set. Fold in 1/2 cup whipped topping.

Spoon pudding into two dessert dishes. Garnish with remaining whipped topping; drizzle with caramel topping and sprinkle with almonds. **Yield:** 2 servings.

Nutrition Facts: 2/3 cup equals 117 calories, 1 g fat (trace saturated fat), 2 mg cholesterol, 362 mg sodium, 22 g carbohydrate, 2 g fiber, 4 g protein. **Diabetic Exchanges:** 1 starch, 1/2 fat-free milk.

Stir-Fried Green Beans

Heidi Wilcox • Lapeer, Michigan

In no time at all, I can stir-fry fresh green beans with garlic and this variety of herbs.

✓ Uses less fat, sugar or salt. Includes Nutrition Facts or Diabetic Exchanges.

1 garlic clove, minced
1 tablespoon butter
1-1/2 cups cut fresh green beans
1 teaspoon minced fresh parsley
1/2 teaspoon dried basil
1/4 teaspoon salt
1/4 teaspoon dried oregano
1/8 teaspoon cayenne pepper

In a large nonstick skillet or wok, stir-fry garlic in butter for 1 minute. Add the beans; stir-fry 3 minutes longer. Stir in the parsley, basil, salt, oregano and cayenne; stir-fry for 2-3 minutes or until beans are crisp-tender. **Yield:** 2 servings.

Nutrition Facts: 3/4 cup equals 77 calories, 6 g fat (4 g saturated fat), 15 mg cholesterol, 358 mg sodium, 6 g carbohydrate, 3 g fiber, 2 g protein. **Diabetic Exchanges:** 1 vegetable, 1 fat.

Garlic-Herb Red Snapper

Nancy Mueller • Menomonee Falls, Wisconsin

My husband often prepares the main course at dinnertime. He likes to grill seafood, and this yummy entree is a favorite of both of ours.

✓ **Uses less fat, sugar or salt. Includes Nutrition Facts or Diabetic Exchanges.**

- 2 tablespoons lemon juice
- 2 red snapper fillets *or* orange roughy fillets (7 ounces *each*)
- 2 teaspoons grated lemon peel
- 1/2 teaspoon salt
- 1/2 teaspoon garlic powder
- 1/2 teaspoon dried chervil
- 1/4 teaspoon dill weed
- 1/4 teaspoon pepper

Spoon lemon juice over both sides of fillets. Combine the lemon peel and seasonings; sprinkle over fillets.

If grilling the fish, coat grill rack with nonstick cooking spray before starting the grill. Grill fish, uncovered, over medium heat or broil 4-6 in. from the heat for 3 minutes on each side or until fish flakes easily with a fork. **Yield:** 2 servings.

Nutrition Facts: One fillet equals 146 calories, 1 g fat (trace saturated fat), 40 mg cholesterol, 716 mg sodium, 2 g carbohydrate, trace fiber, 29 g protein. **Diabetic Exchange:** 4 very lean meat.

Couscous Pepper Cups

Nancy Mueller • Menomonee Falls, Wisconsin

We often double this recipe so that we have two pepper cups to eat at dinner and two to freeze for a meal on a busy night. The cups also make a nice addition to chicken suppers.

✓ **Uses less fat, sugar or salt. Includes Nutrition Facts or Diabetic Exchanges.**

- 2 large sweet red peppers
- 1/2 cup chopped onion
- 1/4 cup sliced fresh mushrooms
- 1/4 cup sliced celery
- 1/4 cup chopped peeled apple
- 1 garlic clove, minced
- 3/4 cup reduced-sodium chicken broth
- 1/4 teaspoon salt
- 1/4 teaspoon ground cumin
- 1/4 teaspoon pepper
- 1/8 teaspoon ground turmeric, optional
- 1/2 cup uncooked couscous
- 1 teaspoon olive oil
- 2 tablespoons golden raisins
- 1 tablespoon pine nuts, toasted
- 1 tablespoon minced fresh parsley

Cut tops off peppers and remove seeds. In a large kettle, cook peppers in boiling water for 3-5 minutes or until crisp-tender. Drain and rinse in cold water; set aside.

In a nonstick skillet coated with nonstick cooking spray, saute the onion, mushrooms, celery, apple and garlic for 4-5 minutes or until the vegetables are tender. Remove from the heat and set aside.

In a saucepan, combine the broth, salt, cumin, pepper and turmeric if desired. Bring to a boil; stir in couscous and oil. Remove from the heat; cover and let stand for 5 minutes. Fluff with a fork. Stir in the vegetable mixture, raisins, pine nuts and parsley. Spoon into peppers.

Place in an 8-in. square baking dish coated with nonstick cooking spray. Cover and bake at 350° for 15 minutes or until heated through. **Yield:** 2 servings.

Nutrition Facts: One serving equals 318 calories, 6 g fat (1 g saturated fat), 0 cholesterol, 553 mg sodium, 61 g carbohydrate, 7 g fiber, 11 g protein.

Mandarin Mixed Green Salad

Nancy Mueller • Menomonee Falls, Wisconsin

I make the salads and bake most of the desserts in our house. Mandarin Mixed Green Salad has a tangy citrus dressing we truly enjoy.

✓ Uses less fat, sugar or salt. Includes Nutrition Facts or Diabetic Exchanges.

2 cups torn mixed salad greens
1/2 cup mandarin oranges
1/4 cup chopped walnuts, toasted
CITRUS VINAIGRETTE:
3 tablespoons orange juice
2 teaspoons balsamic vinegar
1 teaspoon olive oil
1 teaspoon honey
1 teaspoon Dijon mustard
1 teaspoon reduced-sodium soy sauce
1/2 teaspoon minced fresh gingerroot
1 garlic clove, minced

Place greens on two serving plates; top with oranges and walnuts. In a blender, combine the vinaigrette ingredients; cover and process until blended. Drizzle over salads. **Yield:** 2 servings.

Nutrition Facts: One serving equals 181 calories, 11 g fat (1 g saturated fat), 0 cholesterol, 177 mg sodium, 16 g carbohydrate, 2 g fiber, 6 g protein. **Diabetic Exchanges:** 2 fat, 1 vegetable, 1 fruit.

Piled-High Turkey Sandwiches

Prue Thompson • Stuart, Florida

The first time I had this open-faced sandwich was at the Grand Hotel on Mackinac Island in Michigan. That was back in the 1950s, and the recipe has been a staple in my kitchen since.

3   tablespoons mayonnaise
1   tablespoon ketchup
1   teaspoon milk
1/2 teaspoon minced fresh parsley
1/2 teaspoon minced chives
Dash Worcestershire sauce
2   slices bread, toasted
4   slices deli turkey
2   slices tomato

2   slices red onion
1   hard-cooked egg, sliced
2   bacon strips, cooked and halved

In a small bowl, combine the mayonnaise, ketchup, milk, parsley, chives and Worcestershire sauce. Cover and refrigerate for 15 minutes.

Spread 1 tablespoon over each piece of toast. Top each with turkey, tomato, onion, egg and bacon. Dollop with remaining mayonnaise mixture. **Yield:** 2 servings.

Rice 'n' Egg Salad

Christina Moran • Collierville, Tennessee

This savory salad is a mainstay for my mother-in-law and me. I like the fact that it doesn't leave room for leftovers, but the flavor is what keeps it popular in our homes.

3/4 cup cooked long grain rice
1/3 cup chopped celery
1   hard-cooked egg, chopped
1/4 cup sliced ripe olives
2   tablespoons chopped onion
1   tablespoon dill pickle relish
1   tablespoon diced pimientos
2   tablespoons mayonnaise
2   to 4 teaspoons canola oil

2   teaspoons cider vinegar
1   to 2 teaspoons prepared mustard
1/2 teaspoon salt, optional
Dash pepper

In a bowl, combine the first seven ingredients. In a small bowl, combine the mayonnaise, oil, vinegar, mustard, salt if desired and pepper; pour over rice mixture and toss to coat. Cover and refrigerate for at least 20 minutes before serving. **Yield:** 2 servings.

Lemon-Berry Pitcher Punch

Margaret O' Bryon • Bel Air, Maryland

The tangy combination of lemonade and cranberry juice makes this drink a real thirst-quencher on a warm day.

✓ Uses less fat, sugar or salt. Includes Nutrition Facts or Diabetic Exchanges.

1/4 cup sweetened lemonade drink mix
2   cups cold water
1/3 cup cranberry juice, chilled
3/4 cup lemon-lime soda, chilled

In a pitcher, combine the drink mix, water and cranberry juice. Stir in soda. Serve immediately. **Yield:** about 3 cups.

Nutrition Facts: 1 cup (prepared with sugar-free lemonade, reduced-calorie cranberry juice and diet soda) equals 9 calories, 0 fat (0 saturated fat), 0 cholesterol, 3 mg sodium, 1 g carbohydrate, 0 fiber, trace protein.

Curry Lamb Chops

Lois Szemko • East Islip, New York

My husband and I are retired but busy, so I rely on fast and simple dishes like this one. The tender lamb and mouth-watering gravy seem fancy, but they both come together without much work.

✓ **Uses less fat, sugar or salt. Includes Nutrition Facts or Diabetic Exchanges.**

- 4 bone-in lamb loin chops (4 ounces *each*)
- 1 tablespoon canola oil
- 3/4 cup orange juice
- 2 tablespoons reduced-sodium teriyaki sauce
- 2 teaspoons grated orange peel
- 1 teaspoon curry powder
- 1 garlic clove, minced
- 1 teaspoon cornstarch
- 2 tablespoons cold water

Hot cooked rice, optional

In a skillet, brown the lamb chops on both sides in oil; drain. Combine the orange juice, teriyaki sauce, orange peel, curry and garlic; pour over lamb. Cover and simmer for 15-20 minutes or until meat is tender. Remove chops and keep warm.

Combine cornstarch and water until smooth; stir into pan drippings. Bring to a boil; cook and stir for 2 minutes or until thickened. Serve lamb and gravy with rice if desired. **Yield:** 2 servings.

Nutrition Facts: 2 lamb chops with 1/4 cup gravy equals 337 calories, 17 g fat (4 g saturated fat), 90 mg cholesterol, 402 mg sodium, 15 g carbohydrate, 1 g fiber, 30 g protein. **Diabetic Exchanges:** 4 lean meat, 1 fruit, 1 fat.

Tiny Chiffon Cakes

Jan Huszczo • Beverly Hills, Michigan

My father is not a cake lover, but he absolutely loves this treat. In fact, it's the only cake he'll eat. If you don't want to frost the little desserts, just dust them with confectioners' sugar.

- 1/3 cup cake flour
- 3 tablespoons sugar
- 1/4 teaspoon baking powder
- 1/8 teaspoon salt
- 1 egg yolk
- 1 tablespoon orange juice
- 1 tablespoon canola oil
- 1-1/2 teaspoons water
- 1/2 teaspoon grated orange peel
- 2 egg whites
- 1/8 teaspoon cream of tartar

Frosting, optional

Line the bottom of two ungreased 4-in. tube pans with parchment or waxed paper; set aside. In a small mixing bowl, combine the flour, sugar, baking powder and salt. Add the egg yolk, orange juice, oil, water and orange peel; beat until smooth. In another small mixing bowl, beat egg whites and cream of tartar until stiff peaks form. Fold into batter.

Spoon into prepared pans. Bake at 325° for 15-20 minutes or until a toothpick comes out clean. Immediately invert pans to cool. Loosen cake from pan with a knife; remove cakes. Frost if desired. **Yield:** 2 cakes.

Orange Broccoli Florets

Paula Kenny • New Hudson, Michigan

This easy dish appears often on my dinner table. The citrus flavor makes broccoli more special.

✓ Uses less fat, sugar or salt. Includes Nutrition Facts or Diabetic Exchanges.

1-1/2 cups fresh broccoli florets
2 teaspoons butter
1-1/2 teaspoons all-purpose flour
1/4 cup orange juice
1/2 teaspoon grated orange peel

Place broccoli and 1 in. of water in a saucepan; bring to a boil. Reduce heat; cover and simmer for 5-8 minutes or until crisp-tender. Meanwhile, in a small saucepan, melt butter. Stir in flour until smooth. Gradually stir in orange juice. Bring to a boil; cook and stir for 1 minute or until thickened. Stir in orange peel. Drain broccoli; add orange juice mixture and toss to coat. **Yield:** 2 servings.

Nutrition Facts: 1/2 cup (prepared with reduced-fat butter) equals 53 calories, 2 g fat (1 g saturated fat), 7 mg cholesterol, 38 mg sodium, 8 g carbohydrate, 2 g fiber, 2 g protein.

Three-Cheese Grilled Cheese

Terri Brown • Delavan, Wisconsin

When making these sandwiches, my favorite combination is Swiss and cheddar along with the cream cheese. But Mexican cheese is tasty as well, particularly when the sandwiches are served with salsa.

- 2 slices wheat, rye *or* sourdough bread
- 2 tablespoons softened cream cheese
- 2 tablespoons butter, softened
- 2 slices white cheese (brick, Monterey Jack *or* Swiss)
- 2 slices yellow cheese (cheddar, pepper *or* taco)
- 1 red onion slice
- 1 tomato slice

For each slice of bread, spread cream cheese on one side and spread butter on the other. On one side of bread, with cream cheese side up, layer the white cheese, yellow cheese, onion and tomato. Top with the other slice of bread, cream cheese side down.

Toast sandwich for 2-3 minutes on each side or until bread is lightly browned. Remove from the heat; cover until cheese melts. **Yield:** 1 serving.

Potato Salad for One

Ray Klinge • Tulsa, Oklahoma

You don't have to toss together an overwhelming amount of potato salad to enjoy its old-fashioned flavor. Here's how I whip up the popular salad for myself.

- 1/4 cup mayonnaise
- 2 tablespoons chopped celery
- 1 tablespoon chopped onion
- 1 tablespoon pickle relish, drained
- 1-1/2 teaspoons diced pimientos, drained
- 1 teaspoon Dijon mustard
- 1/2 teaspoon cider vinegar

Dash salt and pepper
- 1 medium baking potato, cooked, peeled and cubed

In a small bowl, combine mayonnaise, celery, onion, relish, pimientos, mustard, vinegar, salt and pepper; mix well. Add potato and toss to coat. Chill for 1 hour. **Yield:** 1 serving.

Chocolate Pudding Mix

Lois Miller • New Paris, Indiana

It's wonderful having this mix on hand. Whenever you're in the mood for a chocolate dessert, you can easily turn to the mix and stir up a serving for yourself.

PUDDING MIX:
- 1 cup nonfat dry milk
- 2/3 cup sugar
- 6 tablespoons cornstarch
- 1/3 cup baking cocoa
- 1/4 teaspoon salt

PUDDING:
- 1/2 cup water
- 1/4 cup Pudding Mix (above)
- 2 teaspoons butter

- 1/4 teaspoon almond *or* vanilla extract

Whipped topping and baking cocoa, optional

Combine mix ingredients; store in an airtight container or resealable plastic bag. **Yield:** 1-3/4 cups mix (7 batches of pudding).

To make pudding: Combine water and mix in a small saucepan; bring to a boil over medium heat, stirring occasionally. Cook and stir for 2 minutes. Remove from the heat; stir in butter and extract. Pour into a serving dish. Serve warm or chilled; top with whipped topping and sprinkle with cocoa if desired. **Yield:** 1 serving.

Honey-Pecan Chicken Breasts
Zucchini Provencale

Honey-Pecan Chicken Breasts

Penny Davis • Newman Lake, Washington

We love to entertain, and this is a dish I double to welcome dinner guests.
The nuts add an elegant touch, and it fills the house with a great aroma. Try it tonight!

✓ **Uses less fat, sugar or salt. Includes Nutrition Facts or Diabetic Exchanges.**

  2   **boneless skinless chicken breast halves (6 ounces** *each***)**
1/4   **teaspoon salt**
1/8   **teaspoon pepper**
1/8   **to 1/4 teaspoon cayenne pepper**
  1   **tablespoon butter**
1/4   **teaspoon minced garlic**
  3   **tablespoons honey**
  2   **tablespoons finely chopped pecans**

Flatten chicken to 1/2-in. thickness. Sprinkle with salt, pepper and cayenne. In a large nonstick skillet, brown chicken in butter; add garlic. Reduce heat to medium; cover and cook for 3-4 minutes on each side or until juices run clear. Drizzle honey over chicken; sprinkle with pecans. Cover and cook for 2-3 minutes or until heated through. **Yield:** 2 servings.

Nutrition Facts: 1 serving equals 382 calories, 15 g fat (5 g saturated fat), 109 mg cholesterol, 436 mg sodium, 27 g carbohydrate, 1 g fiber, 35 g protein.
Diabetic Exchanges: 3 lean meat, 2 starch, 1 fat.

Zucchini Provencale

Bobbie Jo Yokley • Franklin, Kentucky

To use up the last of your garden's tomatoes and zucchini, try this mouth-watering, speedy side dish.

✓ Uses less fat, sugar or salt. Includes Nutrition Facts or Diabetic Exchanges.

  2 tablespoons chopped onion
  1 tablespoon canola oil
  1 small zucchini, cubed
  1 small yellow summer squash, cubed
1/4 cup chopped green pepper
  1 garlic clove, minced
1/8 teaspoon salt
Dash pepper
  1 medium tomato, cut into wedges
  1 tablespoon grated Parmesan cheese

In a small nonstick skillet, saute onion in oil until tender. Stir in the zucchini, yellow squash, green pepper, garlic, salt and pepper. Cover and cook over low heat for 5-6 minutes or until vegetables are almost tender. Stir in tomatoes; heat through. Sprinkle with Parmesan cheese. **Yield:** 2 servings.

Nutrition Facts: 1 cup equals 120 calories, 8 g fat (1 g saturated fat), 2 mg cholesterol, 205 mg sodium, 10 g carbohydrate, 3 g fiber, 3 g protein. **Diabetic Exchanges:** 2 vegetable, 1-1/2 fat.

Skillet Cherry Cobbler

Kari Damon • Rushford, New York

Once a week, my husband and I enjoy a candlelight dinner after our two children are fed and in bed. This is a perfectly sized dessert for those special "date nights." Try the stovetop cobbler with apple or blueberry pie filling instead of cherry if you'd like.

✓ Uses less fat, sugar or salt. Includes Nutrition Facts or Diabetic Exchanges.

1/2 cup biscuit/baking mix
1-1/2 teaspoons sugar
1/2 to 1 teaspoon grated orange peel
  2 tablespoons 2% milk
  1 cup cherry pie filling
1/4 cup orange juice

In a small bowl, combine the biscuit mix, sugar and orange peel. Stir in milk just until moistened; set aside.

In a small nonstick skillet, combine pie filling and orange juice; bring to a boil, stirring occasionally. Drop biscuit mixture in two mounds onto boiling cherry mixture. Reduce heat; cover and simmer for 10 minutes. Uncover; simmer 5-7 minutes longer or until a toothpick inserted into a dumpling comes out clean. **Yield:** 2 servings.

Nutrition Facts: 1 serving (prepared with reduced-sugar pie filling) equals 262 calories, 6 g fat (2 g saturated fat), 1 mg cholesterol, 397 mg sodium, 51 g carbohydrate, 1 g fiber, 4 g protein.

Skillet Cherry Cobbler

Speedy Ham Slice

Heather Campbell • Lawrence, Kansas

The recipe for this citrus and ginger entree comes in handy when the kids stay with their Grandma and only the two of us are home for dinner. Best of all, it's made in the microwave

1/4 cup orange juice
1 tablespoon brown sugar
1/2 teaspoon grated orange peel
1/8 teaspoon ground ginger
1/2 pound fully cooked ham slice, cut in half
1/2 teaspoon cornstarch
1 teaspoon water

In a microwave-safe baking dish, combine the orange juice, brown sugar, orange peel and ginger. Add ham slice, turning to coat with sauce. Cover and refrigerate for 15 minutes.

Cover and microwave on high for 1 minute on each side. Microwave at 50% power for 2 minutes, spooning sauce over ham once. Remove ham and keep warm.

Combine cornstarch and water until smooth; stir into cooking juices. Microwave, uncovered, at 50% power for 10 seconds; stir. Cook 20 seconds longer or until thickened. Serve over ham. **Yield:** 2 servings.

Editor's Note: This recipe was tested in a 1,100-watt microwave.

Vegetable Couscous

Taste of Home Test Kitchen • Greendale, Wisconsin

Sauteed vegetables add texture and crunch to quick-cooking couscous for this easy dish.

✓ **Uses less fat, sugar or salt. Includes Nutrition Facts or Diabetic Exchanges.**

3/4 cup water
1/2 cup uncooked couscous
1/2 cup chopped carrot
1/2 cup chopped onion
1 tablespoon butter
1/2 cup chopped zucchini
1 green onion, thinly sliced
1/2 teaspoon salt
Dash to 1/8 teaspoon white pepper

In a saucepan, bring water to a boil. Stir in couscous; cover and remove from the heat. Let stand for 5 minutes.

In a small skillet, saute the carrot and onion in butter for 3-4 minutes or until crisp-tender. Add zucchini and green onion; saute 2-3 minutes longer or until tender. Sprinkle with salt and pepper. Fluff couscous with a fork; add vegetable mixture and toss to combine. **Yield:** 2 servings.

Nutrition Facts: 1 cup equals 249 calories, 7 g fat (4 g saturated fat), 15 mg cholesterol, 666 mg sodium, 43 g carbohydrate, 4 g fiber, 8 g protein.

VERY VERSATILE

Not only is couscous a fast favorite, but you can add just about anything to it. Clean out the refrigerator by stirring last night's vegetables into cooked couscous. Add leftover bits of cooked beef, chicken, pork or even shrimp for a no-fuss main course.

Creamy Chocolate Pudding

Mary Ann Gove • Cottonwood, Arizona

*Ten minutes are all you need to whip up this all-time favorite that's pared down for two.
It has the creamy texture of pudding that's cooked on the stove.*

1   **tablespoon cornstarch**
1   **cup milk**
1/2 **cup milk chocolate *or* semisweet
      chocolate chips**
1/4 **cup whipped topping**

In a microwave-safe bowl, combine cornstarch and milk until smooth. Add chocolate chips.

Microwave on high for 2-1/2 to 3 minutes or until thickened and bubbly, stirring twice.

Pour into dessert dishes. Serve warm or refrigerate until serving. Just before serving, dollop with whipped topping. **Yield:** 2 servings.

Editor's Note: This recipe was tested in a 1,100-watt microwave.

COOKIES, BROWNIES & BARS

Need a tempting treat but don't want to fit 3 or 4 dozen snacks into your cookie jar? You've come to the right place. These recipes yield fewer servings than most, so they're perfect when hosting a small get-together or when you only have to satisfy a sweet tooth or two.

Mint Brownie Pie
p. 275

Fudgy Pecan Tartlets
p. 277

Dipped Coconut
Shortbread p. 281

Chocolate Pecan
Thumbprints p. 274

Orange Cranberry Bars
p. 268

Orange Cranberry Bars

Nell June Wheeler • Warrenton, Virginia

My sister, who's a great baker, passed this recipe on to me. The buttery bars are studded with cranberries, pecans and coconut. They're great for fall and pretty enough for Christmas.

✓ **Uses less fat, sugar or salt. Includes Nutrition Facts or Diabetic Exchanges.**

1/4	cup all-purpose flour
1-1/2	teaspoons sugar
2	tablespoons cold butter
2	tablespoons chopped pecans

TOPPING:

2	tablespoons beaten egg
1-1/2	teaspoons milk
3/4	teaspoon grated orange peel
1/4	teaspoon vanilla extract
1/3	cup sugar
1-1/2	teaspoons all-purpose flour
1/4	cup chopped fresh *or* frozen cranberries
2	tablespoons flaked coconut
2	tablespoons chopped pecans

In a bowl, combine flour and sugar; cut in butter until mixture resembles coarse crumbs. Stir in pecans. Press into an 8-in. x 4-in. x 2-in. loaf pan coated with nonstick cooking spray. Bake at 350° for 15 minutes.

Meanwhile, in a bowl, combine the egg, milk, orange peel and vanilla. Combine sugar and flour; gradually add to egg mixture and mix well. Fold in the cranberries, coconut and pecans. Spread over crust. Bake for 15-20 minutes or until golden brown. Cool on a wire rack. **Yield:** 8 bars.

Nutrition Facts: One bar equals 117 calories, 6 g fat (3 g saturated fat), 21 mg cholesterol, 37 mg sodium, 14 g carbohydrate, 1 g fiber, 1 g protein.

Giant Spice Cookies

Giant Spice Cookies

Sandy Pyeatt • Tacoma, Washington

I heard this cookie recipe over the radio sometime around 1950—shortly after my husband and I were married. The goodies remain my favorite to this day.

1	package (18-1/4 ounces) spice cake mix
1/2	teaspoon ground ginger
1/4	teaspoon baking soda
1/4	cup water
1/4	cup molasses
6	teaspoons vanilla extract

In a bowl, combine the cake mix, ginger and baking soda. Stir in water, molasses and vanilla; mix well. With floured hands, roll into 10 balls.

Place 3 in. apart on greased baking sheets; flatten slightly. Bake at 375° for 13-15 minutes or until surface cracks and cookies are firm. Remove to wire racks to cool. **Yield:** 10 cookies.

Caramel Fudge Brownies

Caramel Fudge Brownies

Priscilla Renfrow • Wilson, North Carolina

These brownies are so yummy, you'll never guess they're actually lighter than most. The caramel topping is a nice surprise that folks enjoy.

✓ **Uses less fat, sugar or salt. Includes Nutrition Facts or Diabetic Exchanges.**

- 4 **squares (1 ounce *each*) unsweetened chocolate**
- 3 **egg whites, lightly beaten**
- 1 **cup sugar**
- 2 **jars (2-1/2 ounces *each*) prune baby food**
- 1 **teaspoon vanilla extract**
- 1/2 **teaspoon salt**
- 1/2 **cup all-purpose flour**
- 1/4 **cup chopped walnuts**
- 6 **tablespoons fat-free caramel ice cream topping**
- 9 **tablespoons reduced fat-whipped topping**

In a microwave or saucepan, melt chocolate; stir until smooth. In a bowl, combine the egg whites, sugar, melted chocolate, prunes, vanilla and salt; mix well. Stir in flour until just moistened.

Pour into an 8-in. square baking pan coated with nonstick cooking spray. Sprinkle with walnuts. Bake at 350° for 30-32 minutes or until the top springs back when lightly touched. Cool on a wire rack. Cut into squares; drizzle with caramel topping and dollop with whipped topping. **Yield:** 9 servings.

Nutrition Facts: One piece equals 251 calories, 10 g fat (5 g saturated fat), 0 cholesterol, 170 mg sodium, 42 g carbohydrate, 3 g fiber, 4 g protein. **Diabetic Exchanges:** 2 starch, 2 fat, 1/2 fruit.

PB&J Bars

Mitzi Sentiff • Alexandria, Virginia

Big and little kids alike will love these four-ingredient bars that offer a cookie crust, a layer of jam and a crunchy peanut butter and granola topping.

1	package (18 ounces) refrigerated sugar cookie dough, *divided*
2/3	cup strawberry jam
3/4	cup granola cereal without raisins
3/4	cup peanut butter chips

Line a 9-in. square baking pan with foil and grease the foil. Press two-thirds of the cookie dough into prepared pan. Spread jam over dough to within 1/4 in. of edges. In a mixing bowl, beat the granola, peanut butter chips and remaining dough until blended. Crumble over jam.

Bake at 375° for 25-30 minutes or until golden brown. Cool on a wire rack. Using foil, lift out of pan. Cut into bars and remove from foil. **Yield:** 9 servings.

PB&J Bars

Coconut Lemon Crisps

Segarie Moodley • Longwood, Florida

We had these cookies at our wedding reception, where they brought smiles and compliments. Since then, this pared-back version has become our anniversary dinner trademark.

7	tablespoons butter, softened
1/4	cup sugar
1/2	teaspoon vanilla extract
1	cup all-purpose flour
1	egg white, beaten
1/2	cup flaked coconut

FILLING:

1/3	cup sugar
4-1/2	teaspoons cornstarch
3/4	cup water
2	tablespoons lemon juice
1	egg yolk, beaten
3	tablespoons butter, softened

In a mixing bowl, cream butter, sugar and vanilla. Gradually add flour. On a lightly floured surface, roll out half of the dough to 1/8-in. thickness. Cut with a 2-in. round cookie cutter. Repeat with remaining dough, using a 2-in. doughnut cutter so the center is cut out of each cookie.

Place 1 in. apart on lightly greased baking sheets. Brush egg white over cookies with cutout centers; sprinkle with coconut. Bake at 350° for 8-10 minutes. Remove to wire racks to cool.

In a small saucepan, combine sugar and cornstarch. Stir in water and lemon juice until smooth. Add egg yolk and butter; cook and stir over medium heat until thickened. Cool. Spread a teaspoonful on the bottom of each solid cookie; place coconut topped cookie over lemon filling. Store in the refrigerator. **Yield:** 1-1/2 dozen.

Spice Bars

Brooke Pike • Durham, North Carolina

These bars smell so good while they are baking—the spicy aroma brings everyone to the kitchen in a hurry!

6	tablespoons buttermilk
1/3	cup packed brown sugar
1/4	cup molasses
3	tablespoons butter, melted
1	egg
1	teaspoon vanilla extract
1-1/4	cups all-purpose flour
3/4	teaspoon ground cinnamon, *divided*
1-1/4	teaspoons Chinese Five Spice
1/2	teaspoon baking powder
1/4	teaspoon baking soda
1/4	teaspoon salt
1/3	cup raisins
1	tablespoon confectioners' sugar

In a medium mixing bowl, combine the buttermilk, brown sugar, molasses, butter, egg and vanilla; mix well.

Combine the flour, 1/2 teaspoon cinnamon, Chinese Five Spice, baking powder, baking soda and salt; add to buttermilk mixture and beat until smooth. Stir in raisins.

Pour into a 9-in. square baking pan coated with nonstick cooking spray. Bake at 350° for 18-20 minutes or until a toothpick inserted near the center comes out clean. Cool on a wire rack. Combine confectioners' sugar and remaining cinnamon; sprinkle over bars. **Yield:** 1 dozen.

Cookie Ice Cream Sandwiches

Melissa Stevens • Elk River, Minnesota

Here's an icebox specialty that won't hog all of the room in your freezer. Wrapped individually, the no-bake sandwiches make great, anytime snacks for small homes.

Peanut butter
- 12 oatmeal raisin cookies
- 1 pint vanilla ice cream *or* flavor of your choice

Miniature chocolate chips

Spread peanut butter over the bottom of six cookies. Top with a scoop of ice cream. Top with another cookie; press down gently. Roll sides of ice cream sandwich in chocolate chips. Wrap in plastic wrap. Freeze until serving. **Yield:** 6 servings.

Cookie Ice Cream Sandwiches

Giant Cherry Oatmeal Cookies

Giant Cherry Oatmeal Cookies

Irene McDade • Cumberland, Rhode Island

These colossal cookies taste best when they are golden around the edges and moist and chewy in the center. With a glass of milk, they're polished off in no time by my grandchildren.

1/2	cup shortening
1/2	cup butter, softened
3/4	cup packed brown sugar
1/2	cup sugar
2	eggs
1	teaspoon vanilla extract
2-1/2	cups old-fashioned oats
1-1/3	cups all-purpose flour
2	teaspoons apple pie spice
1/2	teaspoon baking powder
1/4	teaspoon baking soda

1/4	teaspoon salt
1-1/2	cups dried cherries, chopped
1/2	to 1 teaspoon grated orange peel

In a large mixing bowl, cream shortening, butter and sugars. Beat in the eggs and vanilla. Combine the oats, flour, apple pie spice, baking powder, baking soda and salt; gradually add to the creamed mixture. Stir in cherries and orange peel.

Drop by 1/3 cupfuls onto an ungreased baking sheet. Press to form a 4-in. circle. Bake at 375° for 9-12 minutes or until golden brown. Let stand for 1 minute before removing to wire racks to cool. **Yield:** 1 dozen.

Hedgehog Cookies

Sandi Pichon • Slidell, Louisiana

These little snacks are as cute as they can be, and they are delicious, too. A lady from my garden club shared this recipe one Christmas, but they're perfect for any occasion. They're a hit with little kids and grown-ups alike.

1	cup finely chopped walnuts
1/2	cup finely chopped dates
1/2	cup packed brown sugar
1	cup flaked coconut, *divided*
1	egg, lightly beaten

In a bowl, combine the walnuts, dates and brown sugar. Add 1/2 cup coconut and the egg; mix well. Shape into 1-in. balls; roll in remaining coconut. Place on greased baking sheets. Bake at 350° for 12-13 minutes or until lightly browned. Remove to wire racks to cool. **Yield:** about 1-1/2 dozen.

Easy Company Bars

Ruby Lee Hughes • Lynchburg, Virginia

When my husband and I were newlyweds, he had the habit of inviting friends to our house at the spur of the moment for coffee. I had to come up with a recipe both good and quick to fix. After testing these bars a few times, I could make them shortly after the coffee was brewed.

2	tablespoons butter, melted
2	eggs
1	cup packed brown sugar
1	teaspoon vanilla extract
1/3	cup all-purpose flour
1/8	teaspoon baking soda
1	cup finely chopped nuts
Confectioners' sugar	

Coat the bottom of an 8-in. square baking pan with melted butter. In a mixing bowl, beat eggs. Gradually beat in brown sugar and vanilla just until combined. Combine flour and baking soda; stir into the egg mixture. Fold in nuts.

Pour batter evenly over butter; do not stir. Bake at 350° for 25 minutes or until bars test done with a toothpick. Cool slightly; dust with confectioners' sugar and cut. Cool completely. **Yield:** 1-1/2 dozen.

Chocolate Pecan Thumbprints

Jim Ries • Milwaukee, Wisconsin

Every Christmas for over 30 years, I have rolled, cut, shaped and baked batches of cookies. These melt-in-your-mouth morsels, with a dollop of chocolate in the center, are among my favorites.

1/2   **cup plus 1 tablespoon butter, softened,** *divided*
1/4   **cup packed brown sugar**
1   **egg yolk**
1   **teaspoon vanilla extract**
1   **cup all-purpose flour**
1   **egg white, lightly beaten**
3/4   **cup finely chopped pecans**
3/4   **cup semisweet chocolate chips**

In a mixing bowl, cream 1/2 cup butter and brown sugar. Beat in egg yolk and vanilla. Gradually add flour; mix well. Cover and refrigerate for 2 hours or until easy to handle.

Roll dough into 1-in. balls. Dip in egg white, then coat with pecans. Place 2 in. apart on greased baking sheets. Using the end of a wooden spoon handle, make a 1/2-in. indentation in the center of each ball. Bake at 325° for 10 minutes. Press again into indentations with the spoon handle. Bake 10-15 minutes longer or until pecans are golden brown. Remove to wire racks to cool.

In a microwave-safe bowl, heat the chocolate chips and remaining butter until melted; stir until blended and smooth. Spoon into cooked cookies. **Yield:** about 1-1/2 dozen.

Fruity Cookie Tarts

Fruity Cookie Tarts

Beverly Coyde • Gasport, New York

Sliced strawberries, kiwi and whipped topping dress up two prepared cookies in this no-stress recipe. A little melted chocolate makes the delectable dessert fancy enough for special dinners and casual snacks alike.

1/2   **cup whipped topping**
2   **large soft chocolate chips cookies**
1   **kiwifruit, peeled and sliced**
4   **large strawberries, sliced**
1/4   **cup semisweet chocolate chips**
1/2   **teaspoon shortening**

Spread whipped topping over cookies. Top with the kiwi and strawberries. In a microwave or heavy saucepan, melt chocolate chips and shortening; stir until smooth. Drizzle over fruit. Serve immediately. **Yield:** 2 servings.

Quick Elephant Ears

Terry Lynn Ayers • Anderson, Indiana

Our children loved helping make these sweet crunchy treats. We fried flour tortillas for a few seconds in oil, then sprinkled with cinnamon and sugar. I usually did the frying, then had one of the older kids add the coating.

1-1/2   cups sugar
   2   teaspoons ground cinnamon
Oil for frying
  10   flour tortilla (7 inches)

Combine sugar and cinnamon in a shallow bowl or large plate; set aside. In a skillet, heat 1/2 in of oil. Place one tortilla at a time in skillet, cook for 5 seconds; turn and cook 10 seconds longer or until browned. Place in sugar mixture and turn to coat. Serve immediately. **Yield:** 10 servings.

Quick Elephant Ears

Mint Brownie Pie

Karen Hayes • Conneaut Lake, Pennsylvania

When I served slices of this layered treat to my family on St. Patrick's Day, it was an instant success.

  6   tablespoons butter
  2   squares (1 ounce *each*) unsweetened chocolate
  1   cup sugar
  2   eggs, beaten
1/2   teaspoon vanilla extract
1/2   cup all-purpose flour
FILLING:
  1   package (8 ounces) cream cheese, softened
3/4   cup sugar
1/2   teaspoon peppermint extract
Green food coloring, optional
  1   carton (8 ounces) frozen whipped topping, thawed
1/4   cup semisweet chocolate chips, melted
Additional whipped topping and chocolate chips, optional

In a saucepan, melt butter and chocolate. Stir in sugar until well blended. Add eggs and vanilla; mix well. Stir in flour until well blended. Pour into a greased 9-in. springform pan.

Bake at 350° for 18-20 minutes or until a toothpick inserted near the center comes out clean. Cool on a wire rack.

In a mixing bowl, beat cream cheese and sugar until smooth. Add extract and food coloring if desired; mix well. Fold in whipped topping. Spread evenly over brownie layer. Cover and refrigerate for at least 1 hour.

Remove sides of pan just before serving. Melt chocolate chips; drizzle over the top. Garnish with whipped topping and chocolate chips if desired. **Yield:** 8 servings.

Coconut Macaroons

Coconut Macaroons

Nancy Tafoya • Ft. Collins, Colorado

*I keep the ingredients for these easy-to-make cookies in my pantry.
That way I can have a freshly made batch in minutes whenever we feel like it.*

2-1/2   **cups flaked coconut**
1/3   **cup all-purpose flour**
1/8   **teaspoon salt**
2/3   **cup sweetened condensed milk**
1   **teaspoon vanilla extract**

In a bowl, combine the coconut, flour and salt. Add milk and vanilla; mix well (batter will be stiff).

Drop by tablespoonfuls 1 in. apart onto a greased baking sheet. Bake at 350° for 15-20 minutes or until golden brown. Remove to wire racks. **Yield:** 1-1/2 dozen.

COOKIE CLUES

Instead of baking a full-size batch of cookies, consider saving a portion of the dough and freezing it in small balls. When the munchies come calling, bake as many of the frozen dough balls as you'd like.

Fudgy Pecan Tartlets

Maggie Evans • Northville, Michigan

A friend sent me this recipe over 25 years ago. I usually bake a dozen for the holidays, but they are a hit regardless of when I serve them. Everyone loves them!

1/4	cup butter, softened
3	tablespoons cream cheese, softened
1/2	cup all-purpose flour

FILLING:

1	egg yolk
3	tablespoons sugar
1-1/2	teaspoons butter, melted
1-1/2	teaspoons 2% milk
1/2	teaspoon vanilla extract
1/2	cup semisweet chocolate chips, melted and cooled
12	pecan halves

In a small mixing bowl, cream butter and cream cheese until light. Gradually add flour, beating until blended. Roll into 1-in. balls. Press onto the bottom and up the sides of miniature muffin cups coated with nonstick cooking spray.

For filling, in a bowl, combine the egg yolk, sugar, butter, milk and vanilla; gradually stir in melted chocolate. Fill tart shells three-fourths full. Top each with a pecan half.

Bake at 375° for 18-22 minutes or until lightly browned and filling is set. Cool for 10 minutes before removing to a wire rack. **Yield:** 1 dozen.

Dipped Peanut Butter Sandwich Cookies

Jackie Howell • Gordo, Alabama

This is a tempting treat you'll love to try! The recipe is almost too simple to believe as it relies on butter-flavored crackers!

1/2	cup creamy peanut butter
1	sleeve (4 ounces) round butter-flavored crackers
1	cup white, semisweet, *or* milk chocolate chips
1	tablespoon shortening

Spread peanut butter on half of the crackers; top with remaining crackers to make sandwiches. Refrigerate.

In a double boiler over simmering water, melt chocolate chips and shortening, stirring until smooth. Dip sandwiches and place on waxed paper until chocolate hardens. **Yield:** 9 servings.

Dipped Peanut Butter Sandwich Cookies

Coconut Chocolate Chip Cookies

Laura Bankard • Manchester, Maryland

Here is a delicious twist on traditional chocolate chip cookies. They're textured and flavored with coconut, resulting in a cookie that's both crispy and chewy. We think this recipe is a winner.

Coconut Chocolate Chip Cookies

1/2   cup butter, softened
3/4   cup sugar
  1   egg
1/2   teaspoon coconut extract
  1   cup plus 2 tablespoons all-purpose flour
1/2   teaspoon baking soda
1/2   teaspoon salt
  1   cup (6 ounces) semisweet chocolate chips
1/2   cup flaked coconut

In a mixing bowl, cream butter and sugar. Beat in egg and coconut extract; mix well. Combine the flour, baking soda and salt; add to the creamed mixture. Stir in chocolate chips and coconut.

Drop by rounded tablespoonfuls 2 in. apart onto ungreased baking sheets. Bake at 375° for 11-13 minutes or until golden brown. Remove to wire racks to cool. **Yield:** about 1 dozen.

Peanut Butter Kiss Cookies

Dee Davis • Sun City, Arizona

These cookies are great for little tummies, and they keep hungry adults guessing as to how they can be made with only a handful of kitchen staples.

 1   cup peanut butter
 1   cup sugar
 1   egg
 1   teaspoon vanilla extract
24   milk chocolate kisses

In a large mixing bowl, cream peanut butter and sugar. Add the egg and vanilla; beat until blended.

Roll into 1-1/4-in. balls. Place 2 in. apart on ungreased baking sheets. Bake at 350° for 10-12 minutes or until tops are slightly cracked. Immediately press one chocolate kiss into the center of each cookie. Cool for 5 minutes before removing from pans to wire racks. **Yield:** 2 dozen.

Editor's Note: Reduced-fat or generic brands of peanut butter are not recommended for this recipe.

Luscious Lemon Bars

Marina Jines • Enid, Oklahoma

These bars are wonderful as a snack or dessert. But beware...they're habit-forming! The recipe only makes eight bars, and I like to share the extras with a neighbor.

✓ **Uses less fat, sugar or salt. Includes Nutrition Facts or Diabetic Exchanges.**

1/4 **cup butter, softened**
2 **tablespoons confectioners' sugar**
1/2 **cup all-purpose flour**
FILLING:
1 **egg**
1/2 **cup sugar**
2 **tablespoons lemon juice**
1 **tablespoon all-purpose flour**
1/8 **teaspoon baking powder**
1/2 **teaspoon confectioners' sugar**

In a small mixing bowl, cream butter and confectioners' sugar; gradually beat in flour. Press onto the bottom of an ungreased 8-in. x 4-in. x 2-in. loaf pan. Bake at 325° for 14-16 minutes or until set and the edges are lightly browned.

For filling, in a mixing bowl, beat the egg, sugar, lemon juice, flour and baking powder until frothy. Pour over warm crust. Bake for 18-22 minutes or until lightly browned. Cool on a wire rack. Dust with confectioners' sugar. Cut into bars. **Yield:** 8 bars.

Nutrition Facts: One bar equals 149 calories, 6 g fat (4 g saturated fat), 42 mg cholesterol, 70 mg sodium, 22 g carbohydrate, trace fiber, 2 g protein.

Luscious Lemon Bars

Pineapple Almond Bars

Pineapple Almond Bars

Janice Smith • Cynthiana, Kentucky

Oats and almonds are a crunchy complement to the sweet pineapple filling in these yummy almond bars.

☑ **Uses less fat, sugar or salt. Includes Nutrition Facts or Diabetic Exchanges.**

3/4   cup all-purpose flour
3/4   cup quick-cooking oats
1/3   cup packed brown sugar
5   tablespoons cold reduced-fat stick margarine
1/2   teaspoon almond extract
3   tablespoons sliced almonds
1   cup pineapple preserves

In a food processor, combine the flour, oats and brown sugar; cover and process until blended. Add margarine and extract; cover and pulse until crumbly. Remove 1/2 cup crumb mixture to a bowl; stir in sliced almonds.

Press remaining crumb mixture into a 9-in. square baking pan coated with nonstick cooking spray. Spread preserves over crust. Sprinkle with reserved crumb mixture. Bake at 350° for 25-30 minutes or until golden. Cool on a wire rack. **Yield:** 1 dozen.

Nutrition Facts: 1 bar equals 166 calories, 4 g fat (1 g saturated fat), 0 cholesterol, 39 mg sodium, 34 g carbohydrate, 1 g fiber, 2 g protein. **Diabetic Exchanges:** 1 starch, 1 fruit, 1/2 fat.

Dipped Coconut Shortbread

Toni Petroskey • Lorain, Ohio

I usually prepare these impressive shortbread cookies for Valentine's Day, but feel free to bake them up any time of the year.

3/4 cup butter, softened
1/4 cup sugar
2 teaspoons vanilla extract
1-3/4 cups all-purpose flour
1/2 teaspoon baking powder
1 cup flaked coconut
1-1/2 cups semisweet chocolate chips
1 tablespoon shortening

In a mixing bowl, cream butter, sugar and vanilla until light and fluffy. Combine flour and baking powder; gradually add to creamed mixture and mix well. Stir in coconut. Cover and refrigerate for 1 hour or until firm.

On a floured surface, roll out dough to 1/4-in. thickness. Cut with a 2-1/2-in. round cookie cutter. Place 2 in. apart on ungreased baking sheets. Bake at 300° for 20-25 minutes or until edges begin to brown. Cool on wire racks.

In a small saucepan over low heat, melt chocolate chips and shortening. Remove from the heat; dip cookies halfway into chocolate. Place on waxed paper-lined baking sheets until set. **Yield:** about 2 dozen.

Fudgy Saucepan Brownies

Janet Taylor • Mayville, New York

These brownies travel so well that I often bake them in a disposable foil pan for camping. That way, I don't have to worry about lugging a baking pan back home with me.

1/2 cup butter
2 squares (1 ounce *each*) unsweetened chocolate, coarsely chopped
2 eggs, beaten
1 cup sugar
2/3 cup all-purpose flour
1/2 cup chopped nuts
1/2 teaspoon baking powder
1/2 teaspoon vanilla extract
Confectioners' sugar, optional

In a saucepan, combine butter and chocolate. Cook and stir over low heat until the chocolate is melted. Remove from the heat.

Stir in the eggs, sugar, flour, nuts, baking powder and vanilla; mix well. Pour into a greased 8-in. square baking pan. Bake at 350° for 16-20 minutes or until top is set. Cool on a wire rack. Dust with confectioners' sugar if desired. **Yield:** 1 dozen.

Fudgy Saucepan Brownies

Old-Fashioned Cutout Cookies

Elizabeth Turner • Lula, Georgia

These simple cookies are full of the heartwarming flavor you remember as a child. It's hard to eat just one because they're so crisp and buttery. I make them for special occasions and holidays, but they're welcome any time.

- 1/4 cup butter, softened
- 3/4 cup sugar
- 1 egg
- 1 teaspoon milk
- 1/2 teaspoon vanilla extract
- 1-1/2 cups self-rising flour
- Additional sugar

In a small mixing bowl, cream butter and sugar. Beat in the egg, milk and vanilla. Add flour and mix well.

On a lightly floured surface, roll out dough to 1/8-in. thickness. Cut with 3-in. cookie cutters dipped in flour. Sprinkle with additional sugar.

Place 1 in. apart on greased baking sheets. Reroll scraps if desired. Bake at 375° for 7-8 minutes or until edges are lightly browned. Remove to wire racks to cool. **Yield:** about 1-1/2 dozen.

Editor's Note: As a substitute for 1-1/2 cups self-rising flour, place 2-1/4 teaspoons baking powder and 3/4 teaspoon salt in a measuring cup. Add all-purpose flour to measure 1 cup. Combine with an additional 1/2 cup all-purpose flour.

Microwave Oatmeal Bars

Annette Self • Junction City, Ohio

Topped with a layer of chocolate, these hearty oat bars make a nice change of pace from oatmeal cookies. Preparing them in the microwave saves time and doesn't heat up my kitchen.

- 2 cups quick-cooking oats
- 1/2 cup packed brown sugar
- 1/2 cup butter, melted
- 1/4 cup corn syrup
- 1 cup (6 ounces) semisweet chocolate chips

In a bowl, combine oats and brown sugar. Stir in butter and corn syrup. Press into a greased 9-in. square microwave-safe dish. Microwave, uncovered, on high for 2 minutes. Rotate a half turn; microwave 2 minutes longer. Sprinkle with chocolate chips. Microwave at 30% power for 6 minutes or until chips are glossy; spread chocolate evenly over top. Refrigerate 15-20 minutes before cutting. **Yield:** 8-10 servings.

Editor's Note: This recipe was tested with an 850-watt microwave.

Cherry Squares

Mildred Schwartzentruber • Tavistock, Ontario

A scrumptious coconut crust complements cherry pie filling in these quick-to-fix squares. Try them the next time you've invited a friend or two for coffee.

- 1-3/4 cups flaked coconut
- 1/2 cup butter, softened
- 1/2 cup sugar
- 1-1/2 cups all-purpose flour
- 1 can (21 ounces) cherry pie filling

In a mixing bowl, combine first four ingredients. Press half the mixture into the bottom of a greased 9-in. x 9-in. baking pan. Top with the pie filling and sprinkle with remaining crumbs. Bake at 375° for about 40 minutes or until golden brown. **Yield:** 9 servings.

Cream Cheese Swirl Brownies

Heidi Johnson • Worland, Wyoming

I'm a chocolate lover, and this treat has satisfied my cravings many times. The rich chocolate taste of the brownies can't be beat. My family requests them often, and I'm happy to oblige.

✓ **Uses less fat, sugar or salt. Includes Nutrition Facts or Diabetic Exchanges.**

- 3 eggs
- 6 tablespoons reduced-fat stick margarine
- 1 cup sugar, *divided*
- 3 teaspoons vanilla extract
- 1/2 cup all-purpose flour
- 1/4 cup baking cocoa
- 1 package (8 ounces) reduced-fat cream cheese

Separate two eggs, putting each white in a separate bowl (discard yolks or save for another use); set aside. In a small mixing bowl, beat margarine and 3/4 cup sugar until crumbly. Add the whole egg, one egg white and vanilla; mix well. Combine flour and cocoa; add to egg mixture and beat until blended. Pour into a 9-in. square baking pan coated with nonstick cooking spray; set aside.

In a mixing bowl, beat cream cheese and

Cream Cheese Swirl Brownies

remaining sugar until smooth. Beat in the second egg white. Drop by rounded tablespoonfuls over the batter; cut through batter with a knife to swirl. Bake at 350° for 25-30 minutes or until set and edges pull away from sides of pan. Cool on a wire rack. **Yield:** 1 dozen.

Nutrition Facts: 1 brownie equals 167 calories, 7 g fat (3 g saturated fat), 28 mg cholesterol, 108 mg sodium, 23 g carbohydrate, trace fiber, 4 g protein. **Diabetic Exchanges:** 1-1/2 starch, 1 fat.

Editor's Note: This recipe was tested with Parkay Light stick margarine.

Apple Nut Bars

Karen Nelson • Sullivan, Wisconsin

For big apple taste packed into a yummy bar, try these sweets. Best of all, you don't even have to peel the apples.

✓ **Uses less fat, sugar or salt. Includes Nutrition Facts or Diabetic Exchanges.**

- 2 egg whites
- 2/3 cup sugar
- 1/2 teaspoon vanilla extract
- 1/2 cup all-purpose flour
- 1 teaspoon baking powder
- 2 cups chopped unpeeled tart apples
- 1/4 cup chopped pecans

In a bowl, whisk egg whites, sugar and vanilla for about 1-1/2 minutes. Add flour and baking powder; whisk for 1 minute. Fold in the apples and pecans.

Pour into an 8-in. square baking pan coated with nonstick cooking spray. Bake at 350° for 25-30 minutes or until the bars test done. Cool. **Yield:** 1 dozen.

Nutrition Facts: 1 bar equals 73 calories, 2 g fat (0 saturated fat), 0 cholesterol, 50 mg sodium, 14 g carbohydrate, 0 fiber, 1 g protein. **Diabetic Exchange:** 1 starch.

AFTER-DINNER DELIGHTS

Old-fashioned fruit pies...bubbling berry crumbles... piled-high cream puffs. Now it's easier than ever to set dessert on the table without dealing with leftovers. The sweet specialties that follow are sized right for small households, so bake up a tantalizing treat tonight!

Chocolate Chip Coffee Ring p. 292

Crustless Almond Cheesecake p. 305

Glazed Pineapple Sundaes p. 291

Cookie 'n' Almond Parfaits p. 307

Peaches 'n' Cream Dessert
p. 286

Frozen Raspberry Cheesecakes

Vicki Melies • Glenwood, Iowa

With the delectable taste of cheesecake, this frosty, layered dessert serves as an elegant ending to any meal. A church friend originally made a version with lime sherbet. I loved the taste, but this is a fun variation.

1/2   cup crushed shortbread cookies
2   tablespoons butter, melted
3   ounces cream cheese, softened
6   tablespoons sweetened condensed milk
2   tablespoons lemon juice
2/3   cup raspberry sherbet, softened
1/2   cup fresh raspberries

In a small bowl, combine the cookie crumbs and butter. Press onto the bottom of two 4-in. springform pans coated with nonstick cooking spray. Freeze for 10 minutes. In a bowl, combine the cream cheese, milk and lemon juice until blended. Spread the cream cheese mixture over each crust. Freeze for 2 hours or until firm.

Spread sherbet over cream cheese layers; freeze 2 hours longer. Top with raspberries. **Yield:** 2 servings.

Frozen Raspberry Cheesecakes

Peaches 'n' Cream Dessert

Karen Oakes • Wichita, Kansas

This chilled, no-bake treat is wonderful on warm summer evenings and when peaches are ripe. The creamy filling is made with help from marshmallows and your microwave.

2/3   cup graham cracker crumbs
4-1/2   teaspoons sugar
2   tablespoons butter, melted
10   large marshmallows
2   tablespoons orange juice
4-1/2   teaspoons confectioners' sugar
1/2   cup heavy whipping cream
1   cup chopped peeled fresh *or* frozen unsweetened peaches, thawed

Line an 8-in. x 4-in. x 2-in. loaf pan with plastic wrap; coat with nonstick cooking spray. In a small bowl, combine the cracker crumbs, sugar and butter. Reserve 2 tablespoons for topping. Press remaining crumb mixture into prepared pan; set aside.

In a microwave-safe bowl, melt marshmallows with orange juice; stir until smooth. Cool. Whisk in confectioners' sugar until smooth. In a small mixing bowl, beat cream until stiff peaks form. Fold into marshmallow mixture. Fold in peaches.

Pour over crust. Sprinkle with reserved crumb mixture. Cover and refrigerate overnight. Using plastic wrap, lift dessert out of pan; cut into four pieces. **Yield:** 4 servings.

Mocha Cream Puffs

Aimee Kirk • Jacksonville, Alabama

Looking for a special-occasion dessert that's easy to fix? Try these golden puffs with a chocolaty filling. Unlike other cream puff recipes that yield too many to store for long, this one makes only four of the sensational goodies.

1/4   **cup water**
2   **tablespoons butter**
1/4   **cup all-purpose flour**
1/8   **teaspoon salt**
1   **egg**
FILLING:
2/3   **cup heavy whipping cream,** *divided*
3   **tablespoons semisweet chocolate chips**
2   **teaspoons sugar**
Dash salt
1/2   **teaspoon vanilla extract**
1/2   **teaspoon instant coffee granules**
Confectioners' sugar

In a small saucepan over medium heat, bring water and butter to a boil. Add flour and salt all at once; stir until a smooth ball forms. Remove from the heat; let stand for 5 minutes.

Add egg; beat until smooth. Drop batter into four mounds 3 in. apart on a greased baking sheet. Bake at 425° for 20-25 minutes or until golden brown. Remove puffs to a wire rack. Immediately cut a slit in each for steam to escape; cool.

For the filling, combine 3 tablespoons cream, the chocolate chips, sugar and salt in a small saucepan. Cook over low heat until the chips are melted; stir until blended. Remove from the heat; gradually stir in vanilla, coffee and remaining cream.

Transfer to a small mixing bowl. Refrigerate until chilled. Just before serving, split puffs and remove soft dough. Beat filling until stiff. Fill cream puffs; replace tops. Dust with confectioners' sugar. **Yield:** 4 cream puffs.

Mocha Cream Puffs

Easy Boston Cream Cake

Taste of Home Test Kitchen • Greendale, Wisconsin

Why make a Boston cream pie from scratch when this cake version is so simple and perfectly sized? Preparing the pudding with half-and-half cream instead of milk gives the dessert an added richness that's hard to beat.

1-1/2	cups cold half-and-half cream
1	package (3.4 ounces) instant vanilla pudding mix
1	loaf (10-3/4 ounces) frozen pound cake, thawed
3/4	cup confectioners' sugar
2	tablespoons baking cocoa
4	to 5 teaspoons hot water

In a bowl, whisk together cream and pudding mix; let stand for 5 minutes.

Split cake into three horizontal layers. Place bottom layer on a serving plate; top with half of the pudding. Repeat layers. Top with third cake layer. In a small bowl, combine the confectioners' sugar, cocoa and enough water to reach a spreading consistency. Spread over top of cake, letting glaze drizzle down sides. **Yield:** 4-6 servings.

Easy Boston Cream Cake

Plum Kuchen

Gretchen Berendt • Carroll Valley, Pennsylvania

My mother made plum kuchen but never followed a recipe. This version tastes a lot like hers.

2	eggs
1/3	cup milk
3	tablespoons butter, melted
1	cup all-purpose flour
1/2	cup plus 2 tablespoons sugar, *divided*
1	teaspoon baking powder
1-1/4	teaspoons ground cinnamon, *divided*
1/4	teaspoon salt
1/4	teaspoon ground nutmeg
6	medium plums, pitted and halved

Whipped cream and additional ground nutmeg, optional

In a mixing bowl, beat the eggs, milk and butter. Combine the flour, 1/2 cup sugar, baking powder, 3/4 teaspoon cinnamon, salt and nutmeg; add to the egg mixture and beat just until combined.

Pour into a greased 9-in. round baking pan. Place plums cut side up over batter. Combine remaining sugar and cinnamon; sprinkle over the top. Bake at 375° for 20-25 minutes or until a toothpick inserted near the center comes out clean. Cool for 10 minutes before removing from pan to a wire rack to cool completely. Serve with whipped cream and sprinkle with nutmeg if desired. **Yield:** 6 servings.

Minty Baked Alaska

Brenda Mast • Clearwater, Florida

I've made this dessert on a few special occasions. My husband just loves it. It's so simple, but it looks and tastes like you spent all day in the kitchen. Crushed peppermint candy adds a special taste and decorative touch that never fail to impress.

2	egg whites
1/4	cup sugar
1/4	teaspoon cream of tartar
1/4	teaspoon vanilla extract

Dash salt

1	tablespoon crushed peppermint candy
2	individual round sponge cakes
2/3	cup mint chocolate chip ice cream

In a double boiler, combine the egg whites, sugar and cream of tartar; with a portable mixer, beat on low speed for 1 minute. Continue beating over low heat until the mixture reaches 160°, about 12 minutes. Remove from the heat.

Add vanilla and salt; beat until stiff peaks form, about 2 minutes. Fold in peppermint candy.

Place sponge cakes on an ungreased foil-lined baking sheet; top each with 1/3 cup ice cream. Immediately spread meringue over ice cream and cake, sealing meringue to the foil. Broil 8 in. from the heat for 3-5 minutes or until lightly browned. Serve immediately. **Yield:** 2 servings.

Easy Trifle for Two

Betty Kibbe • Albuquerque, New Mexico

Since there are just the two of us in the house now, I need to "keep it small" where my cooking is concerned. This trifle helps me do just that. The vanilla wafers work perfectly for small-portion desserts.

16	vanilla wafers
2	tablespoons raspberry preserves
1/2	cup prepared vanilla pudding
2	tablespoons flaked coconut, toasted
1/3	cup prepared tapioca pudding

Spread the flat side of 12 wafers with 1/2 teaspoon raspberry preserves each. Crumble remaining wafers and set aside.

Place five wafers each around the edges of two 4- to 6-oz. dishes, preserves side facing in. Place one wafer in the bottom of each dish, preserves side up. Spoon vanilla pudding in the center; sprinkle with wafer crumbs and half of the coconut. Top with tapioca pudding and remaining coconut. Cover and refrigerate for at least 3 hours. **Yield:** 2 servings.

Easy Trifle for Two

Mini Apple Pie

Mini Apple Pie

Edna Hoffman • Hebron, Indiana

I like to try new recipes when apples are in season, and this one was a keeper. Golden Delicious apples are our favorites, so I bake up this little pie regularly.

1/4 cup golden raisins
1/3 cup apple juice
2 large Golden Delicious apples (about 1 pound), peeled and sliced
2 tablespoons sugar
2 tablespoons brown sugar
1 tablespoon all-purpose flour
1/4 teaspoon ground cinnamon
Pastry for single-crust pie (9 inches)

In a saucepan over medium heat, cook raisins in apple juice for 5 minutes. Add apples; cook, uncovered, for 8-10 minutes or until tender. Remove from the heat; cool.

Combine the sugars, flour and cinnamon; add to apple mixture. On a floured surface, roll out half of the pastry to fit a 20-oz. baking dish. Place pastry in dish; trim to edge of dish. Add filling.

Roll out the remaining pastry to fit top of pie; place over filling. Trim, seal and flute edges. Cut slits in pastry. Bake at 400° for 35-40 minutes or until golden brown and bubbly. Cool on a wire rack. **Yield:** 2 servings.

Candy Bar Ice Cream

Myra Innes • Auburn, Kansas

Three items are all you need to create this frozen delight for two. It's so easy, yet it tastes just like it came from a real ice cream parlor.

2-1/2 cups vanilla ice cream, softened
1 tablespoon fudge ice cream topping
2 Snickers candy bars (2.07 ounces *each*), chopped

In a blender, combine the ice cream and fudge topping; cover and process until smooth. Stir in the candy bars.

Transfer to a freezer container; freeze for 4 hours or until firm. May be frozen for up to 2 months. **Yield:** 2 servings.

Glazed Pineapple Sundaes

Dawn Czysz • New Berlin, Wisconsin

Topped with a mildly spiced sauce, these frozen-yogurt sundaes are always a much-anticipated treat!

✓ **Uses less fat, sugar or salt. Includes Nutrition Facts or Diabetic Exchanges.**

2 fresh pineapple slices (1/2 inch thick)
1 tablespoon 100% apricot spreadable fruit
Sugar substitute equivalent to 1 teaspoon sugar
Dash ground cinnamon
1 cup reduced-fat frozen vanilla yogurt

Place pineapple slices on a baking sheet; brush with spreadable fruit. Broil 4 in. from the heat for 5-6 minutes or until bubbly. Combine the sugar substitute and cinnamon; sprinkle over pineapple. Top with frozen yogurt. **Yield:** 2 servings.

Nutrition Facts: 1 sundae equals 137 calories, 1 g fat (1 g saturated fat), 5 mg cholesterol, 59 mg sodium, 27 g carbohydrate, trace fiber, 5 g protein. **Diabetic Exchanges:** 1 starch, 1 fruit.

Editor's Note: This recipe was tested with Splenda No Calorie Sweetener.

Chocolate Chip Coffee Ring

Anne Betts • Kalamazoo, Michigan

My husband often requests this moist and rich cake. It's great when sharing coffee with a friend or two or when hosting a small dinner party.

1/4 cup butter, softened
1/2 cup sugar
1 egg
1/2 cup sour cream
1/2 teaspoon vanilla extract
1 cup all-purpose flour
1/2 teaspoon baking powder
1/2 teaspoon baking soda
1/4 teaspoon salt
1/2 cup semisweet chocolate chips

TOPPING:
1/4 cup all-purpose flour
1/4 cup packed brown sugar
3/4 teaspoon baking cocoa
1/4 cup cold butter
1/4 cup chopped pecans

GLAZE:
1/2 cup confectioners' sugar
1 to 2 teaspoons milk

In a small mixing bowl, cream butter and sugar. Beat in egg. Beat in sour cream and vanilla. Combine the flour, baking powder, baking soda and salt; add to creamed mixture. Stir in chocolate chips. Pour into an 8-in. fluted tube pan coated with nonstick cooking spray.

For topping, combine the flour, brown sugar and cocoa in a bowl. Cut in butter until mixture resembles coarse crumbs. Stir in pecans; sprinkle over batter. Bake at 350° for 35-40 minutes or until a toothpick inserted near the center comes out clean. Cool for 15 minutes before removing from pan to a wire rack to cool completely.

In a small bowl, combine glaze ingredients until smooth. Drizzle over cake. **Yield:** 8 servings.

Quick Ambrosia

Quick Ambrosia

Eleanor Lock • Escondido, California

After raising four sons, it wasn't easy to scale down my cooking habits, so I ventured into some new recipes that didn't take a lot of time to prepare. Loaded with fruit, this dessert has appeared after many of our meals.

1/4 cup flaked coconut, toasted
2 tablespoons confectioners' sugar
1 orange, peeled and sectioned
1 firm banana, sliced
1/4 cup orange juice
Maraschino cherries, optional

Combine coconut and confectioners' sugar. Place orange sections and banana slices in two small bowls; pour orange juice over all. Sprinkle with coconut mixture. Chill or serve. Garnish with cherries if desired. **Yield:** 2 servings.

Coconut Creme Brulee

Coconut Creme Brulee

Gloria Jabaut • Red Bluff, California

There's always time for dessert, and this elegant, quick-to-fix treat is one I turn to regularly.
After one bite, you may make it a favorite as well.

☑ **Uses less fat, sugar or salt. Includes Nutrition Facts or Diabetic Exchanges.**

2 **refrigerated vanilla pudding snack cups (4 ounces *each*)**

2 **tablespoons brown sugar**

2 **tablespoons flaked coconut**

2 **teaspoons butter, melted**

Spoon pudding into two 6-oz. ramekins or custard cups. Combine the brown sugar, coconut and butter; sprinkle over pudding. Broil 5-6 in. from the heat for 2-3 minutes or until topping is bubbly and golden brown. Serve warm. **Yield:** 2 servings.

Nutrition Facts: One serving (prepared with fat-free pudding and reduced-fat butter) equals 189 calories, 4 g fat (3 g saturated fat), 9 mg cholesterol, 255 mg sodium, 36 g carbohydrate, trace fiber, 3 g protein.

PIE POINTER

Lucille Jackson of Wyoming, Illinois loves homemade pie but can't finish one by herself. "I slice the pie, leaving a gap between slices," she writes. "Then, I cover and freeze the dessert. The frozen servings are easy to remove one at a time and heat nicely in the microwave."

Strawberry Cheesecake Parfaits

Melanie Qualls • Marysville, Washington

A friend brought these pretty parfaits to a potluck, and I just had to have the recipe. You can substitute your favorite fresh fruit, such as peaches or raspberries.

2	cups sliced fresh strawberries
1	tablespoon sugar
1	package (3 ounces) cream cheese, softened
1/3	cup plus 1 teaspoon confectioners' sugar, *divided*
1/4	cup sour cream
1/2	teaspoon vanilla extract, *divided*
1/8	teaspoon almond extract
1/4	cup heavy whipping cream
2-1/2	cups angel food cake cubes
2	whole fresh strawberries, halved

In a small bowl, combine sliced strawberries and sugar; set aside. In a small mixing bowl, beat the cream cheese and 1/3 cup confectioners' sugar. Add the sour cream, 1/4 teaspoon vanilla and almond extract.

In a small mixing bowl, beat cream until it begins to thicken. Add the remaining confectioners' sugar and vanilla; beat until soft peaks form. Fold into cream cheese mixture.

In two parfait glasses, layer a fourth of the sliced strawberry mixture, cake cubes and cream mixture. Repeat layers. Cover and refrigerate for at least 1 hour. Top each parfait with two strawberry halves. **Yield:** 2 servings.

Cookie Dessert

June Smith • Byron Center, Michigan

This no-bake specialty tastes so good that no one believes how quickly it comes together. The recipe calls for just five items and can easily be doubled or tripled...just use a larger pan.

36	crisp chocolate chip cookies
3/4	cup milk
1	carton (12 ounces) frozen whipped topping, thawed
2	tablespoons chocolate syrup
2	tablespoons chopped pecans

Quickly dip cookies completely in milk. Place 12 of the cookies in an ungreased 8-in. square dish; top with a third of the whipped topping. Repeat layers twice. Cover and refrigerate overnight.

Drizzle with chocolate syrup; sprinkle with nuts. **Yield:** 9 servings.

Editor's Note: This recipe was tested with Chips Ahoy chocolate chip cookies.

Pound Cake S'mores

Grace Yaskovic • Branchville, New Jersey

You don't have to start a campfire to indulge in a classic S'more. Here's a take on the sweet sandwiches that surely satisfies the sweet tooth.

2	slices pound cake
1	tablespoon miniature marshmallows
1	tablespoon miniature semisweet chocolate chips
	Caramel ice cream topping and chopped nuts, optional

Place cake slices on a baking sheet. Sprinkle with marshmallows and chocolate chips. Broil 4-6 in. from the heat for 1-2 minutes or until marshmallows are lightly browned.

Transfer to a serving plate. Drizzle with caramel topping and sprinkle with nuts if desired. **Yield:** 1 serving.

Strawberry Cheesecake Parfaits

Little Lemon Meringue Pies

Kathy Zielicke • Fond du Lac, Wisconsin

Since our sons went off to college, I'm back to cooking for just the two of us. The recipe for these cute lemon pies is supposed to serve two. They're so scrumptious, however, they sometimes only serve one!

1/3	cup all-purpose flour
1/8	teaspoon salt
1	tablespoon shortening
1	tablespoon cold butter
1	teaspoon cold water

FILLING:

1/3	cup sugar
1	tablespoon cornstarch
1/8	teaspoon salt
1/2	cup cold water
1	egg yolk, beaten
2	tablespoons lemon juice
1	tablespoon butter

MERINGUE:

1	egg white
1/8	teaspoon cream of tartar
2	tablespoons sugar

In a bowl, combine flour and salt; cut in shortening and butter until crumbly. Gradually add water, tossing with a fork until dough forms a ball. Divide in half. Roll each portion into a 5-in. circle. Transfer to two 10-oz. custard cups. Press dough 1-1/8 in. up sides of cups. Place on a baking sheet. Bake at 425° for 7-10 minutes or until golden brown.

In a saucepan, combine sugar, cornstarch and salt. Gradually stir in cold water until smooth. Cook and stir over medium heat until thickened and bubbly. Reduce heat; cook and stir 2 minutes more. Remove from the heat.

Stir half of hot filling into egg yolk; return all to the pan. Bring to a gentle boil; cook and stir for 2 minutes. Remove from the heat; stir in lemon juice and butter.

Pour into pastry shells. In a small mixing bowl, beat egg white and cream of tartar on medium speed until soft peaks form. Spread evenly over hot filling, sealing edges to crust. Bake at 350° for 15-20 minutes or until meringue is golden brown. Cool on a wire rack for 1 hour; refrigerate for at least 3 hours before serving. **Yield:** 2 servings.

Coffee Lover's Dessert

Coffee Lover's Dessert

Louise Stuhr • Chatham, New Jersey

This recipe caught my mother's eye back in 1925 after it appeared in a local newspaper. It quickly became my brothers' and my favorite dessert, and I still look forward to it today.

10	to 12 large marshmallows
1/2	cup brewed coffee
1/2	cup heavy whipping cream, whipped

In a heavy saucepan, combine marshmallows and coffee; cook and stir over low heat until melted. Remove from the heat and cool to room temperature.

Fold in whipped cream. Spoon into individual dessert dishes. Chill. **Yield:** 2 servings.

Apricot Berry Shortcake

Marion Lowery • Medford, Oregon

Here is a fun and convenient alternative to traditional strawberry shortcake. It's a delightful dessert that's easy to assemble using purchased sponge cakes.

- 1 cup fresh raspberries *and/or* blackberries
- 1 tablespoon sugar

Dash ground nutmeg

- 1/4 cup apricot jam
- 1 teaspoon butter

Dash salt

- 2 individual round sponge cakes

Whipped cream

In a bowl, combine the berries, sugar and nutmeg. Cover and refrigerate for 1 hour.

In a saucepan, heat jam, butter and salt on low until butter is melted. In a microwave, warm the sponge cakes on high for 20 seconds; place on serving plates. Top with berry mixture; drizzle with apricot sauce. Top with a dollop of whipped cream. **Yield:** 2 servings.

Apricot Berry Shortcake

Comforting Banana Pudding

Opal Hinson • Lubbock, Texas

Homemade pudding is always a treat...especially when it's dressed up with vanilla wafers and fresh fruit. Layered in pretty glasses or bowls, the dessert makes for an impressive presentation, too.

- 1 cup sugar
- 1 tablespoon cornstarch
- 1-1/2 cups milk
- 1 egg, beaten
- 1/4 teaspoon vanilla extract
- 8 vanilla wafers
- 1 large firm banana, sliced

In a saucepan, combine sugar and cornstarch; gradually stir in milk until smooth. Cook and stir over medium-high heat until thickened and bubbly. Reduce heat; cook and stir 2 minutes longer. Remove from the heat.

Stir 1 cup hot mixture into egg; return all to the pan and bring to a gentle boil. Remove from the heat; stir in vanilla.

Refrigerate for 15 minutes. Layer vanilla wafers and banana slices in parfait glasses or bowls. Top with pudding. **Yield:** 2 servings.

Sweetheart Brownie Sundae

Sweetheart Brownie Sundae

Dottie Miller • Jonesborough, Tennessee

I make this special treat for my family whenever there's a birthday or anniversary. Even without a special occasion, it caps off meals with a festive flair. I especially like to prepare the dessert in a heart shape for Valentine's Day.

1/4 cup butter

2 squares (1 ounce *each*) semisweet chocolate

1 egg

1/2 cup packed brown sugar

1 teaspoon vanilla extract

1/4 teaspoon salt

1/4 cup all-purpose flour

1 cup vanilla ice cream, softened

CHOCOLATE SAUCE:

1 cup water

1/2 cup baking cocoa

1/4 cup sugar

2 tablespoons butter

Confectioners' sugar

In a microwave or double boiler, melt butter and chocolate; cool for 10 minutes. In a mixing bowl, beat egg, brown sugar, vanilla and salt. Stir in chocolate mixture. Add flour; mix well.

Line an 8-in. square baking pan with foil and grease the foil. Spread batter evenly into pan (batter will be thin). Bake at 350° for 15 minutes or until a toothpick inserted near the center comes out clean. Cool completely on a wire rack. Cover and refrigerate until firm.

Using a 3-1/2-in. x 3-1/2-in. heart pattern or heart-shaped cookie cutter, mark four hearts on the surface of brownies; cut with a knife. Spread ice cream on two hearts; top each with a second heart. Wrap in plastic wrap; freeze in a single layer overnight.

For chocolate sauce, combine water, cocoa and sugar in a saucepan; bring to a boil over medium heat, stirring constantly. Reduce heat; simmer for 2-3 minutes or until thickened. Remove from the heat; stir in butter until melted.

To serve, dust brownie hearts with confectioners' sugar and drizzle with warm chocolate sauce. Store any leftover sauce in the refrigerator. **Yield:** 2 servings.

Giant Pineapple Turnover

Carolyn Kyzer • Alexander, Arkansas

Fresh apple, canned pineapple and plump raisins make this comforting turnover a surefire hit. Made from refrigerated pie pastry, the crust is as quick as it is tasty.

1   sheet refrigerated pie pastry
1   medium tart apple, peeled and coarsely chopped
1   can (8 ounces) crushed pineapple, well drained
3/4 cup sugar
1/3 cup finely chopped celery
1/3 cup raisins
1/3 cup chopped walnuts
1/4 cup all-purpose flour
Ice cream, optional

Unfold pastry and place on a baking sheet. In a bowl, combine the apple, pineapple, sugar, celery, raisins, walnuts and flour; toss gently. Spoon filling onto half of crust, leaving 1 in. around edge. Fold pastry over filling and seal edge well. Cut slit in top.

Bake at 400° for 30-35 minutes or until crust is golden brown and filling is bubbly. Cool on a wire rack. Cut into wedges. Serve with ice cream if desired. **Yield:** 4 servings.

Chocolate Cappuccino Mousse

Katie Sloan • Charlotte, North Carolina

This decadent dessert is sure to please your favorite chocolate or coffee lover. It's easy to make, and it's great for two-person households.

2   teaspoons instant coffee granules
1   teaspoon hot water
2/3 cup sweetened condensed milk
1/4 cup baking cocoa
4-1/2 teaspoons butter
1   cup heavy whipping cream
1/2 teaspoon ground cinnamon
Additional whipped cream, baking cocoa and ground cinnamon *or* cinnamon sticks, optional

In a small saucepan, dissolve coffee in hot water. Stir in the milk, cocoa and butter. Cook and stir over medium-low heat until blended. Remove from the heat.

Transfer to a large bowl; cool completely. In a small mixing bowl, beat cream and cinnamon until stiff peaks form. Fold a fourth of the whipped cream mixture into cocoa mixture, then fold in the remaining whipped cream mixture. Spoon into dessert dishes. Top with additional whipped cream, cocoa and cinnamon if desired. **Yield:** 2 servings.

Chocolate Cappuccino Mousse

Individual Apple Crisp

Lethea Weber • Newport, Arkansas

You don't have to skip dessert if you're cooking for one. Hot and bubbling from the oven, this satisfying crisp is a great way to treat yourself.

Individual Apple Crisp

- 1 small apple, peeled and sliced
- 1 tablespoon all-purpose flour
- 1 tablespoon brown sugar
- 1 tablespoon quick-cooking oats
- 1/8 teaspoon ground cinnamon

Dash ground nutmeg
Dash salt

- 1 tablespoon cold butter

Half-and-half cream *or* ice cream, optional

Place apple in a small greased baking dish. In a small bowl, combine the dry ingredients; cut in butter until crumbly. Sprinkle over apple. Bake, uncovered, at 375° for 30-35 minutes or until apple is tender. Serve warm with cream or ice cream if desired. **Yield:** 1 serving.

Strawberry Peach Melba

Marion Karlin • Waterloo, Iowa

I get oohs and aahs when setting out this cool, fruity dessert. It combines my three all-time favorites—peaches, strawberries and vanilla ice cream. It's so simple, I can assemble it for friends after everyone finishes the main course.

- 3 cups fresh *or* frozen whole strawberries
- 1 cup confectioners' sugar
- 1/4 cup water
- 1 teaspoon lemon juice
- 2 teaspoons cornstarch
- 1 tablespoon cold water
- 1 teaspoon vanilla extract
- 4 scoops vanilla ice cream
- 1 can (15 ounces) sliced peaches, drained

Whipped topping

In a large saucepan, mash strawberries; add sugar, water and lemon juice. Cook and stir until mixture comes to a boil. Combine the cornstarch and cold water until smooth; stir into the strawberry mixture. Cook and stir for 2 minutes or until thickened and bubbly. Remove from the heat; stir in vanilla. Strain to remove the pulp.

Place the pan in an ice-water bath to cool, stirring occasionally. Serve strawberry sauce over ice cream; top with peaches and whipped topping. **Yield:** 4 servings.

Chocolate Layer Cake

Verna Mae Floyd • Highlands, Texas

You can "halve" your cake and eat it, too, with this chocolaty classic. My mother came up with the dessert after we kids left the nest. Today, I enjoy this tempting, two-layer treat with my husband.

1/4 cup shortening
1 cup sugar
1 egg
1/2 teaspoon vanilla extract
1 cup all-purpose flour
1/4 cup baking cocoa
1 teaspoon baking powder
1 teaspoon baking soda
1/4 teaspoon salt
3/4 cup milk
FROSTING:
1/2 cup butter, softened
2-1/2 cups confectioners' sugar
1/2 cup baking cocoa
1 teaspoon vanilla extract
2 to 3 tablespoons hot water

In a mixing bowl, beat shortening and sugar. Beat in egg and vanilla. Combine the flour, cocoa, baking powder, baking soda and salt; add to creamed mixture alternately with milk.

Pour into a greased and floured 9-in. round baking pan. Bake at 350° for 30-35 minutes or until a toothpick inserted near the center comes out clean. Cool in pan for 10 minutes before removing to a wire rack to cool completely.

For frosting, in a small mixing bowl, cream butter. Gradually beat in the confectioners' sugar, cocoa, vanilla and enough water to achieve spreading consistency.

To assemble, cut cake in half. Place one half on a serving plate. Spread with 1/2 cup frosting. Top with remaining cake. Spread remaining frosting over top and rounded edge of cake. **Yield:** 4 servings.

Chocolate Layer Cake

Gingerbread Cake

Shannon Sides • Selma, Alabama

I drizzle a basic orange sauce over homemade gingerbread for this old-fashioned dessert.
I suggest cutting just the number of squares needed and freezing the rest.

1/2   cup butter-flavored shortening
1/3   cup sugar
  1   cup molasses
3/4   cup water
  1   egg
2-1/3   cups all-purpose flour
  1   teaspoon baking soda
  1   teaspoon ground ginger
  1   teaspoon ground cinnamon
3/4   teaspoon salt
ORANGE SAUCE:
  1   cup confectioners' sugar
  2   tablespoons orange juice
1/2   teaspoon grated orange peel

In a large mixing bowl, cream shortening and sugar. Add the molasses, water and egg. Combine the flour, baking soda, ginger, cinnamon and salt; add to creamed mixture and beat until combined.

Pour into a greased 15-in. x 10-in. x 1-in. baking pan. Bake at 350° for 18-22 minutes or until a toothpick inserted near the center comes out clean. Cool on a wire rack.

In a bowl, combine the sauce ingredients. Serve with cake. **Yield:** 4 servings.

Frosty Summer Dessert

Frosty Summer Dessert

Nicole Bresee • Westport, Ontario

A creamy, fruit-flavored filling tops a chocolate crumb crust in this frozen, after-dinner delight. No baking is involved, and it's oh-so refreshing.

3/4   cup crushed chocolate wafers
  3   tablespoons butter
  4   ounces cream cheese, softened
3/4   cup apple-raspberry juice concentrate
  1   tablespoon confectioners' sugar
  1   cup whipped topping

In a small bowl, combine wafer crumbs and butter. Press onto the bottom of a 6-in. springform pan coated with nonstick cooking spray; set aside.

In a small mixing bowl, beat the cream cheese, juice concentrate and confectioners' sugar until smooth. Fold in whipped topping. Pour over crust. Cover and freeze for 4 hours or until firm. Remove from the freezer 5-10 minutes before serving. **Yield:** 4 servings.

Strawberries 'n' Cream Tarts

Karen Tysdal • Duluth, Minnesota

These pretty tartlets are a yummy dinner conclusion when fresh berries are in season. I always receive rave reviews whenever I make them.

✓ **Uses less fat, sugar or salt. Includes Nutrition Facts or Diabetic Exchanges.**

- 1 package (3 ounces) cream cheese, softened
- 5 teaspoons sugar
- 1/8 teaspoon almond extract
- 1/4 cup heavy whipping cream, whipped
- 1 cup sliced fresh strawberries
- 3 individual graham cracker tart shells

In a mixing bowl, beat cream cheese until fluffy. Beat in sugar and almond extract. Fold in whipped cream; fold in strawberries. Spoon into tart shells. Refrigerate until serving. **Yield:** 3 servings.

Nutrition Facts: 1 tart (prepared with reduced-fat cream cheese, sugar substitute and 1/2 cup fat-free whipped topping) equals 225 calories, 12 g fat (5 g saturated fat), 20 mg cholesterol, 270 mg sodium, 24 g carbohydrate, 2 g fiber, 4 g protein.

Strawberries 'n' Cream Tarts

Fudgy Peanut Butter Cake

Bonnie Evans • Norcross, Georgia

I clipped this slow-cooker recipe from a newspaper years ago. The house smells great while it's simmering. My husband and son enjoy this warm, decadent dessert with vanilla ice cream and nuts on top.

- 3/4 cup sugar, *divided*
- 1/2 cup all-purpose flour
- 3/4 teaspoon baking powder
- 1/3 cup milk
- 1/4 cup peanut butter
- 1 tablespoon vegetable oil
- 1/2 teaspoon vanilla extract
- 2 tablespoons baking cocoa
- 1 cup boiling water

Vanilla ice cream

In a bowl, combine 1/4 cup sugar, flour and baking powder. In another bowl, combine the milk, peanut butter, oil and vanilla; stir into dry ingredients just until combined. Spread evenly into a slow cooker coated with nonstick cooking spray.

In a bowl, combine the cocoa and remaining sugar; stir in boiling water. Pour into slow cooker (do not stir). Cover and cook on high for 1-1/2 to 2 hours or until a toothpick inserted near the center of cake comes out clean. Serve warm with ice cream. **Yield:** 4 servings.

Cinnamon
Mocha Cupcakes

Cinnamon Mocha Cupcakes

Edna Hoffman • Hebron, Indiana

Like to end a meal with a little sweet? My mocha cupcakes might do the trick. The recipe only makes eight of the treats, but you can freeze whatever is leftover if you wish.

1/4	cup butter, softened
2/3	cup sugar
1	egg
1/2	teaspoon vanilla extract
3/4	cup plus 2 tablespoons all-purpose flour
1/4	cup baking cocoa
1/2	teaspoon baking soda
1/2	teaspoon salt
1/4	teaspoon baking powder
1/4	teaspoon ground cinnamon
1/4	cup strong brewed coffee, room temperature
3	tablespoons buttermilk
1	cup chocolate frosting
3/4	teaspoon instant coffee granules
1	teaspoon hot water

In a small mixing bowl, cream the butter and sugar. Beat in egg and vanilla. Combine the flour, cocoa, baking soda, salt, baking powder and cinnamon; add to creamed mixture alternately with coffee and buttermilk.

Coat muffin cups with nonstick cooking spray or use paper liners; fill half full with batter. Bake at 350° for 18-20 minutes or until a toothpick comes out clean. Cool for 5 minutes before removing from pan to a wire rack to cool completely.

Place the frosting in a bowl. Dissolve coffee granules in hot water; stir into frosting until smooth. Frost cupcakes. **Yield:** 8 cupcakes.

Crustless Almond Cheesecake

Molly Seidel • Edgewood, New Mexico

The scrumptious dessert is a tried-and-true favorite. My mother made it for years. It's creamy and satisfying, and folks always ask for the recipe.

✓ Uses less fat, sugar or salt. Includes Nutrition Facts or Diabetic Exchanges.

1	package (8 ounces) cream cheese, softened
1/3	cup sugar
1	egg
1/8	teaspoon almond extract

TOPPING:

1/2	cup sour cream
4	teaspoons sugar
1/2	teaspoon vanilla extract

Assorted fresh fruit, optional

In a small mixing bowl, beat the cream cheese and sugar for 2 minutes or until smooth. Add the egg and almond extract; beat on low speed just until combined.

Pour into a 7-in. pie plate coated with nonstick cooking spray. Bake at 350° for 25 minutes. Remove to a wire rack; cool for 5 minutes.

Combine topping ingredients; spread over cream cheese filling. Bake 7-8 minutes longer or until set. Cool on a wire rack for 10 minutes. Carefully run a knife around edge of pan to loosen; refrigerate for at least 1 hour before serving. Serve with assorted fruit if desired. **Yield:** 4 servings.

Nutrition Facts: One piece (prepared with reduced-fat cream cheese and reduced-fat sour cream) equals 281 calories, 16 g fat (10 g saturated fat), 103 mg cholesterol, 276 mg sodium, 25 g carbohydrate, 0 fiber, 10 g protein.

Cranberry Pear Cobblers

Cranberry Pear Cobblers

Taste of Home Test Kitchen • Greendale, Wisconsin

These individual cranberry-and-pear goodies feature a hint of ginger and cinnamon. Served warm and topped with ice cream, their home-style flavor is sure to satisfy anyone's craving.

2	small pears, peeled and cut into 3/4-inch pieces
1/4	cup dried cranberries
3	tablespoons sugar
1-1/2	teaspoons all-purpose flour
1	teaspoon grated fresh gingerroot
1/4	teaspoon ground cinnamon
1	tablespoon butter

TOPPING:

3	tablespoons sugar
1	teaspoon grated fresh gingerroot
1/2	cup all-purpose flour
1/4	teaspoon baking soda
1/8	teaspoon salt
8	teaspoons cold butter
1/4	cup buttermilk

In a bowl, combine the first six ingredients. Spoon into two 10-oz. custard cups coated with nonstick cooking spray. Dot with butter. Bake at 350° for 15-20 minutes or until hot and bubbly.

For topping, combine sugar and ginger in a blender; cover and process until crumbly. Set aside 1-1/2 teaspoons of the mixture. Add flour, baking soda and salt to the blender; cover and process for 20 seconds or until combined. Add butter; process until mixture resembles coarse crumbs.

Transfer to a small bowl; stir in buttermilk. Drop by rounded tablespoonfuls onto hot fruit filling; sprinkle with reserved sugar mixture. Bake for 30-35 minutes or until topping is golden brown. Serve warm. **Yield:** 2 servings.

Cookie 'n' Almond Parfaits

Carol Hagerty • Upper Arlington, Ohio

These lovely parfaits are simply delectable. The recipe is perfect for two, but you can easily assemble more if you're entertaining company.

25   miniature cream-filled chocolate sandwich cookies
1   egg white
1/3   cup sugar
2   teaspoons water
1/8   teaspoon cream of tartar
1/4   teaspoon almond extract
Dash salt
1/3   cup heavy whipping cream
2   tablespoons slivered almonds, toasted

Set aside four cookies for garnish. Crush the remaining cookies; set aside. In a heavy saucepan, combine the egg white, sugar, water and cream of tartar. With a portable mixer, beat on low speed for 1 minute. Beat over low heat until egg mixture reaches 160°, about 12 minutes. Remove from the heat.

Add almond extract and salt; beat until stiff peaks form. In a mixing bowl, beat cream until stiff peaks form; fold into meringue mixture. Spoon half the cookie crumbs into two parfait glasses; top with half of filling. Repeat layers. Refrigerate for 1-2 hours or until set. Sprinkle with almonds and garnish with reserved cookies. **Yield:** 2 servings.

Cinnamon Apple Wraps

Linda Nealley • Newburgh, Maine

I love to bake, so I trimmed down the recipe for this homey apple dessert to serve just two of us. The results were truly delectable.

3/4   cup all-purpose flour
1/2   teaspoon salt
1/4   cup shortening
2   to 3 tablespoons cold water
2   tablespoons butter, melted, *divided*
2   tablespoons sugar
1/2   teaspoon ground cinnamon
1   large apple, peeled and quartered

Cinnamon Apple Wraps

In a bowl, combine flour and salt; cut in shortening until crumbly. Gradually add water, tossing with a fork until a ball forms. On a lightly floured surface, roll out pastry into a 10-in. square; brush with 1 tablespoon butter. Fold into thirds. Roll into a 10-in. x 6-in. rectangle; cut lengthwise into four strips. Brush with butter.

Combine sugar and cinnamon; sprinkle half over the strips. Place an apple wedge on each; wrap pastry around apple. Line a baking sheet with foil and coat the foil with nonstick cooking spray.

Place wraps on prepared pan. Brush with remaining butter; sprinkle with remaining cinnamon-sugar. Bake at 400° for 28-32 minutes or until golden brown. Serve warm. **Yield:** 2 servings.

General Recipe Index

✓ Recipe includes Nutritional Facts or Diabetic Exchanges.

Alphabetical Index

✓ Recipe includes Nutritional Facts or Diabetic Exchanges.